Signifying as a Scaffold for Literary Interpretation

NCTE Standing Committee on Research

NCTE Research Report No. 26

Signifying as a Scaffold for Literary Interpretation

The Pedagogical Implications of an African American Discourse Genre

Carol D. Lee
School of Education and Social Policy
Northwestern University

National Council of Teachers of English
1111 W. Kenyon Road, Urbana, Illinois 61801–1096

Manuscript Editor: William Tucker
Staff Editor: Marlo Welshons
Cover Design: Susan Huelsing
Interior Book Design: Tom Kovacs for TGK Design

NCTE Stock Number: 44713-3050

Library of Congress Cataloging-in-Publication Data

Lee, Carol D.
    Signifying as a scaffold for literary interpretation : the pedagogical implications of an African American discourse genre / Carol D. Lee.
       p. cm. — (NCTE research report, ISSN 0085-3739 ; no. 26)
    "Reports the results of research conducted in the completion of a doctoral dissertation at the University of Chicago"
—Acknowledgments.
    Includes bibliographical references.
    ISBN 0-8141-4471-3 (pbk.) : $14.00 (est.)
    1. American literature—Afro-American authors—Study and teaching (Secondary) 2. Afro-Americans in literature—Study and teaching (Secondary) 3. Afro-Americans—Education (Secondary) 4. Language and culture—United States. 5. Discourse analysis, Literary.
6. Black English. I. Title. II. Series.
PE1011.N295 no. 26
[PS153.N5]
428'.007 s—dc20
[810.9'896073'07]   93-10347
                                               CIP

Contents

Acknowledgments

This book reports the results of research conducted in the completion of a doctoral dissertation at the University of Chicago. Without the support of the following persons, I could never have completed this project.

Bakari Kelvin Dance, Stephanie Wilson, Sterling Plumpp, and Donda West spent many intense hours reading the students' tests. Bakari and Stephanie read both the pilot and the field tests and gave most unselfishly of their time and skills. Sandy Dolan ran the Rasch statistics, provided a needed sound board for ideas and answered questions about the statistical analysis. Stephanie Foster Crane, Wanda Turks, and Ava Watson extended themselves generously to complete exhaustive typing and transcription.

Although their names are not mentioned in order to protect the anonymity of the participating schools, the principals, department and curriculum chairpersons, and the participating teachers were wonderfully giving. They were consummate professionals, working under difficult conditions, giving thoughtfully and generously to the students they served.

Many friends pitched in to provide special support. Joyce Joyce spent many hours with me thrashing out ideas over the phone lines and was especially supportive in developing the concepts in the test of prior social knowledge. Michael Gipson and F. Leon Wilson were always available to address the many computer problems I faced during this project. Betty Bolden proofread the manuscript all the way from Washington, D.C. My godmother Vivian King proofread, typed, and volunteered whenever I needed her.

Benjamin Wright provided invaluable advice on the use of the Rasch model, and Larry Hedges provided a helpful critique of the results chapter of the book.

Each of the members of my dissertation committee critically supported the evolution of this project. Edgar Epps was the friend I needed to get through my graduate program, offering advice and keeping my focus realistic. Susan Stodolsky helped set the stage early in my graduate career by refining my skills in classroom observation. Peggy Miller stimulated my interest in Vygotsky and continuously offered a unique perspective on my work. Geneva Smitherman inspired much of the focus of this work through her research on Black English. Her recommendations of several early readings provided the focus which refined the scope of the project. Finally, George Hillocks, my committee chairperson, challenged my thinking and forced me to dig deeper than I thought possible. His many readings of versions of this manuscript were invaluable and appreciated. Through his efforts, I was able to obtain the financial support of the Gray Reading Research Fund to support this project.

To each of these persons, I offer deeply felt thanks. Although this project could not have been completed without their help, the support of my family was clearly the buoy which kept me afloat. I thank my children, Laini, Bomani, and Akili, for being resilient and independent over these last three years so that I could devote myself to this work. I thank my mother, Inez Singleton Hall, who became the mother of my children and the rock to which I could always cling. I thank my husband, Haki Madhubuti, for always believing I could do this, for encouraging me both publicly and privately, and for being a man with such big ideas. Finally, I acknowledge the inspiration I have received daily for the past seventeen years from the children and staff of the New Concept Development Center. They were always living proof that cultural knowledge had meaningful cognitive consequences.

1 The Problem

The United States currently faces a literacy crisis. According to the National Alliance of Business (1990), U.S. companies spend $210 billion to provide additional training for an unprepared workforce. The Education Summit called by President Bush in 1989 indicates the national concern over this escalating problem. The data reported from the 1988 National Assessment of Educational Progress (Mullis, Owen, and Phillips 1990) documents its severity. Although students demonstrate competence in basic skills, too few appear to grasp higher-level thinking skills. Many have "substantial difficulty in articulating evidence for whatever understanding they have" of a text (Mullis, Owens, and Phillips 1990, 14). Langer (1984) made similar observations about the 1981 NAEP results. Langer reports that "only 10–15 percent could successfully write an explanation or defense of why they answered [inferential questions] as they did" (115). According to the 1981 NAEP report,

> Students seem satisfied with their initial interpretations of what they have read and seem genuinely puzzled at requests to explain or defend their point of view. (Langer 1984, 115)

The problems of illiteracy and low levels of literacy are particularly acute among Blacks, some minority language groups, and the poor (Kozol 1985; Mullis, Owen, and Phillips 1990; Scribner 1984b). As measured by the reading comprehension section of the 1988 NAEP, the gaps between Whites and Blacks, and Whites and Hispanics, have narrowed. However, the differences in achievement between them remain significant. In recognition of this disparity, the 1989 Education Summit called for U.S. schools to meet this challenge. In meeting this challenge, policy makers called on schools to help students become knowledgeable "about the diverse cultural heritage of this nation and about the world community" (Mullis, Owen, and Phillips 1990, 10).

Some of the problems with reading achievement in U.S. schools have been attributed to the organization and content of instruction in classrooms (Beck and McKeown 1984; Heath 1989; Hillocks 1989; Langer 1984; Mullis, Owen, and Phillips 1990; Purves 1984). At the secondary school level, instruction in reading occurs primarily in English classes, where the study of literature dominates the curriculum. Therefore, any attempts to increase literacy levels should include a focus on the organization and content of literature instruction at the secondary school level.

At least five major criticisms have been raised regarding literature instruction at the secondary level. Critics have argued that little attention is paid to the "rhetoric of the text"—that is, how the specific configuration of words and the structure of the text influence meaning (Purves 1984; Scholes 1985). Teachers often dominate classroom discussion, telling their students a "right" interpretation of the text. In so doing, teachers do not teach interpretive skills that would support students' ability to carry out the interpretive process independently (Hillocks 1989; Marshall 1989; Scholes 1985; Smith and Hillocks 1988). In addition, the texts in units of literature instruction are not sequenced in such a way as to build up a body of genre knowledge (such as how to approach the interpretation of irony, satire, and tragedy) or a knowledge of themes which would extend social knowledge as it may critically be applied to the interpretation of literature (Hillocks 1989; Smagorinsky and Gevinson 1989; Smith 1989; Smith and Hillocks 1988).

Perhaps the most highly debated criticism of literature instruction relates to the scope of texts most commonly taught. Applebee (1989) completed a national survey of book-length works of literature taught in grades 7–12. In the public, private, and Catholic high schools surveyed, the list of book-length works cited as most in use was dominated by white male authors. Of a total of 630 titles listed, fewer than ten African American authors were reported. Although this picture does not include works cited in anthologies, it is clear that African American texts are not a meaningful part of the literature curriculum in U.S. schools.

This study is offered as one example of an instructional approach which speaks to the problems of literacy among African American, and by extension among other ethnically diverse student populations, as well as to the problems that plague literature instruction in U.S. schools.

2 Rationale

The need to redefine literacy is fueled in part by at least three factors: the increasing ethnically diverse student population in U.S. schools, particularly in large urban school districts that have high rates of poverty (Langer, Applebee, Mullis, and Foertsch 1990); the concentration among these populations of low levels of literacy as measured by standardized achievement tests (Mullis, Owens, and Phillips 1990; Lomotey 1990), competence in the workforce, and high school graduation rates (National Alliance of Business 1990; Wilson 1987; Lomotey 1990); and a greater tendency to observe those classroom practices which professional associations of educators have criticized as restrictive and not supporting the development of critical thinking skills (Marshall 1990; Means and Knapp 1991; McNeil 1988; Oakes 1985). Perhaps because of the increasing formal sensitivity to ethnicity, as well as our greater understanding of the cultural contexts of human cognition (Shweder and Levine 1984; Stigler, Shweder, and Herdt 1990), literacy has been redefined as a set of social practices situated in specific sociocultural contexts (Farr 1991; Resnick 1990; Scribner 1984; Scribner and Cole 1981). As a set of social practices, specific literacies are evident in the ways in which people talk, read, write about, and otherwise use a variety of printed texts (Robinson 1988; Heath 1988). Literate behavior involves attitudes toward language and the uses of print which readers in particular communities bring to material they read. These may be ethnic communities, religious communities, work communities, or other configurations, all of which act as interpretive communities as defined by Stanley Fish (1980). Any person may be a member of a variety of such communities and practice a variety of literacy skills.

In defining literacy as a set of social practices, it is important to understand that those practices are influenced by the kind of text being read (Resnick 1990). Literary texts make certain demands on readers as well as offer imaginative possibilities to them. The imaginative possibilities of literary texts, in particular narrative, may be explained by the argument that narrative is a universal phenomenon, a means by which people make sense of their experiences in the world (Bruner 1986; Polkinghorne 1988; Nelson 1989). If this thesis is credible, then literature would seem to hold the possibility of promoting people's thinking about the significance of their own experiences. Langer (1989) posits a theory that the act of reading literature promotes a kind of

3

hypothesizing that is different from what occurs while reading expository texts. Langer maintains that readers of literary texts hypothesize about "a constantly moving *horizon of possibilities* . . . [which focus] on the human situation with all its uncertainties and ambiguities—bringing to bear all that the readers [know] about people, situations, relationships and feelings" (15–16). In reading expository texts, on the other hand, readers' understanding is "constrained by their perceptions of the topic" (Langer 1989, 16). Comparable observations have been made by Vipond and Hunt (1984) and Rosenblatt (1978). In a similar vein, Hynds (1989) has demonstrated that better readers use their social knowledge to interpret characters in short stories.

Thus, reading literature requires social knowledge regarding human relationships, the motivation of people in particular circumstances, and the relationship between human goals and actions. One cannot adequately read the literature of a people without knowing something of the culture and the historical circumstances of that people. Scholes (1985) calls such social and cultural knowledge the cultural codes of a literary text.

In addition to the assumption of social or cultural knowledge, reading literary texts also requires genre knowledge, i.e., knowledge of the literary conventions in which authors couch their language. This tradition within the narrative, for example, may include manipulation by the author of the point of view of narrators or characters, of imagery and detail to create mood and setting, of rhetorical strategies to create ironic effects, as well as the juxtaposition of characters and relationships and events to suggest interpretation beyond surface meaning. Some of these literary conventions are employed by people in everyday conversation when relating stories of personal experience, a point illustrated in detail by Deborah Tannen in *Talking Voices: Repetition, Dialogue, and Imagery in Conversational Discourse* (1989). Literary texts re-present the vividness of social experience through dialogue, imagery, and other stylistic strategies aimed at engaging the emotional involvement of the reader. What some writers of literary texts, especially narrative texts, do is to elevate and hone these strategies of everyday talk so that the talk becomes representational/symbolic, taking on its meaning from the structure and rhetoric of the text.

Thus, if we are to shape effective readers of literary texts, we must make certain students understand the cultural codes of a literary text (i.e., the social knowledge and values upon which it rests) and we must teach the use of specific interpretive strategies that represent the technology, if you will, of interpreting literature (Hillocks et al. 1971; Rabinowitz 1987). By so doing, we can empower students to move from more basic levels of comprehension to the more demanding levels which Scholes (1985) challenges English teachers to approach: interpretation of the significance and meaning of themes in a work of fiction, and criticism, "a critique of the themes . . . and the codes . . . out of which a given text has been constructed" (22–23).

The exchange between the reader and a piece of literature is the result of a dynamic interchange among a number of variables. These variables include prior social and cultural knowledge, genre knowledge about literary conventions and the structure of the text, prior readings, and personal taste. The give and take between reader and text have been explored in cognitive psychology through schema acquisition and modification theories (Rumelhart 1980; Spiro 1980) and in literary criticism through reader-response theories (Tompkins 1980). The reading paradigm which emerges from reader-response and schema theories can support an approach to teaching literature that takes advantage of the cultural and linguistic knowledge which novice readers bring to the classroom.

The levels of congruence between the social knowledge of the reader and the social world of the text can, for novice readers, aid comprehension and interpretation. Thus, in the situation where one wishes to initiate novice readers into the subtleties of allusion and symbolic import that rich texts of fiction offer, the nature of the texts can be important. The levels of congruence between the social knowledge of the reader and the social world of the text may be described as shared spaces. Especially among novice readers, it is possible that these shared spaces may promote dialogic reading depending on three factors:

1. the extent to which a reader empathizes with characters;

2. the extent to which a reader recognizes and construes a meaningful function to the literary conventions used in the text (perhaps because they are consistent with the conventions of his or her own oral style);

3. the extent to which a reader gains insight into the depth of values explored in the literature because the reader has had to grapple with similar or comparable human tensions without benefit of the insights of the author.

For example, when these shared spaces exist, the text may trigger an association perhaps unanticipated by the author but supportable from the text and the reader understands an allusion intended by the author. One can appropriately describe such an interaction between the reader and the author as a kind of dialogue mediated by the text. Citing Vipond, Hunt, Jewett, and Reither (in press), Hynds writes,

> [A] *dialogic* reading . . . [is one in which] readers . . . understand the
> effects a text has on them, what literary conventions define such effects,
> how the text comes to mean in terms of their own personal identities, and

how the text reflects the values, norms, and expectations of particular
cultures. (5)

Thus, the interaction between a reader and a literary text may appropriately be
described as a sociocultural context.

It is important to realize that shared social knowledge is at once necessary
and insufficient by itself to support dialogic reading. For example, when black
students read the story "seemothermotherisverynice" (from Morrison's *The
Bluest Eye* [1970]), it is safe to assume that many are familiar with the
emotions engendered by gospel music in many African American fundamentalist churches. Still, if these readers are not cognizant of certain interpretative
strategies, they will not be sensitive to the details in the story which signal
irony. For example, when Pauline, the adolescent protagonist of the story, is
in church, she listens and dreams:

> Pauline was fifteen, still keeping house, but with less enthusiasm. Fanta-
> sies about men and love and touching were drawing her mind and hands
> away from her work. . . . These feelings translated themselves to her
> in extreme melancholy. She thought of the death of newborn things,
> lonely roads, and strangers who appear out of nowhere simply to hold
> one's hand, woods in which the sun was always setting. In church
> especially did these dreams grow. The songs caressed her, and while
> she tried to hold her mind on the wages of sin, her body trembled for
> redemption, salvation, a mysterious rebirth that would simply happen,
> with no effort on her part. In none of her fantasies was she ever
> aggressive, she was usually idling by the river bank, or gathering berries
> in a field when a someone appeared, with gentle and penetrating eyes,
> who—with no exchange of words—understood; and before whose
> glance her foot straightened and her eyes dropped. The Presence, an
> all-embracing tenderness with strength and a promise of rest. . . . There
> was a woman named Ivy who seemed to hold in her mouth all of the
> sounds of Pauline's soul. Standing a little apart from the choir, Ivy sang
> the dark sweetness that Pauline could not name; she sang the death-
> defying death that Pauline yearned for, she sang of the Stranger who
> *knew* . . .

> > Precious Lord take my hand
> > Lead me on, let me stand
> > I am tired, I am weak, I am worn.
> > Through the storms, through the night
> > Lead me on to the light
> > Take my hand, precious Lord, lead me on.

> Thus it was that when the Stranger, the someone, did appear out of
> nowhere, Pauline was grateful but not surprised. (88–89)

An inexperienced reader who is knowledgeable about the fundamentalist
African American church may empathize with the religious experience and
understand its importance and intensity. Such a reader likely knows the song
"Precious Lord" and realizes that it was a favorite spiritual of Dr. Martin

Luther King, Jr., a song which he acknowledged in his final public speech, just before his death, when he revealed that he had seen the spiritual mountaintop and did not fear death. Such an inexperienced reader, however, is not likely to realize that the tension between what one would expect a religious person to think about and feel when hearing "Precious Lord" sung and the fact that Pauline calls up images of sensuality are warning flags that the author waves. This flag says, "keep this tension in mind as you read further about Pauline because it may help you understand her later in the story." Such readers interpret Pauline as a good, church-going woman at the end of the story, and in making such an evaluation of Pauline completely miss the irony of Morrison's conclusion. Such an inexperienced reader will also not likely think there is any special significance to the song being sung in the early church scene, believing that any spiritual would do. Thus, in this scenario, the reader's prior social knowledge inhibits a sophisticated interpretation of the story. On the other hand, this same prior social knowledge in the hands of an experienced reader—one who understands and uses knowledge of literary conventions—is empowering and may support sophisticated and subtle readings.

A similar case can be made for the difficulties that the chapter "The Threshing-Floor" from James Baldwin's *Go Tell It on the Mountain* (1952) poses to the novice reader. When John, the protagonist, finally gives in to the ritual of religious conversion in his father's fundamentalist church and is possessed by the Holy Ghost, he experiences a dreamlike state. The inexperienced reader may not be aware that the chronology of events in the dream need not be linear and that the narration can move back and forth between John's dream state and reality, between John's point of view and Baldwin's point of view. A reader who does not enter the text with this genre knowledge will likely miss the symbolic import of the scene, despite having an intimate understanding of the rituals of fundamentalist prayer meetings. In fact, the ultimate irony of this novel, I believe, is how the author is intimately consumed by the very church he criticizes. Baldwin cannot criticize the fundamentalist church without entering its very bosom, representing its rituals with such vividness that the reader is drawn into the rituals as a kind of participant observer who, as Baldwin himself, must consciously step back from the experience and intellectually critique the ever-present ironies. And yet, knowing firsthand how the body and emotions are totally consumed by spiritual possession, such an experienced reader, knowledgeable about literary conventions, can be attuned to very subtle details that another reader might not notice. For example, near the end of that same story from *The Bluest Eye* (1970), Morrison says of the mature Pauline, "More and more she neglected her house, her children, her man—they were like the afterthoughts one has just before sleep, the early morning and late evening edges of her day, the dark edges that made the daily life with the Fishers lighter, more delicate, more lovely" (99). I believe the potential symbolic and satiric import of those details are more readily available to an experienced reader who is African American, female, and over twenty-five. A more detailed analysis of this scene can be found in chapter 3.

Smith and Hillocks (1988) observe that students who are able to interpret symbols, recognize irony, and generalize with insight about characters "[note] details, . . . [identify] salient similarities, . . . [and draw] inferences on the basis of the details [of the text]" (47). Davison, King, and Kitchener (1990) say that "the very act of literary reading demands a tolerance of the multiple tensions and disruptions inherent in the literary encounter" (cited in Hynds 1990, 6). These same observations can be made about people who signify.[1] Expert signifiers think analogically, looking for unusual verbal inventions and unapparent similarities between events, objects, and/or people. When teaching students who are good at signifying, but not proficient at interpreting literature, the challenge is to help them become conscious of the sensibilities and strategies they unconsciously apply when signifying. They should also be given opportunities to apply those sensibilities and strategies to a body of literature about which they have significant prior social and linguistic knowledge.

The complex relationships between ethnicity and/or culture and thinking have been investigated in cross-cultural studies. Some researchers have specifically looked at the links between everyday practice and schooling. Their cross-cultural investigations have provided in-depth pictures of social practices outside of traditional Western schooling which have cognitive consequences that these researchers have identified and measured: Vai literacies in three scripts (Scribner and Cole 1981; 1988), Brazilian children's candy selling (Saxe 1988; 1991), the uses of literacy and the interplay of oral and written mediums in a southern African American and a white working-class community (Heath 1983; 1988), the construction of mathematical strategies in the work environment of a dairy factory (Scribner 1984a), the mathematical strategies of dieters while shopping and preparing meals (de La Rocha 1985)—to name a few. From the standpoint of anthropology and psychology, these studies provide meaningful insights into the texture and nuances of the interplay of culture and cognition—how, as Saxe (1991) suggests, culture and cognition co-construct one another. What is missing, however, in terms of enriching the links between everyday practice and schooling, are specific descriptions of the knowledge structures taught in school as they relate to the knowledge structures constructed within non-school social settings. The interplay between structures of knowledge constructed through social activity outside classrooms and structures of knowledge embedded in school learning is potentially powerful because the resulting network of associations is richer in both its specificity and its generalizability. This interaction can be viewed in Vygotskian terms as the cross-fertilization of scientific and spontaneous concepts (Vygotsky 1986). The purpose of this study is to examine one such link between a social practice and a school task. The social practice is signifying, a ritualized form of talk in the African American community, and the school task is teaching literary interpretation.

The voices of America's diverse ethnic communities each have a linguistic power that too often only the creative writer—the novelist, the poet, the dramatist, the creative essayist—hears and appreciates. This study offers an example of the voice of one such community and the craft with which the talk of that community is sculpted and re-created at another level by creative writers. In this study, I do not simply join the ranks of those who agitate for the positive self-esteem that black students can gain from reading African American literature or that Mexican American students can gain from reading Chicano literature. Instead, I propose that this union of novice readers and ethnic literature may support the development of critical strategies for interpreting literature.

Literateness within the African American community includes an attitude toward language use. Whether the text is an oral sermon, political oratory, autobiographical narrative, or simply a good story, language use must demonstrate flair and style, rhythm through selective repetition, and indirection articulated through the use of figurative language. Smitherman (1977), Gates (1988), Mitchell-Kernan (1981), and Kochman (1972), among others, have made similar observations. This sense of style as a purveyor of meaning, a sense of rhetoric, is one aspect of literateness shared across social classes within the African American community.

Many texts of African American literature reflect the oral culture of African Americans. This literature traditionally reflects the historic and personalized experiences of African Americans. Many African American writers have publicly avowed their role as tellers of the stories of the people, as interpreters of the sociopolitical realities which the people experience, and as maintainers and shapers of the language: W.E.B. DuBois (1903), Alain Locke (1925), James Weldon Johnson (1932), Richard Wright (1926), Ralph Ellison (1964), the many contributors to *The Black Aesthetic* (Gayle 1971), and Alice Walker (1983), to name just a few.

Henry Louis Gates, in *The Signifying Monkey* (1988), explicates with grace and details the links between the talk of the people and what he calls the "speakerly text." The discourse practices of signifying within the African American community and the genre strategies of at least one significant and powerful body of African American literature are bridged not only by socially meaningful motifs, but also by an intimate overlay of rhetoric that links the oral talk and the literary language. By focusing on the pedagogical relation-

ships between signifying and a certain body of African American literature, I
hope to address in a practical way the challenge issued by Heath (1989) when
she noted,

> The school has seemed unable to recognize and take up the potentially
> positive interactive and adaptive verbal and interpretive habits learned by
> Black American children (as well as other nonmainstream groups), rural
> and urban, within their families and on the streets. These uses of lan-
> guage—spoken and written—are wide ranging, and many represent
> skills that would benefit all youngsters. (370)

Signifying

In the article "Oral and Literate Traditions Among Black Americans Living in
Poverty," Heath (1989) characterizes the skills demonstrated by African
American children's use of language as

> keen listening and observational skills, quick recognition and nuanced
> roles, rapid-fire dialogue, hard-driving argumentation, succinct recapitu-
> lation of an event, striking metaphors, and comparative analyses based
> on unexpected analogies. (370)

In that same article Heath bemoaned what she observed as a decline in the
amount and complexity of verbal interaction between young mothers in an
urban housing project and their young children. An African American ethnog-
rapher who situated himself (as Heath had done in the work that led up to
Ways With Words [1983]) as an intimate participant/observer in a housing
project community in Chicago made a very different set of observations
(Potts 1989). Potts, by contrast, did not observe a decline in the amount and
complexity of verbal interaction in regard to narratives constructed by pre-
school-aged children and narratives co-constructed between youngsters and
their parents. In any case, Heath goes on to observe that despite the dearth of
language stimulation in the earlier years, adolescents in this housing project
community somehow had become experts at signifying.

Signifying has been formally defined by many scholars, writers, and activ-
ists (Abrahams 1970; Andrews and Owens 1973; Brown 1969; Cooke 1984;
Gates 1984, 1988; Hurston 1935; Kochman 1972; Major 1970; Mitchell-
Kernan 1981; Smitherman 1977). Some define its characteristics in structural
terms as a speech act with delineated functions (Abrahams 1970; Kochman
1972). Others define it as a rhetorical stance, an attitude toward language, and
a means of cultural self-definition (Cooke 1984; Gates 1984, 1988; Mitchell-
Kernan 1981; Smitherman 1977). Both definitions are necessary to the argument of this research. An understanding of signifying as a rhetorical stance,
an attitude toward language, and a means of cultural self-definition, is impor-

tant in assessing the value given to signifying as an art form within the African American community. It is precisely because it is so highly valued and so widely practiced that signifying has the potential to serve as a bridge to certain literacy skills within a school environment. In many social settings within the African American community, the adolescent, in particular, who cannot signify has no status and no style, is a kind of outsider who is incapable of participating in social conversation. Signifying is a traditional form of African American discourse which has been maintained across generations and across both rural and urban environments and easily can be traced back to the period of the "African-American Holocaust," known to many as slavery (Gates 1988).

Both Gates (1984, 1988) and Mitchell-Kernan (1983) point to the specialized meanings attributed to the word "signify" within the African American community. Both contrast the Eurocentric dictionary-based definition of signification with the Afrocentric definition. To signify within the African American community means to speak with innuendo and double meanings, to play rhetorically upon the meaning and sounds of words, and to be quick and often witty in one's response. There is no parallel usage of the terms to signify or signification within other ethnic or English-speaking communities. Gates punctuates the difference in the use of the term in the two communities by capitalizing the first letter to identify *Signifying* as a specialized concept of language use within the Black community.

Signifying may be either called or classified by many names. The family of related discourse forms

> subsumed under signifying would include "marking," "loud-talking," "specifying," "testifying," "calling out" (of one's name), "sounding," "rapping" and "playing the dozens". (Gates 1984, 286)

Other terms include "shucking" (as in "shucking and jiving") and "talking shit." However, as my students reminded me recently, these terms are old-fashioned. The current labels include the terms "disin'" and "mackin'"! Still, the fundamental taxonomy of forms remains stable.

Mitchell-Kernan (1981) describes signifying as a "way of encoding messages or meanings which involves, in most cases, an element of indirection" (311). She emphasizes that dictionary meanings of words in an act of signifying are not sufficient for constructing meaning. One must recognize "... implicit content or function, which is potentially obscured by the surface content or function" (314). Ralph Ellison (1964) talks about "ironic signifying—'signifying' here meaning, in the unwritten dictionary of American Negro usage, 'rhetorical understatements'" (249–50). Smitherman (1977) summarizes the formal properties of signifying as follows:

> indirection, circumlocution; metaphorical-imagistic (but images rooted in the everyday, real world); humorous, ironic; rhythmic fluency and

sound; teachy but not preachy; directed at persons or persons usually
present in the situational context (siggers do not talk behind yo back);
punning, play on words; introduction of the semantically or logically
unexpected. (121)

Popular categories of signifying include playing the dozens (i.e., talking
about yo' mama), and cappin' or sounding (out-performing in a verbal duel of
friendly insults):

Dozens—Yo mamma so skinny, she do the hula hoop in a Applejack!

Cappin' or sounding—Someone says, "I went to your house and
wanted to sit down. A roach jumped up and said 'Sorry, this seat is
taken.'" You respond, "I went in yo house and stepped on a match and
yo mama said, 'Who turned off the heat?'"

Signifying can be metaphoric and serve other functions than to insult. The
following example is taken from Mitchell-Kernan (1981):

(Grace has four kids. She had sworn she was not going to have any more
babies. When she discovered she was pregnant again, she wouldn't tell
anybody. Grace's sister came over and they had the following conversation.) *Rochelle:* Girl, you sure do need to join the Metrecal for lunch
bunch. *Grace:* (noncommitally) Yea, I guess I am putting on a little
weight. *Rochelle:* Now look here girl, we both standing here soaking wet
and you still trying to tell me it ain't raining. (323)

Signifying can also be ironic. This second example also comes from Mitchell-
Kernan (1981). A young man has approached the researcher. She tells him
about her research on signifying. He raps (i.e., talks flirtatiously) to her. In the
midst of their signifying dialogue, he says,

Baby, you a real scholar. I can tell you want to learn. Now if you'll just
cooperate a li'l bit, I'll show you what a good teacher I am. But first we
got to get into my area of expertise. (323)

African American adolescents regularly produce and interpret such figurative
and ironic talk. African American creative writers in the "speakerly text"
tradition appropriate and re-figure this attitude toward language and discourse
form.

These properties of signifying may be broadly classified under the scope
of metaphoric or figurative language and ironic talk. Signifying is replete with
figurative language. Gates (1988) has minimally identified the following
rhetorical tropes as used in various categories of signifying: irony, metaphor,
synecdoche, metonymy, and metalepsis. If one broadly categorizes the cognitive processes required to participate in signifying discourse, one process
would require metaphoric reasoning, and the second would require ironic
reasoning. To reason or infer metaphorically involves establishing an unstated

relationship between the topic and the vehicle of the metaphor, and then building levels of parallel associations that extend to the topic of the metaphor (Booth 1974; Winner 1988). For example, when the protagonist Janie Starks of Zora Neale Hurston's *Their Eyes Were Watching God* (1937) proclaims that her new lover, Vergible Tea Cake Woods, could be a "bee to a blossom," the reader must process an unstated relationship metaphorically. The reader must identify a variety of relationships between a bee and a blossom and must then link which of those relationships may parallel other relationships in the novel. These would include not only the relationship between Janie and Tea Cake, but also between Janie and her deceased husband, Joe Starks, who would not allow Janie, among other things, to participate in the community signifying which ritually occurred on the front porch of Joe Starks's store. There are a number of possible and applicable relationships between a bee and a blossom that may apply to this situation and such reasoning can generate multiple layers of generalizations about the evolution of Janie as a woman, about the depth of Tea Cake as a man, as well as the evolution of their relationship. This kind of metaphoric reasoning in the context of fiction proceeds almost effortlessly for the expert reader. On the other hand, Janie's words would more likely than not be simply overlooked or simplistically processed by the novice reader. Discovering how to reach the novice reader of fiction is the goal of this study.

Ironic reasoning differs from metaphoric reasoning in that the reader must reject the surface meaning of the passage and then construct levels of meaning that are in contrast or even contradiction to the literal interpretation of the text. Wayne Booth (1974) describes this process of interpreting irony as building levels of meaning below the surface of the literal floor, whereas the process of interpreting metaphor requires building levels of meaning that are in addition to or above the literal floor. Irony in literature is not only pervasive but is also quite difficult, for novice readers in particular, to understand (Booth 1974; Smith 1987; Smith and Hillocks 1988). Signifying requires quick processing of the intended meaning of dialogue that is always either metaphoric, ironic, or both. It is students' knowledge of the purposes and rituals of this discourse form as well as their social knowledge of the persons involved in the dialogue (one does not signify with strangers) that in part allows them to process so quickly. This knowledge parallels the knowledge that the expert reader of a text of fiction brings to bear in literary interpretation: knowledge of the genre, knowledge of the author, and knowledge of the social world of the text as it unfolds.

I propose that novice African American adolescent readers bring into classrooms a powerful intellectual tool which goes unnoticed, devalued, and untapped. Signifying is not merely a discourse form, but also serves as a medium for the internal organization of experience and a heuristic for problem solving that requires analogical reasoning, be it metaphoric or ironic. Thus the problem of transfer must focus not only on the process of such reasoning, but the content over which one reasons. In the context of reading fiction, the content and cultural milieu of the text, as well as the language in which layers of implied meanings are situated, are critical factors to consider in scaffolding. Many texts of African American literature which Gates (1988) calls "speakerly texts" are appropriate for the kind of scaffolding I advocate. Such texts make use of Black English to give voice to characters and/or the narrator. Such texts brim with figurative language that conveys themes, motifs, and symbols in the works. The research which I will describe involves such a pedagogical marriage between texts of African American fiction and the discourse of signifying. Henry Louis Gates (1988) set the precedent regarding the function of signifying in African American fiction. I have merely tried to extend that analysis to its pedagogical implications.

In the only works of their kind that I am aware of, Taylor (1982), and Ortony, Turner, and Larson-Shapiro (1985) investigated whether there was any relationship between the predominance of figurative talk in the African American community, specifically what they called "sounding," and comprehension of figurative language in school texts. The studies indicate that, for white students, comprehension of figurative language is directly related to general verbal ability. For black students, however, "black language ability affects sounding skill, which in turn [directly] affects figurative language comprehension" (Delain et al. 170). Ortony, Turner, and Larson-Shapiro (1985) investigated how skill in sounding could be used to improve the quality of writing. They concluded that "skills acquired 'in the streets,' so to speak, do transfer to school settings" (Delain et al. 171). However, the problem with the implications of these findings for school achievement was the evidence that teachers generally do not respect or in any way support any demonstrations of Black English in classrooms (Delpit 1990; Rist 1970; Smitherman 1977; Taylor 1982). I have attempted to extend the findings of Delain et al. to focus on not only comprehension of literary texts, i.e., "speakerly" texts of African American literature, but also to extend the expected skills in interpreting figurative language and ironic verbal constructions to the acquisition of a new and more complex skill, namely the interpretation of what Hillocks (Hillocks and Ludlow 1984) has identified as a core set of inferential skills used in the analysis of fiction.

I have demonstrated elsewhere (Lee 1990) that it is possible to use the strategies an expert reader would employ to interpret an ironic text in order to generate the intended meaning in an extended signifying dialogue. This is appropriate because in the extended signifying dialogue the text is essentially ironic throughout; neither speaker means exactly what the words appear to mean when literally interpreted. Wayne Booth (1974) and Michael Smith

(1987) divided these expert strategies into those used to identify a passage as ironic and those used to reconstruct the intended meaning. The process of reconstructing the intended ironic meaning depends heavily on appropriate social knowledge, knowledge of the genre, and knowledge about the author. In extended signifying, the discourse form of signifying is the genre and the social knowledge about the community and the individual participants is an absolute prerequisite to reconstructing the intended meaning of each speech turn. Booth says that in order for the author and reader to engage each other in a shared understanding of the irony of a passage, they must agree on at least three areas of common experience:

1. their common experience of the vocabulary and grammar of English . . . along with understanding of rules which allow for and control verbal inventions;

2. their common cultural experience and their agreement about its meaning and value;

3. their common experience of literary genres, a potentially large (but almost certainly finite number of shared grooves or tracks into which reading experience can be directed). (100)

For many African American students (and others whose community culture and/or language patterns differ markedly from mainstream school culture), these areas of experience are not shared understandings, particularly when reading literature which does not reflect common experiences with vocabulary and grammar, cultural values which are not part of the students' experience, and literary genres with which the students are explicitly unfamiliar. On the other hand, in an act of signifying it is safe to assume that a majority of African American students will share common understandings of language conventions and meaning, values around the import of the ritual of the act, and understandings about the rules of the game which I believe may be analogous to expectations regarding literary genres.

As I continue to construct this Vygotskian framework, it is equally important to investigate how these oral strategies (which include a high use of figurative and ironic talk within the discourse form of signifying) play out in the expert domain of literature. Gates employs the term "speakerly text" to refer to works of African American literature in which Black English, the language of the people, with its flair for figuration and innuendo, its flair for verve and style, and its relish for playing on the meanings of words, is elevated as art. The term was originally coined by Zora Neale Hurston, who perhaps remains the master of this voice.

In my analysis of Hurston's *Their Eyes Were Watching God*, I have identified one hundred forty statements which I have classified as either metaphoric, proverbial, or oxymorons that carry the implicit themes, symbols, and ironies. Each of these statements would fall within the purview of the indigenous oral tradition of African American discourse typified by signifying. This text, as many others within the speakerly tradition (see Smitherman 1977, and Gates 1988, for other specific examples), is replete with signifying. Signifying as a speech act, in fact, becomes the metaphor for the empowerment of the female protagonist, Janie, and the ironic pettiness as well as largesse of the ordinary people the reader meets between the pages. Hurston refers to the signifers as "big picture talkers . . . using a side of the world for a canvas," and describes the talk of the ordinary folk who signify on the porch as "words walking without masters; walking altogether like harmony in a song" (2). In her description, Hurston captures not only the essential characteristics of signifying as figuration and exaggeration, but also its functions in the African American community. She accurately portrays signifying as empowering and culturally self-defining.

Note

1. Signifying is a form of social discourse within the African American community which may involve ritual insult, but always involves a high use of figurative language.

3 Signifying in African American Fiction

Signifying provides the basis for the instructional unit on which this study focuses. Signifying is important because it is employed as a literary device in works of African American literature. It is also important because the metaphoric and ironic nature of signifying is applicable to literature in the more general sense. The purpose of this chapter is to demonstrate how signifying is employed as a literary device in several works of African American literature and to demonstrate how metaphor and irony in these texts are embedded in African American Vernacular English. Additional examples of signifying in African American literature are well explicated in the works of Gates (1984, 1988) and Smitherman (1977). Additional examples of how African American Vernacular English and aspects of the oral tradition of storytelling and the musical tradition of the blues are embedded in African American texts may be found in Baker (1980), Morrison (1989), and Jones (1991).

Perhaps the most classic example of signifying in a text of African American fiction is Zora Neale Hurston's *Their Eyes Were Watching God* (1935). Gates (1988) makes a thorough analysis of Hurston's use of signifying. My own analysis of Hurston is an attempt to build on Gates's analysis, not simply to replicate it. Hurston begins the novel with a scene of ordinary folk in Eatonville sitting on the front porch signifying in raucous verbal duels and eventually signifying about the protagonist, Janie Woods. Janie has returned, apparently empty handed, after running off with her lover, Tea Cake, who was considerably younger than Janie. Hurston says of these people,

> These sitters had been tongueless, earless, eyeless conveniences all day long. Mules and other brutes had occupied their skins. But now, the sun and the bossman were gone, so the skins felt powerful and human. They became lords of sound and lesser things. They passed nations through their mouths. They sat in judgment. . . . They made burning statements with questions, and killing tools out of laughs. It was mass cruelty. A mood come alive. Words walking without masters; walking altogether like harmony in a song. (1–2)

This passage is replete with metaphor and sets the motif of signifying into play. It also establishes a sociocultural context for the massive presence of signifying in the African American community. Signifying in the novel is the symbol for power plays both within the black community and between the black and white communities. It is the conduit through which the reader can gauge both Janie's oppression and her personal liberation. Janie's second husband, Joe Starks, who, to use Hurston's words, was "too full of his own big self," refuses to allow her to participate in the signifying conversations primarily of men, but also of some women, who sat on the front porch of his store. Because he is mayor of Eatonville, Joe feels that it is socially beneath his wife to participate in such low-down talk, even though he participates in this powerful world of verbal dueling. But, we are told, "Janie loved the conversation" (47), conversation that "was a contest in hyperbole and carried on for no other reason" (55).

Participation in signifying talk is an index of Janie's sense of her own power and self-worth. The scenes in chapter 6 where the menfolk go on at length to signify about Matt Bonner's mule are viciously funny:

> ". . . at mule uh yourn, Matt. You better go see 'bout him. He's bad off."

> "Where 'bouts? Did he wade in de lake and uh alligator ketch him?"

> "Worser'n dat. De womenfolks got yo' mule. When Ah come round de lake 'bout noontime mah wife and some others had 'im flat on de ground usin' his sides fuh uh wash board."

> The great clap of laughter that they have been holding in, bursts out. Sam never cracks a smile. "Yeah, Matt, dat mule so skinny till de women is usin' his rib bones fuh uh rub-board, and hangin' things out on his hock-bones tuh dry." (46)

Janie sympathizes with the mule, who is symbolic of not only her plight but that of women. Janie's grandmother earlier had said that the Black woman is the mule of the world. Janie then suggests to her husband, Mayor Joe Starks, that he buy the mule from Matt Bonner in order to get the mule some needed rest. Joe Starks takes Janie's idea, buys the mule, gets praises for his generosity from the men on the porch, but never acknowledges to anybody that this was, in fact, Janie's idea. A major foreshadowing of Janie's impending powerful voice comes when she subtly signifies on Joe Starks for usurping her thoughts and not giving her credit:

> Janie stood still while they all made comments. When it was all done she stood in front of Joe and said, "Jody, dat wuz uh mighty fine thing fuh you tuh do. 'Tain't everybody would have thought of it, 'cause it ain't no everyday thought. Freein' dat mule makes uh mighty big man outa you. Something like George Washington and Lincoln. Abraham Lincoln, he had the whole United States tuh rule so he freed de Negroes. You got uh town so you freed uh mule. You have tuh have power tuh free things and dat makes you lak a king uh something."

> Hambo said, "Yo wife is uh born orator, Starks. Us never knowed dat befo'. She put jus' de right words tuh our thoughts."

> Joe bit down hard on his cigar and beamed all around, but he never said a word. (51)

Voice is the metaphor of empowerment. Shortly thereafter, Joe Starks verbally lashes out at Janie in front of the menfolk in the store. Janie had thrust herself into the signifying conversation. When Joe begins to signify about Janie no longer looking like a young girl, Janie fires back:

> "You big-bellies round here and put out a lot of brag, but 'tain't nothin' to it but yo' big voice. Humph! Talkin' 'bout me lookin' old! When you pull down yo' britches, you look lak de change uh life."

> "Great God from Zion!" Sam Watson gasped, "Y'all really playin' de dozens tuhnight" (68–69)

Janie's voice has the effect of a killing tool and Joe Starks literally dies as a result. Joe attempts to control Janie through his repression of her signifying voice. In contrast, Janie's new lover and soon-to-be husband in fact pampers and supports Janie's becoming a part of the people. Their life together in the swamps of Florida and his ironic empowerment of Janie by teaching her to shoot a rifle ultimately lead to his untimely and tragic death.

Early in Janie and Tea Cake's relationship, signifying becomes the indicator that her life with Tea Cake is going to be very different from her life with Joe Starks. In this very early conversation between Tea Cake and Janie, she breaks the restrictive mold Joe Starks had set for her and playfully signifies with Tea Cake:

> [*Tea Cake*] "Evenin' Mis' Starks. Could yuh lemme have uh pound uh knuckle puddin' till Saturday? Ah'm sho tuh pay yuh then."

> [*Janie*] "You needs ten pounds, Mr. Tea Cake. Ah'll let yuh have all Ah got and you needn't bother 'bout payin' it back." (83)

After Tea Cake and Janie are married and move to Florida to pick crops on the muck, we are told,

> The men held big arguments here like they used to on the store porch. Only here, she could listen and laugh and even talk some herself if she wanted to. She got so she could tell big stories herself from listening to the rest. (112)

Thus, in *Their Eyes Were Watching God* Hurston quintessentially defines signifying, employs the discourse as motif, symbol, and an index of the protagonist's transformation.

In addition to these more obvious uses of signifying, Hurston plays with figurative language throughout the novel. Hurston defines the essential elements of signifying as "crayon enlargements of life," "a contest in hyperbole," "pass[ing] around pictures of their thoughts," "burning statements with questions, and killing tools out of laughs." These elements of signifying parallel the consistent observations that innuendo, indirection, metaphor, and irony are associated with signifying. Often a clue that a statement is intended as signifying can be found where an obvious contradiction is stated, as in the previously cited dialogue where one sister says to the other, "We both here soaking wet and you trying to tell me it ain't raining." I have identified one hundred forty statements or passages in this novel which I classify as either statements of obvious contradiction, irony, metaphors or imagistic allusions, or proverbial statements. Each of these categories shares the characteristics which have been attributed to signifying. These characteristics are all the more salient when one thinks about the Delain et al. study (1985), which linked skill in sounding (i.e., a form of signifying) and skill in interpreting figurative language.

A few brief examples of each category are offered below. These statements carry many levels of embedded meaning and are keys to the major themes in the novel:

Obvious Contradictions

They mocked everything human in death. (53)

She sent her face to Joe's funeral, and herself went rollicking with the springtime across the world. (76)

Irony

Ah done had six chillun—wuzn't lucky enough tuh raise but dat one—and ain't never had uh nigger tuh even feel mah pulse. White doctors always gits mah money. (117)

[Mrs. Turner, a mulatto looking woman, has tried to get Janie romantically interested in her light-skinned brother. In order to show Mrs. Turner that he's in control, he hits Janie. His friend on the Florida muck suggests that Tea Cake hit Mrs. Turner.] 'Knock her teeth down her throat.' 'Dat would look like she had some influence when she ain't. Ah jus' let her see dat Ah got control. (122)

Metaphor/Image

Mah tongue is in my friend's mouf (9). [Janie tells her story to her dear friend Phoeby who vows never to tell anyone else what Janie has confided to her.]

She [Granny] saw Johnny Taylor lacerating her Janie with a kiss (14). [Janie's first innocent kiss which sent her grandmother into a rage of fear.]

[Joe was] . . . building a high chair for her to sit in and overlook the world and she here pouting over it (54). [The high chair is both the literal chair for the baby who pouts and the symbol of Joe's desire to keep her above the common folk.]

Proverbial

Us colored folks is branches without roots. (17)

Take a stand on high ground. (18) [Janie's grandmother, Nanny, wanted material wealth and a man to protect Janie from the cruelty, racism and sexism of the world. Ironically, the high ground of material wealth represented by Janie's first two husbands, Logan Killicks and Jody Starks, does not protect Janie from oppression nor fulfill the dream of love and oneness with the ordinary folk, the dream which Janie's grand-mother had tried so desperately to erase from Janie's being. There is further irony in that once Janie has immersed herself in the world of the common folk on the muck in Florida and has found her true love in Tea Cake Vergible Woods, there is no literal high ground to save her from the thrashes of the wind and water of the hurricane. Saving Janie for the literal high ground ultimately costs Tea Cake his life.]

All she found out was that she was too old a vessel for new wine (100).

Signifying and, by extension, figuration become critical mechanisms in the work of Zora Neale Hurston. It was Hurston's specific desire to represent the talk of her people in her literary work. Hurston received much criticism from such literary giants of the Harlem Renaissance as James Weldon Johnson, and later from Richard Wright, for her use of Black English Vernacular in her novels and short stories.

Alice Walker consciously walks in the shadow of Zora Neale Hurston. She says that Hurston haunted her throughout the writing of *The Color Purple.* About *Their Eyes Were Watching God,* Walker (1979) writes,

> ... it speaks to me as no novel, past or present, has ever done; and that the language of the characters, that "Comical nigger 'dialect'" that has been laughed at, denied, ignored, or "improved" so that white folks and educated black folks can understand it, is simply beautiful. There is enough self-love in that one book—love of community, culture, tradi-tions—to restore a world. Or create a new one. (2)

The issue of using African American English Vernacular as a creative tool was important to both Walker and Hurston. Both writers realized not only the metaphoric tenor of the language, but also appreciated its capacity for com-municating depth of thought with a terse yet pungent use of imagery. Like Hurston, Walker received criticism from members of the black community for the language she placed stage-front in this novel. On the issue of the signifi-cance of the language in *The Color Purple,* Walker (1988) writes:

> Celie speaks in the voice and uses the language of my step-grandmother, Rachel, an old black woman I loved. Did she not exist; or in my memo-ries of her, must I give her the proper English of, say, Nancy Reagan?

And I say, yes, she did exist, and I can prove it to you, using the only thing that she, a poor woman, left me to remember her by—the sound of her voice. Her unique pattern of speech. Celie is created out of language. In *The Color Purple,* you see Celie because you "see" her voice. To suppress her voice is to complete the murder of her. And this, to my mind, is an attack upon the ancestors, which is, in fact, war against ourselves.

For Celie's speech pattern and Celie's words reveal not only an intelligence that transforms illiterate speech into something that is, at times, very beautiful, as well as effective in conveying her sense of her world, but also what has been done to her by a racist and sexist system, and her intelligent blossoming as a human being despite her oppression demonstrate why her oppressors persist even today in trying to keep her down. . . .

She has not accepted an alien description of who she is; neither has she accepted completely an alien tongue to tell us about it. Her being is affirmed by the language in which she is revealed, and like everything about her it is characteristic, hard won and authentic. (63–64)

Walker also employs signifying in *The Color Purple* as an index of Celie's will. In the beginning of the novel, Celie presents a naive, frightened, and passive exterior. However, among the details which foreshadow the assertive will that later emerges are small instances of signifying of which only Celie and the reader are aware. Early in her marriage to Mr. _____, two of his sisters come to visit. They criticize Annie Julia, Mr. _____'s deceased ex-wife, for keeping a nasty house. The background information that Mr. _____ was repeatedly unfaithful to Annie Julia and he flaunted his relationship with Shug Avery before his wife is important. One of the sisters, Carrie, says of the dead wife, "And cook. She wouldn't cook. She act like she never seen a kitchen" (20). Celie signifies in her response written in her letter to God: "She hadn't never seen his" (20). Later in that same letter, the sisters begin to talk about Shug Avery. The sister, Kate, says, "I'm sick of her too. . . . And you right about Celie, here. Good housekeeper, good with children, good cook. Brother couldn't have done better if he tried" (21). Again, Celie signifies in her written response, "I think about how he tried." These early evidences of signifying are stances that Celie takes, internally revealing only to herself and God. She has not yet found the voice to make public that which is evolving internally.

As her fascination with Shug Avery develops, Celie begins to signify not only through the public silence of her written voice, but also through action which remains private and written. When he comes to visit, Mr. _____'s daddy maligns Shug Avery. In the process it becomes clear that in his relationship with his son, Harpo, Mr. _____ is merely reenacting his own dilemma with his father. Mr. _____ refuses to accept Harpo's marriage to a woman who does not fit his stereotype of the good woman, just as Mr. _____'s daddy would not accept Shug Avery when Mr. _____ was young, unmarried, and courting Shug.

> Old Mr. _____ say to Mr. _____ , Just what is it bout this Shug Avery anyway, he say. She black as tar, she nappy headed. She got legs like baseball bats.
>
> Mr. _____ don't say nothing. I drop little spit in Old Mr. _____'s water. (56)

In this scene, Celie seems to follow the admonition of Alice Walker that ". . . women did not have to speak when men thought they should, that they would choose when and where they wish to speak because while many women had found their own voices, they also knew when it was better not to use it" (Washington 1990, xii). The irony of this signifying scene is not only that Celie signifies on Old Mr. _____, but that her action overpowers her public silence and demonstrates that she is not only more powerful than Mr. _____ in the presence of his father, but that ironically she stands up for him, a subtle foreshadowing of Mr. _____'s transformation at the end of the novel. In that same passage, Old Mr. _____ signifies on Shug, "And her mammy take in white people dirty clothes to this day. Plus all her children got different daddys. It all just too trifling and confuse" (57). Celie signfies with her inner voice, "Next time he come I put a little Shug Avery pee in his glass. See how he like that" (57).

The voices of signifiers are voices of power and assertiveness. Sofia and Shug Avery represent a reformulation of the traditional feminine role. When Sofia returns after having left Harpo and visits Harpo's juke joint, or bar, Celie recounts in her letter,

> Oh, Miss Celie, she cry. It so good to see you again. It even good to see Mr. _____ , she say. She take one of his hands. Even if his handshake is a little weak, she say. (84)

In that same scene,

> Mr. _____ whisper to Sofia. Where your children at?
> She whisper back. My children at home, where yours? (85)

Celie observes that these two women who signify with the best of the men "talk and act sometimes like a man. Men say stuff like that to women" (85).

If signifying serves as the metaphor through which we gauge Celie's growth, then the major transition occurs when Celie signifies on God. In a critical letter, Celie recounts her conversation with Shug Avery about the nature of God. This conversation is important because it supports one interpretation of the significance of the title of the book and is the first explicit reference to what will become the philosophy of life assumed by Celie and the transformed Mr. _____. Shug signifies on the idea that God is white:

> Nettie say somewhere in the bible it say Jesus' hair was like lamb's wool, [Celie] say.
> Well, say Shug, if he [God] came to any of these churches we talking bout he'd have to have it conked before anybody paid him any attention. The last thing niggers want to think about they God is that his hair kinky. (202)

In Celie's very next letter, she writes not to God, but to Nettie, her sister.

> When I told Shug I'm writing to you instead of to God, she laugh. Nettie don't know these people, she say. Considering who I been writing to, this strike me funny. (205)

For Celie to signify on the only one outside of Shug Avery to whom she has been able to confide her frightening secrets for almost two decades is a clear statement that she has initiated her own emancipation and that she has begun to internalize a philosophy of life in which God is not an old white man who will protect you, but rather a creative force that exists within all of creation. This transition is epitomized in the scene which so clearly parallels the scene in *Their Eyes Were Watching God* in which Janie kills Joe Starks with the power of her voice. Celie's voice at this juncture encompasses her realization that God is within all of creation and is within her, just as God is in the small, insignificant, purple flower, and God is "pissed off" if you do not pay attention to it. When she announces to the family, and most importantly to Mr. _____, that she is leaving with Shug Avery, Celie's killing words signify:

> You a lowdown dog is what's wrong, I say. It's time to leave you and enter into Creation. And your dead body just the welcome mat I need. (207)

This classic confrontation in which Celie signifies not silently, but loudly— not merely internally, but publicly—is the verbal bridge over which she struts to release herself from his mental, emotional, physical, and sexual oppression.

Like Hurston, Walker not only uses signifying as a motif and symbol in the novel, but also uses metaphor and imagery in the context of Black English Vernacular to convey multiple levels of meaning in the text. Like Hurston, Walker makes extensive use of natural imagery. Trees represent one such natural image which serves as an index of the symbiotic relationship between humanity and nature, a relationship which is at the core of Walker's philosophy in the novel. This relationship is evident in the important conversation between Celie and Shug about the nature of God. Shug says that her "first step from the old white man was trees. Then air. Then birds. Then other people . . . " (203). "The old white man" is the reference to an image of God as a white man. Celie imagines when she first meets Shug that because of the beauty she perceives in Shug that the trees stand up in Shug's presence. When Mr. _____ beats her, Celie says she turns herself into a tree. Thus, it is proper that when Celie lays her killing words on Mr. _____ the words are given to her by the trees:

> Until you do right by me, I say, everything you even dream about will fail. I give it to him straight, just like it come to me. And it seem to come to me from the trees. (213)

Celie's power, now interwoven with the trees and nature itself, is exercised through her voice. The curse befalls Mr. _____ because Celie *says* it will.

Walker creates a story in Africa with Celie's sister Nettie that parallels many aspects of the African American story. Within that parallel story the image of trees has symbolic value. The Olinka people use the leaves of the roofleaf tree to make roofs for their homes. We are told, "Where roofleaf had flourished from time's beginning, there was cassava. Millet. Groundnuts" (159). Foreshadowing the saving grace of the roofleaf is the description of the effects of a great storm during one rainy season:

> For six months the heavens and the winds abused the people of Olinka. Rain came down in spears, stabbing away the mud of their walls. . . . Soon the village began to die. By the end of the rainy season, half the village was gone. (159)

Recognizing the intimate and symbiotic relationship between nature, humans, and God, Nettie reflects on the significance of the roofleaf for the Olinka people:

> We know a roofleaf is not Jesus Christ, but in its own humble way, is it not God? (160)

This tree represents the sacred relationship between Olinka man/woman and God, and stands in stark contrast to the foreign rubber tree which the British colonialists bring. The rubber tree is imported and planted on Olinka soil not for the benefit of the people but for the profits of the British Empire. The planting of the rubber trees is the surgery that aborts the Olinka life and opposes Creation as it is culturally represented by the worldview of the Olinka people. Thus, trees in this novel are images which act as a leitmotif, similar to signifying as motif. Both serve as indices of the inner well-being of the characters; both are metaphorical, carrying multiple layers of indirect meaning.

The most powerful signifier in the novel, however, is the transformation of purple, purple-black, black-black—the many associations with the color purple—*The Color Purple*. Purple is associated in the novel with royalty. Because Celie thinks Shug Avery is like a queen, she imagines Shug would wear

purple. Purple is associated with blackness, and with pain, when, after she
is beaten so badly by the police, we are told Sofia's face looks like an
eggplant. The image of black-black, like the purple-black of the eggplant, is
re-presented as the image of African beauty when Nettie, in amazement, is
dazzled by the elegant beauty of the blue-black Senegalese people. Nettie's
first visit to Africa redefines black for her.

> These are the blackest people I have ever seen, Celie. They are black like
> the people we are talking about when we say, "So and so is blacker than
> black, he's *blue*black." They are so black, Celie, they shine. Which is
> something else folks down home like to say about real black folks. But
> Celie, try to imagine a city full of these shining, blueblack people wear-
> ing brilliant blue robes with designs like fancy quilt patterns. Tall, thin,
> with long necks and straight backs. Can you picture it at all, Celie?
> Because I felt like I was seeing black for the first time. And Celie, there
> is something magical about it. Because the black is so black the eye is
> simply dazzled, and then there is the shining that seems to come, really,
> from moonlight, it is so luminous, but their skin glows even in the sun.
> (147)

This instantiation of black stands as politicized contrast to Old Mr. _____'s
diminution of Shug Avery when he calls her black as tar and nappy headed.
Squeak, Harpo's second wife, a mulatto-looking woman, realizes that the high
admiration of physical characteristics which are closest to the ideal of white
beauty is just the reverse side of the coin which belittles black. Squeak asks
Harpo, ". . . do you really love me, or just my color?" (102). Just like the
gramophone which "sit in the corner a year silent as the grave. Then you put
a record on, it come to life" (103), the once quiet and passive Squeak makes
public the contradiction. She sings:

> They calls me yellow
> like yellow be my name
>
> But if yellow is a name
> Why ain't black the same
>
> Well, if I say Hey black girl
> Lord, she try to ruin my game. (104)

Purple is associated with assertiveness when Celie decides that the first
pants she makes for Sofia should be purple and red (a color she has previously
associated with happiness). Celie writes, "I dream Sofia wearing these pants,
one day she was jumping over the moon" (223). Purple is associated with that
which we underappreciate and undervalue in life when Shug says, "I think it
pisses God off if you walk by the color purple in a field somewhere and don't
notice it" (203). Purple becomes the color of transformation, the color of the
breadth of human experience and the representation of the power of the human

will. It becomes, by the end of the novel, Celie's favorite color. In her home, her entire room is decorated in purple and red. As an indicator of Mr. _____'s transformation, he gives Celie a purple frog which he carved especially for her.

The image of purple and its family of associated colors is the vehicle through which Alice Walker signifies upon a culture thick with racism. She plays on purple/black and reverses its intended meaning, expanding its meaning from a reaction to a pro-active stance which enriches life and all of humanity. The dictionary meanings of black as "soiled, dirty; evil, wicked, harmful; disgraceful; full of sorrow or suffering; disastrous; sullen or angry," the related family of blackball, blackguard, blacklist, black magic, blackmail, black mark, black sheep," (from *Webster's New World Dictionary*) belong to another constellation. They are not part of the constellation redefined in *The Color Purple*.

Besides looking at how signifying is utilized and transformed within the texts which made up this instructional unit, it is also important to see how signifying is employed in the two stories which were used for pre- and post-testing. Both stories were excerpted from *The Bluest Eye* by Toni Morrison (1970). The two excerpts were chosen because the dialogue includes both Black English Vernacular and the more standard English. The registers switch back and forth, with the narrator in each story using standard English and the characters speaking in BEV. There are aspects of signifying which all the literary texts in this unit shared: (1) ritual insults that are stylized and metaphoric; (2) rich metaphoric language and images which serve as vehicles for conveying multiple layers of meaning.The story that served as the reading material upon which the pre-test was based is taken from the chapter entitled "Winter." It is the story of the confrontation over values between two sisters, Freida and Claudia, and a well-to-do, light-skinned, beautiful by popular standards, new girl in school, Maureen Peal. Freida and Claudia are poor. When Maureen enters school, everyone, including the teachers, lavishly pours attention on Maureen. The complex and subtle theme of this story is capsulized in the closing passage:

> We were sinking under the wisdom, accuracy, and relevance of Maureen's last words. If she was cute—and if anything could be believed, she was—then we were not. And what did that mean? We were lesser. Nicer, brighter, but still lesser. Dolls we could destroy, but we could not destroy the honey voices of parents and aunts, the obedience in the eyes of our peers, the slippery light in the eyes of our teachers when they encountered the Maureen Peals of the world. What was the secret? What did we lack? Why was it important? And so what? Guileless and without vanity, we were still in love with ourselves then. We felt comfortable in our skins, enjoyed the news that our senses released to us,

admired our dirt, cultivated our scars, and could not comprehend this
unworthiness. Jealousy we understood and thought natural—a desire to
have what somebody else had; but envy was a strange, new feeling for
us. And all the time we knew that Maureen Peal was not the Enemy and
not worthy of such intense hatred. The *Thing* to fear was the *Thing* that
made *her* beautiful, and not us. (57–58)

Freida is a very strong-willed and assertive child. Her aptitude and willingness to signify at the drop of a hat signal the strength of her character. She
calls Maureen "Six-finger-dog-tooth-meringue-pie." When a group of boys
surround their friend Pecola, taunting her with "Black e mo Black e mo Ya
daddy sleeps nekked," Freida fires back, "You shut up, Bullet Head." One of
the boys responds, "You want a fat lip?" Freida signifies, "Yeah. Gimme one
of yours." Morrison builds another layer of evidence to support the story's
theme when she, the author, signifies through Maureen. Maureen tells the
story of a girl named Audrey who had gone to the beauty shop and asked
that her hair be fixed like Hedy Lamarr's. As Maureen tells the story, the
hair dresser responded, "Yeah, when you grow some hair like Hedy Lamarr's."

Perhaps more important, for the purposes of this instructional approach,
than the examples of pure signifying are the uses of metaphor and image to
carry multiple layers of meaning. This is the domain onto which signifying
knowledge was to be mapped. Winter and spring are two central metaphors in
this story. The story opens with a paragraph which compares the sisters' father
to aspects of winter. The description is rich in imagery and is there to serve
metaphoric purposes:

> My daddy's face is a study. Winter moves into it and presides there. His
> eyes become a cliff of snow threatening to avalanche; his eyebrows bend
> like black limbs of leafless trees. His skin takes on the pale, cheerless
> yellow of winter sun. . . . Wolf killer turned hawk fighter, he worked
> night and day to keep one from the door and the other from under the
> windowsills. A Vulcan guarding the flames, he gives us instructions
> about which doors to keep closed or opened for proper distribution of
> heat. . . . And he will not unrazor his lips until spring. (47)

This opening paragraph is difficult for novice readers precisely because the
father is not involved in the story as an active character, and because its
significance is clearly not literal, but metaphoric. Winter is the metaphor for
the life of poverty which Freida and Claudia live, for the cold tensions of
growing up, and for the harshness of a racist society which these black girls
must learn to negotiate. Winter stands in contrast to spring "when there could
be gardens," a time of hope and replenishment:

> By the time this winter had stiffened itself into a hateful knot that nothing
> could loosen, something did loosen it, or rather someone. A someone

who splintered the knot into silver threads that tangled us, netted us, made us long for the dull chafe of the previous boredom. (47)

We are told it was a false spring day when Maureen "pierced the shell of a deadening winter." Maureen is like a false spring day. The silver threads are metaphors for the tinsel beauty and signs of material wealth which Maureen brings as an ideal into the girls' lives. The girls had at first been jealous of the attention Maureen received because of her perceived beauty and wealth. Yet, they too were drawn to Maureen and had hoped that the inner Maureen was as nice, friendly, and caring as the outward persona they perceived. Later, when Maureen reveals her true colors, so to speak, Claudia and Freida are drawn into a web of tension and self-doubt. All of these layers of meaning are embedded in the images and metaphors of the opening page of the story. The ability of students to explore these metaphors and images is tested in several of the questions in the pre-test.

The story on which the post-test is built is the chapter entitled "seemother-motherisverynice." The significance of the orthography of the title can only be gleaned from reading the entire novel, which begins with a mimicking of the stereotyped Dick and Jane school reader.

As in "Winter," the narrator uses a standard English and the protagonist, the only other speaking character, speaks in Black English Vernacular. There is only one instance where Pauline, the protagonist, signifies. Pauline has been doing day-work for a white "family of slender means." Pauline doesn't really like the woman and signifies about the family's dependence on her:

> None of them knew so much as how to wipe their behinds. I know, cause I did the washing. And couldn't pee proper to save their lives. Her husband ain't hit the bowl yet. (101)

As in the other stories, signifying serves as an index of a character's transformation, sense of self-worth, and assertiveness. It stands as the yardstick by which the reader judges how much Pauline has changed by the end of the story. In the later scene, Pauline is again doing day-work, but now for a well-to-do white family. The irony of Pauline's transformation is reflected in the narrator's crisp observation that Pauline had become "what is known as an ideal servant, for such a role filled practically all of her needs" (108). The irony of Pauline's transformation is punctuated by the narrator's observing that

> When she bathed the little Fisher girl, it was in a porcelain tub with silvery taps running infinite quantities of hot, clear water. She dried her in fluffy white towels and put her in cuddly night clothes. Then she brushed the yellow hair, enjoying the roll and slip of it between her fingers. No zinc tub, no buckets of stove-heated water, no flaky, stiff, grayish towels washed in a kitchen sink, dried in a dusty backyard, no

tangled black puffs of rough wool to comb. Soon she stopped trying to
keep her own house. (109)

In the context of the entire story, then, the signifying scenes convey those
layers of meaning which in fact constitute the major theme of the work.

In addition to the signifying by the protagonist which fits the more traditional oral model, Morrison signifies subtly through the voice of the narrator.
The language is standard in register, but the innuendo is there, the killing cut
is there, and the metaphor is the action she satirizes. The narrator comments
further on the extent to which Pauline has abandoned her own family and
internalized values of beauty, family life, and material well-being that the
Fishers represent:

> More and more she neglected her house, her children, her man—they
> were like the afterthoughts one has just before sleep, the early morning
> and late-evening edges of her day, the dark edges that made the daily life
> with the Fishers lighter, more delicate, more lovely. (109)

The image of "late-evening edges of her day, the dark edges" is a metaphor
that is ironic and profoundly black. Pauline has been hurt as a child and all her
life limped with a foot that flopped. She dreams as a child of a "Stranger" who
will come and sweep her away with an ideal romantic love. When she meets
Cholly, Pauline believes he is that romantic ideal lover. After they are married,
the couple move north. In much of African American literature, the move
north assumes mythic proportions and often forbodes danger, the promised
land becomes the ironic usurper of tradition and continuity, the move from
hell to another hell. As one would expect, their marriage begins to deteriorate,
and Pauline takes refuge in the movies. She looks at the prophetically black-
and-white movie screen and tries to make herself look like the Jean Harlow
she idealizes, and wishes Cholly would be the Clark Gable of the black-and-
white screen. While in the movie watching Jean Harlow and Clark Gable,
Pauline bites into a piece of candy and her tooth falls out. After that, any hope
of emulating the white ideal of beauty and the silver screen image of material
wealth, romantic love, and family life becomes impossible for Pauline. After
this, Pauline turns devotedly to the church and her life as the ideal servant for
the Fishers. Within this complex context, Morrison's words, her reference to
the dark edges that her family has come to represent, is metaphorically related
to the nappy edges of the black woman's hair, the traditional "kitchen"[1] (an
ironic twist if ever there was one). When black women attempt to straighten
their hair by either applying heat or chemicals, the process is only temporary.
During the historical time frame of this novel, black women would straighten
their hair by applying heat. Any humidity or physical activity which resulted
in sweat would revert the "dark edges" back to their original kinky texture. In
this sense, then, Morrison is signifying not only on Pauline for abandoning

her family, but she is also signifying on the ideal for which Pauline has abandoned her family. Her family has become that part of her natural being which she so desperately wishes to change—but no matter how hard she tries, she can't! This interpretation of the metaphor, this signifying metaphor, represents a reading based on prior social knowledge that is distinctively cultural. It is the kind of subtle interpretation that even novice African American readers can bring to such a text once they realize that a literary stance is similar to a signifying stance. The two stances are similar in that they both presume an underlying and unstated relationship between two situations, people, or objects. They both require a kind of analogical reasoning and a sensitivity to subtle details.

Note

1. "Kitchen" is a vernacular, although dated, term used by African American women referring to the hair along the neckline.

4 Prior Research on Culture and Comprehension

The rationale for this research has so far been based on theoretical and philosophical warrants rather than empirical evidence. It is difficult to address the issue of what empirical research supports the line of reasoning I have undertaken, because no prior studies of which I am aware directly address the question of how culture affects comprehension of literature. There are, however, domains of empirical research which relate to the hypothesis of this research. These domains include the following:

1. reading research on the relationship of prior knowledge and the uses of schemata in reading comprehension;
2. the relationship of culture to reading comprehension and the acquisition of concepts in mathematics;
3. and finally research which has specifically sought to relate the teaching of literature and/or comprehension to Black English or African American culture.

In this chapter, I offer a brief review of related literature in each of these domains and explain how each has not been sufficient to answer the question which this research addresses.

An accepted tenet in reading research is that prior knowledge plays a critical role in the comprehension of texts (Afflerbach 1990). High prior knowledge about specific content or topics has been positively correlated with comprehension (Bransford and Johnson 1973; Chiesi, Spilich, and Voss 1979; Johnston 1984; Pearson, Hansen, and Gordon 1979; Voss, Vesonder, and Spilich 1980; Helen 1980; Louise 1980; Stein and Trabasso 1982). Prior knowledge about content or topics has been assessed by vocabulary probes based on a Guttman scale or free-association tasks (Anderson and Freebody 1981).

Research on prior knowledge has focused on its interaction with specific aspects of comprehension. Pearson and Johnson (1978) investigated whether prior knowledge facilitates comprehension of particular question types. Their classification scheme of question types is similar to that of Hillocks (Hillocks and Ludlow 1984). The following parallels may be made between the two classification schemes: Textually Explicit questions parallel key detail, basic stated information, and stated relationship questions; Textually Implicit questions parallel to some degree simple implied relationship questions; Scriptally Implicit questions do not parallel the specificity of Hillocks's scheme but share broad characteristics with complex implied relationships and author's generalization questions. Pearson and Johnson conclude that Scriptally Implicit "questions/answers are more influenced by prior knowledge than other question types" (Johnston 1984, 223).

Prior knowledge of content or topic is important for effective comprehension, but it is also mediated by knowledge of textual conventions (particularly in literary texts), by the demands of the text structure, by the constraints of the reader's belief system (Read and Rossen 1981), and by the reader's view of acceptable ways of interacting with a text. Trabasso, Stein, and Johnson (1981) found that what they call "procedural knowledge to activate story schemata" (what I would call "genre knowledge") is another form of prior knowledge that is necessary to comprehend narrative, particularly complex literary texts. Ohlhausen and Roller (1988) further established that both content schemata and text structure schemata are used by readers to select important information and to use that important information to map onto or amend existing knowledge (see Ohlhausen and Roller 1988 for a full review of relevant literature). Gaunt (1989) found that prior knowledge of text structure helps recall when the information in the text is less familiar.

The expansive body of research on the relationship between prior knowledge and the processes of comprehension has proven informative for this research. Two of the measures used in this analysis, the test on signifying and the test on prior social knowledge, are direct results of research on prior knowledge and schema theory. Langer (1984) established a prototype for creating an instrument to measure prior knowledge that was passage specific and part of an instructional design for classroom use. There are, however, several limitations which this research tradition has for the question I address. First, this body of research primarily defines comprehension as recall of gist and detail. As such, it does not begin to address the subtlety of interpretation that is assumed when one speaks of literary interpretation or literary engagement with a text (Vipond, Hunt, and Wheeler 1987). Second, reading researchers traditionally create short, artificial texts, whether narrative or expository, that demonstrate some characteristic which the researcher is investigating. Because of these restrictions, traditional reading research on prior knowledge and inferencing has only limited application to the problems of teaching literature.

Schema acquisition has widespread acceptance among reading researchers as a major variable influencing how prior knowledge is used in the process of comprehension (Anderson and Pearson 1984; Rumelhart 1980; Schank and Abelson 1977). Schemata may be defined as knowledge structures held in long-term memory which in the case of reading are used to organize chunks of information from texts. The argument is that readers map the content of the text onto existing structures (Voss, Vesonder, and Spilich 1980), or they adjust existing structures in order to accommodate new information in the text (Rumelhart 1980). Schemata may help the reader to determine the importance of text components (Afflerbach 1990) or to generate inferences (Anderson and Pearson 1984; Nicholas and Trabasso 1981).

Norris and Phillips (1987) raise a critical question about the explanatory power of schema theory. Although Rumelhart (1980) addresses the issue of schema acquisition and modification, Norris and Phillips claim that schema theory does not explain how we come to understand, say in reading comprehension, when we don't know where we're going. This question was illustrated by one study, among many, which asked subjects to interpret an ambiguous passage in which the topic is simply not clear (Bransford and Johnson 1973). Subjects were confused until they were given a title which indicated the paragraph was about sorting laundry. Once readers knew what the passage was about, they were able to retrieve appropriate schema or script through which to interpret the passage. The question Norris and Phillips (1987) raise is how do readers go about figuring out what such an ambiguous, de-contextualized text is about without the aid of existing content-based schema. They argue that critical thinking theory more appropriately explains how readers go about finding a way through a novel maze. Still, it seems reasonable to argue that knowledge of problem-solving strategies may in itself represent significant and powerful schemata. Certainly the research tradition in metacognition would suggest this.

In the most fundamental sense, this is the problem English teachers face in trying to teach novice readers to become independent interpreters of literature. It is, of course, the same question that Socrates raises in *Meno*. Norris and Phillips propose a process of critical thinking that involves the following stages:

1. Lack of understanding is recognized;

2. alternative interpretations are created;

3. judgment is suspended until sufficient evidence is available for choosing among the alternatives;

4. available information is used as evidence;

5. new information is sought as further evidence;

6. judgments are made of the quality of interpretations, given the evidence;

7. and interpretations are modified and discarded based on these judgments and, possibly, new alternative interpretations are proposed, sending the process back to the third step. (300)

Their explanation of processes involved in critical thinking closely mirrors Dewey's (1966) discussion of experimental thinking. In a literature review of current research on teaching reading comprehension, Dole, Duffy, Roehler, and Pearson (1991) discuss similar processes that good readers use.

In order to carry out the reader strategies which, according to Vipond, Hunt, and Wheeler (1987), are involved in literary reading, these steps in critical thinking would likely be used by a reader, especially a novice reader. Vipond, Hunt, and Wheeler claim the following strategies are requisites of a literary reading:

(a) imputing intentionality to the text; that is, treating the text as the product of an intending author;

(b) assuming that the text, as the product of an intending author, is finished and coherent;

(c) assuming, because the text is finished and complete, that apparent gaps or inconsistencies are to be treated as opportunities or invitations to make connections, supply inferences, or fill gaps;

(d) assuming, for the same reason, that details or textual features that do not immediately seem necessary or functional should not be ignored or dismissed. (152)

Norris and Phillips (1987) indicate that prior knowledge of content or topic is necessary but not sufficient for comprehension of novel texts. The implication, then, is that procedural knowledge (Smith and Hillocks 1988) of the conventions of narrative, for example, must be taught. Smith (1989) made similar observations about the inferencing strategies of a group of ninth graders. Smith (1989) argued that students should be specifically taught strategies for recognizing, understanding, and applying the ramifications of an unreliable narrator in their interpretations of a series of short stories. At the same time, Smith concluded from his observations that "more successful readers tended to make greater use of their personal knowledge" (19).

Morse (1989) and Earthman (1989) also found that less skilled readers did not make connections between their personal experiences and fictional texts. The literary reading, the social engagement with the text which Vipond, Hunt, and Wheeler (1987) define requires both content knowledge which in the reading of fiction includes personal experience, knowledge of human intentionality, and specific cultural values, and it also requires knowledge of literary conventions which the author uses.

Within the present research design, the focus on signifying is an attempt to tap existing knowledge in order to teach specific critical-thinking strategies and textual conventions. The focus on the relationship between the prior social knowledge of the students and the content of the literary texts is an attempt to extend the findings of contemporary research on prior knowledge, schema, and inferencing.

Cultural Schemata

One direction of the research into the uses of schemata in reading comprehension bears directly on the hypothesis of this study. It has to do with what Malik (1990) calls "cultural schemata." These studies look at the effects that culturally familiar, as opposed to culturally unfamiliar, texts have on reading comprehension. Reynolds, Taylor, Steffensen, Shirley, and Anderson (1982) explain the relationship between culture and reading comprehension this way:

> Readers acquire meaning from text by analyzing words and sentences against the backdrop of their own personal knowledge of the world. Personal knowledge, in turn, is conditioned by age, sex, race, religion, nationality, occupation—in short, by a person's culture. . . . our hypothesis is that culture influences knowledge, beliefs, and values; and that knowledge, beliefs and values influence comprehension processes. (354)

Although empirical research on this relationship is limited, its history goes back to the original research of Bartlett (1932) which is considered the genesis of the concept of schema. Bartlett probed a group of educated Englishmen to paraphrase the North American Indian folktale, *The War of the Ghosts.* The Englishmen modified their recall of the story to fit their own cultural expectations. Apparently the implications of this aspect of the now classic Bartlett study did not receive significant attention until Kintsch and Greene (1978).

Before discussing the findings of the series of studies which have followed, I will outline some of the basic design issues which have attended this research. Steffensen, Joag-Dev, and Anderson (1979) criticize the Kintsch and Greene (1978) design for not having a comparable native group to compare interpretations. Kintsch and Greene had a group of university students read selected stories from Boccaccio's *Decameron* and an Apache folk tale *Tar Baby.* Kintsch argued that any group of Apaches who might read the Apache folk tale would be bicultural and would be aware of the structure of the western stories. Steffensen et al. (1979) attempted to rectify the shortcoming in the Kintsch and Bartlett designs of having only one ethnic group. Steffensen et al. included subjects from the United States and India who read letters about an Indian and an American wedding. All subsequent studies have employed a cross-cultural design which includes subjects from two different cultures reading culturally familiar and culturally unfamiliar texts. Reynolds et al. (1982) have been among the few researchers to compare cultural groups within the United States (see also Parrish 1974, and Singer and Zaggara

1982). I have been able to identify only three studies which look at African American readers and it is interesting to note that all three include Marsha Taylor DeLain in her work primarily with Richard Anderson at the Center for the Study of Reading at the University of Illinois at Urbana-Champaign (Reynolds et al. 1982; DeLain et al. 1985; Taylor 1982).

Another critical issue in studies on the relationship between cultural knowledge and comprehension has been differences in focus. Some studies look at cultural expectations around text structure or story structure (Kintsch and Greene 1978; Bartlett 1932). Others look at cultural knowledge around belief systems, social conventions, and values (Malik 1990; Steffensen et al. 1979; Reynolds et al. 1982). Steffensen et al. (1979) make it very clear that their study "must be interpreted in terms of 'content' schemata rather than 'textual' schemata" (27). This present study seeks to link cultural knowledge around belief systems, social conventions and values to expectations around text structure. My study also differs from prior work in this field because it is not a study of what a cultural group of readers do with that knowledge while reading in the absence of instruction; rather this study is an application which seeks to inform practitioners about how cultural knowledge can be directly used in teaching. None of the existing research on culture and comprehension relates directly to the practice of teaching, although Reynolds et al. (1982) say they hope their work has some implications for removing cultural bias from textbooks and standardized tests.

Most of the cross-cultural studies which focus on cultural schemata for content compare cultural groups across national borders. Steffensen et al. (1979) ask adult subjects from India and from the United States to read two letters. The letters were analyzed for comparability in difficulty based on syntactic complexity and idea units. One letter described a wedding in India and the second letter described a wedding in the United States. The researchers found that subjects had greater recall and "more culturally appropriate elaborations" for the native passage and more culturally based distortions for the foreign passage. The researchers conclude, "the schemata embodying background knowledge about the content of a discourse exert a profound influence on how well the discourse will be comprehended, learned, and remembered" (19).

Fritz (1987) extends Steffensen et al. (1979) and in one sense creates a link between the studies of readers within and across national borders. This study involved four groups of students: Americans in the United States, Americans who lived in India, Indians in India, and Indians living in the United States. Each child read four stories: one story about a birthday celebration in the United States and another about a birthday celebration in India. The second set of stories were about a wedding, one in India and one in the United States. Verbal protocols were used, asking students to make predictions while reading the story. Students were asked interpretive questions after their readings. Fritz found significant differences according to the subject's native culture as opposed to where the subject was living.

Malik (1990) focused on the oral reading of English as a Second Language learners. The subjects were Iranian university students studying in the United States who were proficient readers and proficient in English. They were given expository passages from the *Encyclopaedia Britannica,* one based on Iranian belief systems and one on Japanese belief systems. Comparisons of the two passages were made concerning reading comprehension, reading process, and strategies, as well as reading speed. Malik found that cultural schemata of the subjects allowed them to differentiate important information from less important information and to make culturally appropriate elaborations and inferences about familiar texts. Malik also found that readers used the same oral reading speed and the same reading process on both texts, even when they failed to integrate the nonfamiliar text. This finding may have important implications for reading instruction with minority students at the elementary level which often emphasizes literal interpretation at the sentence level, phonics and decoding at the word level, but misses appropriate instruction for integration at the level of the whole text (Means and Knapp 1991).

Other recent studies have found similar results (Pritchard 1987; Tantiwong 1988). Tobin (1989) looked at the influence of cultural knowledge on literary interpretation. Tobin had a group of seventh-grade white students from a middle-class suburb in Australia listen to oral readings and to read from a novel and short story by Australian children's author Patricia Wrightson. Wrightson uses Aboriginal folklore as an integral part of her stories. Tobin found that the lack of knowledge of Aboriginal folklore and cultural experiences interfered with the students' ability to interpret the multiple textual cues that indicated the Aboriginal context. In fact, 40 percent of the students placed the setting of the story outside of Australia.

Reynolds et al. (1982) accurately note that too little work has been done comparing what they call culturally distinct sub-groups within a country, such as the United States. The critical warrant that justifies linking the results of the Reynolds et al. study and those studies comparing cultural groups across national borders is the argument that ethnically cohesive populations within the United States, such as African Americans, Mexican Americans, or Chinese Americans, not only share important features of the common culture but also share within their group distinct cultural experiences, language use, and values.

Reynolds et al. (1982) asked a group of black and a group of white eighth-grade students to read a letter in which a student describes an incident during lunch where he and another student exchanged verbal insults. White students interpreted the passage as being about physical aggression. Black students interpreted the passage as an example of sounding or playing the dozens, a specific form of signifying. The researchers conclude that cultural schemata can influence interpretation.

The two studies which focus on text structure as being culturally explicit look at stories, whereas the studies which focus on cultural content use short expository texts which embed a narrative episode (two of these are letters about personal experiences). The implication of the two studies which presume differences in text structure is that the structure of stories may be culturally explicit.

Investigating the question of the culturally explicit structures of stories, Brewer (1985) has attempted to identify universal properties of the story schema. Clearly the dominant body of work on story schema (Rumelhart 1975; Stein and Glenn 1979; Mandler and Johnson 1977) presumes such universality. Brewer makes a very important critique of studies which claim to investigate the question of a universal story schema. He says that any "cross cultural study using stories as stimuli and [finding] a difference between culture X and culture Y" must be able to distinguish whether the "two cultures differed at the level of event and plan schemata, at the level of narrative schemata, or at the level of story schemata" (176–77). Steffensen and Colker (1982) asked Australian Aboriginal women and women from the United States to recall two narratives, one about a sick child being treated by Western medical practices and the other about a sick child being treated by Aboriginal native medicine. As expected, they found better recall for the same-culture narrative. Brewer (1985) explains that "each group was using culture-specific knowledge about the intentions and goals of the actors to interpret the action sequences described in the narratives" (178). This is an example of what Brewer calls culture-specific properties of stories at the level of event.

To illustrate cultural distinctions at the level of narrative structure, Brewer cites the work of Labov (1972). Labov noted the difference in the structure of stories of personal experience related by middle-class Whites and inner-city Blacks. Middle-class white speakers "interrupted the narrative and made explicit comments about their feelings or emphasized the point they were trying to make." The inner-city black narrators "did not interrupt the narrative, but got information across by using exact quotations or by describing an external action that would act as a sign of an internal state" (Brewer 1972, 178).

At the level of story schema, Brewer distinguishes between oral stories and written stories. He offers numerous examples of oral story conventions around openings, settings, characters, resolutions, epilogues, closings, and narrators. Brewer describes these story conventions as universal properties of a story schema. His discussion of the variety of conventions within the oral story tradition of different cultures is more complete and specific than his discussion of the written story. He says his discussion of written stories does not include literary genres because most people have not read widely enough to have developed schemata for literary genres. Certainly, one goal of literature instruction, however, is to help students develop schemata for literary genres.

Brewer supports the claim that there are universal properties to story schema. He argues for a universal story schema based on his observations that all peoples create stories which attribute human intentionality to characters and their actions or the preponderance of ritualized openings in oral stories. However, Brewer also acknowledges that these universal properties are broad:

> Story schema universals in oral traditions reflect more abstract charac-
> teristics of stories, such as the use of affect to produce enjoyment and the
> use of repetition and parallel structure. (190)

The information needed by the reader or the listener to process such conventions is highly culture specific. That is, the less you know about the culture from which a story emerges, the more likely you are to misread and interpret in ways that a native reader would identify as mistakes in interpretation. Of importance to the present study is Brewer's recognition that there are both universal and culture-specific properties to stories:

> [The] analytic framework . . . that distinguishes between event schemata,
> narrative schemata, and story schemata . . . provides an initial account to
> the nature of universal and culture specific story schemata. (190)

Although Brewer applies this framework primarily to oral stories, I believe it may be applied to cross-cultural studies of written stories.

Brewer's analysis of written stories looks only at the Western tradition. Because Brewer does not contrast written stories from non-Western cultures, it is difficult to infer universal versus culture-specific properties within the written tradition. The question itself is further complicated by the fact that much written literature that emerges out of a particular cultural or national context is influenced by the native oral tradition. The question is also complicated because the level of cross-cultural communication and interaction (both voluntary and interaction as a result of colonial conquest) has resulted in cultures borrowing and sharing ideas and literary conventions. In some sense, one might argue that African American literature fits such an amalgam. African American literature is part of the American/Western tradition and yet still culturally distinct. A similar analysis may be made of much of modern African literature which may be written in either English or French but which clearly employs culturally specific conventions, symbols, and narrative structures. The point is that stories may share universal characteristics and culturally specific properties, as well as sharing oral and literate conventions.

The relevance of this discussion to the point of this study is the necessity of teaching both traditional conventions for reading fiction as well as drawing

upon cultural knowledge which readers bring to texts. The reading of literature requires event and plan schemata, narrative schemata, and story schemata. When there is cultural distance between the reader and the fiction,
teachers need to determine whether the nature of this distance may be at the
level of event and plan schemata, narrative schemata, or story schemata. In
this sense, Brewer's distinctions are useful for practitioners.

The empirical base for claiming a relationship between cultural schemata
and comprehension is consistent in its findings. The fuzziness comes when
one tries to distinguish the source of the relationship—whether the match is
between the reader and her cultural expectations around text structure or
whether the match is between the reader and her knowledge of cultural
content, events, and social intentions. The strongest case to date is for cultural
knowledge of content, events, social conventions, social intentions, and goals.
Although none of the cultural content studies to date have looked specifically
at stories, i.e., literature, their results do have implications for the interpretation of literature. The case for prior knowledge as an aid to reading comprehension has rested primarily on prior knowledge of content, topics, or subject
domain. Although reading literature is different from reading expository texts
(Rosenblatt 1978; Vipond and Hunt 1984; Langer 1989), there is certainly no
question that there are basic processes of reading comprehension that are
applicable to all texts (Dole, Duffy, Roehler, and Pearson 1991). The prior
knowledge research, along with the cultural schemata research, defines comprehension primarily as recall of the gist of a text or as localized inferences.
Although my concerns in terms of literary analysis go beyond these more
limited notions of comprehension, no discussion of more subtle and elaborate
aspects of literary interpretation can proceed without achieving these more
basic elements of comprehension.

Culture and Learning Mathematics

The final body of empirical research which has influenced this study is work
that looks at relationships between knowledge acquired in cultural contexts
and the acquisition of concepts in mathematics. In fact, although at one level
it may appear to be the line of research most distant from this study, it is the
work that initially inspired the thinking that led to this research design.
Whereas all the research on prior knowledge and cultural schemata looks at
how knowledge is used independently outside of the school setting, the
cultural mathematics research has more often looked at how cultural knowledge interacts with or impacts knowledge acquired in school settings. This
viewpoint, I believe, is the cutting edge of the present study.

Stigler and Baranes (1989) provide a comprehensive and critical overview
of research on the interactions between culture and the acquisition of mathe-

matical knowledge. Even to begin to summarize the diverse findings reported in this study is beyond the scope of this literature review. Rather, I will focus solely on those studies which shed some light on how mathematical knowledge that is acquired in the practical contexts of community and family life may relate to mathematical knowledge acquired in school settings. What interested me were the studies which looked at the possible symbiotic relationship between what Vygotsky (1986) called the interaction between spontaneous and scientific concepts (Petitto 1982; Ginsburg, Posner, and Russell 1981; Petitto and Ginsburg 1982; Saxe 1982, 1988, 1991; Carraher, Carraher, and Schliemann 1985, 1987).

Lave (1977), and Reed and Lave (1981) investigated the question of transfer of skill in a practical arena to skill in a school context. They gave a group of schooled and a group of unschooled Liberian tailors two sets of problems. One set involved mathematical problems that would arise out of tailoring and another set of school-type problems. Schooled and unschooled tailors had comparable performance on the tailoring problems; however, on the non-tailoring problems, the schooled tailors outperformed the unschooled tailors. The unschooled tailors had a mean average of 70 percent correct on non-tailoring problems and tailors with one to four years of schooling had 74 percent of the non-tailoring problems correct. Lave (1977) argued that this level of performance was evidence that the practical experiences and apprenticeship of the unschooled tailors provided "general problem solving principles" (179).

Stigler and Baranes (1989) raise the question which Lave did not address, namely how then do you account for the differences between unschooled and schooled tailors. They astutely point out,

> Like the schooled bookies, the schooled tailors were successful in solving the nonpractical problems not because experience with formal schooling allowed them to solve decontextualized problems nor because schooling provided them with general problem-solving skills, but because the nonpractical problems were similar to school problems, and, after years of schooling, they had become skillful school-problem solvers. The point here is that the problems themselves must be carefully examined, as well as the practical experience of the subjects ... all practical experiences are not necessarily equivalent, and some experiences may allow for better performance on school tasks than others. (282)

It is precisely this perspective that has informed my research. It is precisely this perspective that distinguishes this study from others who argue for the inclusion of culturally sensitive literature in schools (with the notable exception of Taylor 1982).

Using Culturally Familiar Texts in Classrooms

I have been able to identify only a few studies which look directly at teaching culturally sensitive texts, specifically texts of African American literature to African American students. To my dismay, each of the studies has serious limitations. It is no wonder that no empirical evidence has been garnered in support of this position.

Harris (1989) reports the results of a study conducted with a group of third-, fourth-, and fifth-grade students who were primarily African American. The study was based on the basic premises of reader-response theory and evaluated student engagement with selected texts of African American children's literature based on the response typology of Purves and Rippere (1968). Harris looked at four broad categories of responses: engagement; perception of the work as an object distinct from the reader; interpretation, i.e., generalizing about the work; and finally evaluation, i.e., statements about what the reader thinks is good and/or bad about the work. Harris was only able to report that students liked the readings and that responses were generally at the level of engagement or involvement.

One limitation of this study is its lack of any control group with which to contrast the responses of the children. There is no way of determining whether the children's responses of engagement or involvement would be any different with other texts which fell into the same genre categories, i.e., adventure stories, scary stories, etc. In addition, the strategies used by the teacher were not aimed at eliciting responses at the levels of interpretation and evaluation as identified by Harris. Even children as young as third through fourth graders can and need to be taught some interpretive strategies for reading stories, poems, and folktales—strategies that go beyond simple recall of plot episodes and emotional responses of like or dislike. Certainly, engagement, liking the literature, is an important variable in language-arts instruction. However, if the only point of a literature curriculum, even at the elementary school level, is to provide students with opportunities to read literature they would like, libraries should be sufficient for this aspect of schooling.

The ethnographic analysis of literature study groups of fifth- and sixth-grade students by Eeds and Wells (1989) provides not only a stark contrast to the purely recitative, teacher-dominated talk reported in Harris's study, but Eeds and Wells (1989) also provide one among many reported models of middle school students engaging literary texts with sophistication, subtlety, and depth. The instructional design for presenting works to students reported in the Harris study was apparently only aimed at engagement.

Scott (1989) investigated whether the selection of literature would significantly influence literal and inferential comprehension of tenth-grade students.

Although the Scott (1989) study did not deal directly with the question of African American or other ethnically rooted literature, I looked at the study because the question of literature content was relevant to my concerns. Scott's hypothesis was not confirmed, again due to an incomplete research design. There did not appear to be any direct relationship between the nature of the instruction around the texts in question and the instruments used to measure achievement along the variables of literal and inferential comprehension. Certainly, Hillocks (Hillocks and Ludlow 1984) has provided convincing evidence that both literal and inferential comprehension have significant distinctions within each category. The second weakness of this study was that measures were taken before and after instruction, but no mention is made of any information, field notes or otherwise, which account for what went on between the pre- and post-tests.

BEV and Reading Comprehension

During the decades of the 1960s and 1970s, questions about relationships between proficiency in Black English Vernacular (BEV) and reading achievement abounded. The preponderance of the research assumed that proficiency in Black English Vernacular was a handicap to reading and writing achievement, even when the linguistic perspective was one of difference rather than deficit (Baratz 1969; DeStefano 1977; Hall and Freedle 1975; Stewart 1969). The present study stands in contrast to that tradition in that it posits proficiency in Black English Vernacular as a strength rather than a weakness.

In a recent study, Hobson (1987) looked at whether proficiency in Black English Vernacular would interfere with achievement in reading among third- and fourth-grade students. The research did not confirm her hypothesis that Black English Vernacular speakers would not have greater difficulty becoming successful readers of Standard English than those who spoke Standard English. The results were mixed.

The study was seriously flawed. The hypothesis of the research presumes a simplistic relationship between proficiency in Black English Vernacular and achievement in reading (for excellent overviews of this question, see Hall and Guthrie 1980; Delpit 1990; and Farr 1991). The study does not appear to take into account the capacity of students to switch registers and dialects. Proficiency in Black English Vernacular was measured by the Black Language Assessment Test. A measure on the Black Language Assessment Test used in this study does not necessarily preclude mastery of so-called Standard English. It does not appear that any comparative measures were used to assess students' strengths in both BEV and Standard English. The only two variables reported in the design of the study were scores on the Black Language

Assessment Test and student reading achievement scores. Students were selected with above, on, and below grade-level reading scores. Without any naturalistic observation of reading classes in which these students participated or the collection of data about other possibly relevant variables which might impact reading achievement, any statistical correlations obtained between proficiency in Black English Vernacular and standardized scores of reading achievement are incomplete. As the design stands, there is no way of determining what variables might mediate any statistical relationship between proficiency in Black English Vernacular and scores on a reading achievement test.

This tradition of research differs from my own in that it focuses on the phonology, syntax, and lexicon of Black English Vernacular, while the present study focuses on broader discourse features. This body of research and the Hobson study are still relevant, however, because they place the on-going concerns about Black English Vernacular and reading achievement in a historical perspective. In addition, reactions to signifying in classroom contexts will inevitably be associated with the attitudes of practitioners toward Black English Vernacular.

Bloome (1981) completed an ethnographic investigation of the reading activities of six black junior high school students. Although Bloome's study does not consider the issue of achievement, of importance is its assertion that the socio-communicative context of reading activities is an important variable in planning instruction and evaluation. For the purposes of this study, Bloome's work is significant because classroom observations revealed that signifying was not only part of the texts the students read, but was also a fundamental part of their classroom interactions. Such interactional patterns may cause discomfort for some teachers, especially novice teachers and teachers who are not African American. In contrast to such negative valuations of BEV patterns, Paznik (1976) analyzed what she called the artistic or aesthetic dimensions of Black English and argued that the discourse model she describes would be useful in developing curriculum. However, the recommendations she makes for curriculum were not empirically tested.

From this diverse body of research, two fundamental precepts emerge: Cultural knowledge and language use are important variables in successful reading, and text conventions need to be mastered for successful reading. Any argument for the efficacy of ethnically rooted literature in school curriculum must address both of these variables with specificity and must emerge from research which is carefully designed and evaluated.

5 Research Design and Implementation

Hypotheses

This study investigated the implications of signifying, a form of social discourse in the African American community, as a scaffold for teaching skills in literary interpretation. This investigation is related to the larger question of the efficacy of culturally sensitive instruction. The study was aimed at providing insights into the following questions:

1. Do prior social knowledge and knowledge of signifying affect students' range of skills in reading and interpreting fiction?
2. Using their prior social knowledge and skill in signifying, how do students construct generalizations about African American "speakerly" texts based on an analysis of the figurative language of such texts?
3. What roles do the organization and focus of instruction play in helping students use their skill in signifying and their prior social knowledge?
4. How do teachers support this scaffolding process?

The hypotheses of this research are that students' prior social knowledge of the themes, values, and social conventions on which the texts are based and their skill in signifying may be productively drawn upon to teach skills in literary analysis. The skills in literary analysis are based on "A Taxonomy of Skills in Reading and Interpreting Fiction" developed by Hillocks (Hillocks 1980; Hillocks and Ludlow 1984). The hypotheses assert that students with appropriate prior social knowledge and skill in signifying will make gains in the broad category of inferential levels of comprehension. Specifically, I hypothesize that students will achieve gains in the difficult reading category of complex implied relationships. Hillocks (Hillocks 1980; Hillocks and Ludlow 1984) has shown that this skill is more difficult to master because the generalizations are not stated in any one passage, but rather must be constructed by generalizing across multiple passages. In addition, the reader must be able to identify those passages which are relevant to the issue under question. The ability to carry out such analytical processes has not been mastered by the majority of American students (Mullis, Owens, and Phillips 1990; Langer 1984; Purves 1984).

The argument rests on three core assumptions:

1. the cultural codes of the literary texts provide a potential advantage for interpretation;

2. the socio-cultural knowledge base of the students and the cultural codes of the texts are only a potential affinity, not an automatically operable relationship. This potential may most effectively be actualized through inquiry-based instruction (Hillocks 1982, 1986, 1987);

3. the prior social and linguistic knowledge must be specifically and explicitly tapped through instruction.

Design

A total of six classes participated in the project. Four classes were taught an experimental instructional unit, the objective of which was to build upon the signifying skill of the students in order to teach strategies for interpreting fiction. Two classes served as controls or no-treatment classes and maintained their normal curricular routines.

All classes were given three tests before any instruction began: one test on a story they had never read, with questions that reflect the Hillocks hierarchy of reading skills applicable to the interpretation of fiction; a test which reliably estimated their knowledge of and skill in signifying; and a test which attempted to measure the kinds of prior social knowledge they brought to the texts. At the end of the instructional period, another test was given on a story they had never read, with questions again reflecting the same hierarchy of reading skills applicable to the interpretation of fiction. Students read the stories in class and were encouraged to support their answers with examples from the text.

Change scores by treatment from pre- to post-test were subjected to one-tailed T tests to ascertain significance. Three sets of regressions were done with change score, pre-test, and post-test scores, each serving as the dependent variable in each equation. A one-way analysis of variance (ANOVA) was carried out to determine the statistical significance of the correlations generated out of the regression analyses. Scores on signifying and prior knowledge were the independent variables in each analysis. Additional analyses were conducted with high and low scores on signifying and prior knowledge regressed on pre-, post-, and change scores. This was done in order to distinguish any differential effects among groups.

Staff

I taught one experimental class in each of the two schools. Four other teachers, regular employees of the district, participated in the project. Two teachers taught the two experimental classes and the other two taught the two control classes. Table 1 below provides data on the experience and training of all teachers. All teachers participating in the project volunteered. The teachers were recruited by the chairperson of the English department in Corrigan High School (pseudonym) and the director of curriculum in Fairgate High School (pseudonym). All participating teachers were veterans in the system and all had advanced professional degrees in their field.

The Schools

Over a period of six weeks, six classes from two urban high schools participated in this project. Fairgate School and Corrigan School were in an urban center and suffered from the typical problems of urban schools: low achievement scores in reading, high absenteeism, low graduation rates relative to the size of the freshman class that entered four years prior, and problems keeping the violence of the surrounding community out of the school. Table 2, Table 3, and Table 4 summarize data from the most recent state report card on each

Table 1

Experience and Training of Participating Teachers

	Exp 1	Exp. 2	Control 1	Control 2
Degrees (major)	B.A. (English)	B.S. (Speech)	B.A. (English)	B.A. (English)
		M.S. (Reading)	M.S. (English)	M.A. (English)
		M.S. (Admin. and Supervision)	Ph.D. (English)	M.A. + 15 (Writing)
Years teaching	25	25	17	25
Years at present school	19	12	10	21

Table 2

Profile of Student Population of Participating Schools
(in percent)

	Fairgate High School	Corrigan High School
Racial/ethnicity (black)	99.9	100.0
Low income	34.0	26.4
Attendance rate	83.0	87.0
Student mobility	23.5	22.4
Graduation rate	39.8	50.9

school. As Table 2 indicates, both schools have student populations that are practically all African American. The relatively low graduation rates are comparable to that of the district and to graduation rates of other large urban districts with high proportions of minority and poor students (Lomotey 1990; Wilson 1987). The attendance rates of 83 percent and 87 percent mask the problems of class cutting. Finally, the moderate percentage (34 percent and 26.4 percent) of low-income families in the two schools belies the stereotyped notion that problems of school achievement and school climate are primarily the result of poverty.

Table 3

Standardized Test Data on Participating Schools
Percentage of Student Population by Quartile
Grade 11–State Goal Assessment by Progress (GAP)
Reading (1988 Norms)

	Fairgate High School (%)	Corrigan High School (%)
Top 25 percent	6.5	12.3
3rd 25 percent	17.7	21.5
2nd 25 percent	39.7	35.4
Bottom 25 percent	36.2	30.8

Table 4

Standardized Test Data on Participating Schools
Percentage of Student Population by Quartile
Test of Achievement and Proficiency (TAP)*
Grade 11–Reading Comprehension (1988 Norms)

	Fairgate High School (%)	Corrigan High School (%)
Top 25 percent	1.6	3.1
3rd 25 percent	11.8	12.2
2nd 25 percent	31.8	27.8
Bottom 25 percent	54.9	56.9
Percentage taking test	63.0	89.4

* Published by the University of Iowa.

Tables 3 and 4 summarize the results of mandated achievement tests. The GAP is a state-mandated test,[1] while the Test of Achievement and Proficiency (TAP) is a district-mandated test. At every quartile, students perform better on the GAP. The two tests are organized around different principles of test construction: the TAP is the more traditional design, while the GAP includes longer reading passages and the choice of more than one right answer. In addition, a student's score takes into consideration what prior knowledge the student has about the topic of a passage.

Participating Students

Reading scores were one dimension used to evaluate where students were at the beginning of instruction. Figure 1 shows the overall trend for the entire population. Although scores were not available for 28 percent of the entire population, the distribution for the remaining students was negatively skewed. Most of the remaining students scored below the 50th percentile rank. Forty-one percent of the students scored in the first quartile, that is, with percentile ranks in reading at the 25th percentile or below. Unfortunately, these trends are typical not only of this urban school district, but of most school districts in large urban areas (Langer, Applebee, Mullis, and Foertsch 1990). Figure 2 shows virtually no overall difference between the reading scores of the control and experimental groups.

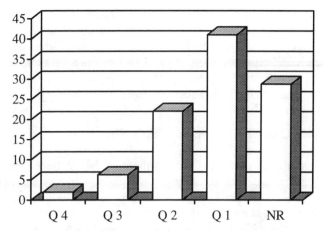

Figure 1. Reading Percent Across Groups by
Quartile. National Percentile Ranks.

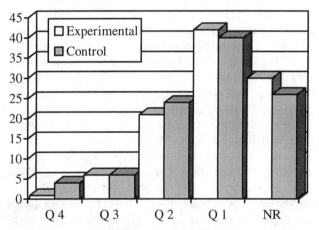

Figure 2. Reading Scores by Treatment Group
National Percentile Ranks by Quartile

One of the experimental classes was called "Topics in World Literature."
The students enrolled in this class had poor academic records and many had
previously failed some English class during their high school careers. The
control class, which turned out to constitute the vast majority of control
students to take both the pre- and post-tests, had been held together as a cohort
across their four years of high school because of their motivation and hard

work in school. This class had five students (17.8 percent) with reading scores from the district's standardized achievement test above the 50th national percentile rank, but the vast majority of these students had reading scores which were consistent with the pattern of low scores across all six classes. Only one experimental class had a comparable number of students with reading scores above the 50th percentile (four, or 13.3 percent).

Instructional Unit for Experimental Treatment

The instructional unit was designed with four phases. In the first phase students examine data sets. Teachers provide students with samples of signifying dialogues. These dialogues serve as data sets for examination by the students. The students respond to the following four questions: (1) Does each speaker mean exactly and literally what each says? (2) How do you know? (3) What does each speaker actually mean? (4) How do you know?

The teacher lists the strategies students articulate as answers to the questions of how they know that the speaker doesn't mean what the words appear to mean when interpreted literally and what the speaker actually does mean. The teachers need to state strategies as generalizations rather than simply as observations of a particular instance. For example, in the dialogue where the husband who works as a garbage man tells his wife he's going to work in a suit and tie, the student is expected to generalize that the man is acting out of the ordinary rather than only to describe the specific discrepancies of this one case. The purpose of this phase of the instructional unit is to tap explicitly students' prior social and linguistic knowledge. The examination of data sets in order to generate strategies and concepts is a fundamental part of inquiry-based instruction (Hillocks 1982, 1986, 1987).

In the second phase of the instructional unit, the goal is to expand the students' metalinguistic knowledge about signifying and its properties. Students read two expository articles, one about signifying, "Signifying, Loud Talking and Marking," by Mitchell-Kernan (1981) and "Nobody Mean More to Me Than You and the Future Life of Willie Jordan," by Jordan (1988). Students learn names and characteristics of different categories of signifying. In the third phase, students work in small groups to write their own signifying dialogues.

The fourth phase of the instructional unit involves application. The students apply the strategies they articulate in the first phase of the unit to the short story, "My Man Bovanne," by Toni Cade Bambara, and the opening chapter of *Their Eyes Were Watching God,* by Zora Neale Hurston. The purpose of this activity is to focus students' attention on determining what details they should pay attention to and how they should interpret those details. The design of the unit presumes that the interpretive strategies generated by the students may be used to detect and interpret significant figurative details. Students use worksheets to record details they deem important. The four sets of worksheets cover the following: monitoring important relationships between characters; following the unfolding of a character's personality; following important figurative language; and monitoring images, colors, sounds, and textures. The assumption behind this and the final phase of the instructional unit is that the focus of the first two phases will prepare students to actualize the potential link between the cultural codes of the texts and their own social and linguistic knowledge.

In the final stage of application, students read and interpret two novels, *Their Eyes Were Watching God* by Hurston (1935) and *The Color Purple* by Alice Walker (1982). Working in both whole and small groups, students talk and write about inferential questions aimed at promoting a close reading of the text. Students also generate questions of their own about the texts and discuss these questions in small groups.

The instructional unit is characterized by the following:

1. small-group discussions;
2. discussions focusing on student-generated questions (samples of student-generated questions on *The Color Purple* are discussed in Chapter 9);
3. the articulation of a set of criteria by which students would deem a passage worthy of additional investigation;
4. reading about, talking about, and thinking about signifying;
5. focus on the talk in the text—either by characters or the narrator—which is assumed to convey generalizations necessary to the construction and evaluation of themes, symbols, and significant relationships; such talk in the works in question is characterized as figurative language (metaphorical or proverbial talk);
6. emphasis in whole- and small-group discussion on students justifying interpretations through reference to both the text and real world knowledge, emphasis on elaboration of support for points of view by both much talk and writing.

Researcher's Role as Participant-Observer

My role as participant-observer was influenced by the reservations expressed by Barr (1986) about university-based classroom research. Barr asserts that experimental studies of classroom reading instruction should also include naturalistic observations in order to document both student and teacher strate-gies, as well as how new teaching strategies are incorporated. Barr is particu-larly concerned that experimental studies which advocate new instructional strategies be sensitive to the complex realities of everyday teaching.

I served as a teacher in order to provide a model for other teachers in the project, drawing on the research supporting peer coaching as an effective tool for teacher in-service (Garman 1986, 1987; Goldhammer, Anderson, and Krajewski 1980; Schon 1983, 1987). I reasoned that active teaching would allow me to anticipate problems in implementation. I anticipated problems in how to use the signifying dialogues, how to handle the problems of discussing raunchy dialogue in the signifying as well as in both novels, especially the sexually explicit scenes and descriptions in *The Color Purple*. Even though I had piloted the instructional unit with students who had just graduated from high school and were enrolled in an Upward Bound program in a local university, this experience was not the same as working in a high school. Secondly, I expected that establishing a peer bond with the other instructors would help to allay the experimental teachers' hesitations about the amount of reading required by the unit. Finally, as a researcher I would get to know firsthand what was required and involved in implementing such a program.

As an observer, I would make audiotapes of class sessions in order to document the differences between the experimental and control groups. Audiotapes and observations were made of each of the experimental classes and weekly observations and tapes were made of the control classes. Audio-tapes were partially coded. The coding structure looked at the nature of the teacher's scaffolding, how students refined, extended, supported, and chal-lenged one another, how students used both the text as well as prior social and linguistic knowledge to construct generalizations about the text as well as comments made by the students about the nature and pace of the instruction. Transcripts of classroom sessions would serve as a source of details about small-group interactions and about how students used and transformed their knowledge about signifying as well as social knowledge to interpret these "speakerly" texts.

I would also directly observe both experimental and control classrooms. The teachers whose classes I taught would serve as observers of those classes. Classroom observations were to include tallies of student turns at talk as well as the content and timing of classroom episodes and activity segments (Stodolsky 1989). Classroom episodes focus on the content and objectives of instruction while activity segments focus on the structure of activities in which both teachers and students are engaged. Field notes were to be kept of discussions with teachers and any general observations or personal reflections.

I regularly met with the two teachers participating in the experimental instruction in order for us to share observations on one another's classes, to evaluate the pace and effectiveness of the instruction, and to adjust teaching plans as needed. I met at least weekly with the two teachers whose classes were involved in the project as control classes in order to understand their instructional plans and to determine when it was best for me to observe their classes.

Note

1. The complete name of this test would identify the state. Since I choose to keep the district anonymous, I have withheld the full name of this state-mandated test.

6 Measurement Instruments

In order to test the hypotheses of this research, four measurement instruments were used: pre- and post-measures of achievement in literary interpretation and a measure of prior social knowledge were developed; a measure of skill in signifying was adapted from a prior study (Taylor 1982).

The pre- and post-measures of achievement in literary interpretation were modeled after the taxonomy of skills in reading and interpreting fiction developed by George Hillocks (1980, 1984). The pre- and post-tests were piloted for two reasons: in order to field questions which would form a hierarchical scale of difficulty and to find out if the pre- and post-forms proposed were comparable. To maximize the number of questions which could be piloted in a single sitting, two overlapping forms of the pre- and post-test were administered. Each form contained ten essay questions. Each question reflected one of the interpretive categories outlined by Hillocks. The questions provided for a range of responses and at the upper end would reveal students' ability to deal with the text as a whole. On the two forms, questions were distributed across reading categories as follows: one basic stated information, two key detail, one stated relationship, two simple implied relationship, four complex implied relationship, one structural generalization, one author's generalization, and one application. For the pilot post-test, two stated relationship questions were given. A total of fourteen questions were given on the pilot pre-test and a total of fifteen questions on the pilot post-test. Both instruments are included in the appendix. Forms A and B represent the questions piloted for the pre-test. Forms D and E represent the questions piloted for the post-test. As I noted earlier, the story used for the pre-test was excerpted from the chapter entitled "Winter" of *The Bluest Eye* by Toni Morrison (1970) and the story for the post-test was excerpted from the chapter entitled "seemothermotherisverynice" from the same novel.

The Rasch Rating Scale Model

To provide an objective measure of change in the interpretation of "speakerly" texts of African American fiction, I developed sets of literal and inferential questions that represented a hierarchical scale. The Rasch Rating Scale Model

(Wright and Stone 1979; Wright and Masters 1982) provided a model for developing such an instrument. The Rasch model allows one to estimate the difficulty of items as well as the ability of persons relative to the variable being measured such that these estimates might be ordered according to a common linear scale. Accurately generating such a scale is important in order to compare achievement across comparable tests, in this instance to compare achievement from the pre-test to the post-test. This common linear scale allows one to arrange items and persons along a continuum from the most easy items and least able persons to the most difficult items and the most able persons.

The basic measure for item difficulty and person ability is the logit. The Rasch model makes it possible ". . . to state probabilistically, that a person at a given position [along the linear continuum] should succeed on these items and fail on those items" (Hillocks and Ludlow, 17). Smith restates the significance of the logit: ". . . the logit [is] the log of the probability that an individual with ability at the origin of the scale will get the item right divided by the probability that he or she will get the item wrong. The easiest items have the most negative values. The most difficult questions have the highest positive values" (Smith 1987, 99). Calibrations are given in logits for both item difficulty and for person measures or person abilities.

The Rasch Rating Scale also allows one to determine whether a given item or person fits the assertions of the model:

> The basic data for the model are the person and item total correct scores. From these raw scores are computed the expected response for every person on each item. Person by item residuals are the difference between the observed and expected responses. (Hillocks and Ludlow 1984, 17)

A large residual (2 or above) indicates that either a person of high ability unexpectedly missed an easier question or a person of lower ability scored correctly on an item whose degree of difficulty is greater than the measure of the person's ability on that variable. High residuals are associated with either infit or outfit scores. Either indicates that the person or the item does not fit the model and that the test designer must look closely for the probable causes.

In summary, the Rasch Rating Scale Model allows one to test the reliability of a test design and to measure independently both the uniqueness of item difficulties on the test as well as the abilities of the persons taking the test. Standard measures of reading achievement do not focus on the specific skills of literary interpretation of concern in this study. Second, there are no standardized measures of the other two variables. Finally, the Rasch model allowed me to develop a common measure which could be used to compare across the pre- and post-tests and to independently measure each student's ability for each of the three variables.

Establishing the Tests

During the piloting, in two of the three classes, half of the students were given Form A and half Form B for the pre-test. A similar split of Forms D and E were distributed for the post-test during piloting. Once the students' answers to the pilot pre- and pilot post-tests were scored, a difficulty rating calibrated in logits was established for all the questions. In those categories for which only one question was piloted, of course, that question was used. For those categories for which more than one question was piloted, questions were chosen which yielded minimal standard errors and which would maximize the logit difference between categories on a single test and across categories for the two tests.

The purpose in using the Rasch analysis of item difficulties was to equate the pre- and post-tests. At the pilot phase, the eight questions chosen for the pre-test and the eight questions chosen for the post-test were comparable in terms of the mean item calibrations for each test. However, the comparability of item calibrations did not hold up across all eight reading categories. The question then was how to look at the test; how to determine what it would measure. If I looked only at mean difficulty as established by the average of the item calibrations of the eight questions on the pre-test and the eight questions on the post-test, then I could only reliably look at gross change across a single variable, that of reading comprehension of fictional texts. On the other hand, the hypotheses of the research clearly sought to distinguish effects in at least two broad categories of literal versus inferential comprehension and placed particular attention on the more difficult reading category of complex implied relationships. Therefore, it was important to maintain the validity and reliability of the categories. Thus, instead of approaching the tests as if they were comparable, even though in mean item difficulty they were not only comparable but the same for the pilot group, another approach was used. The item calibrations in the field group were anchored to the item difficulties in the pilot tests. This means that the probability of a person in the field group getting a question right or wrong (the basis of the logit calibration in Rasch scaling) was based on the actual item calibration for that item from the pilot tests. A more detailed explanation of the rationale for this move is available in the technical notes of the appendix.

In order to make comparisons within groups, i.e., pilot pre- to pilot post-tests, field pre- to field post-tests, analyses were conducted using only the measures of those persons who took both tests. There was considerable attrition in both the pilot group and the field group due to absenteeism. For the pilot group, only 19 persons completed both the pre- and post-test out of an original group of 43 persons. For the field group, only 77 persons completed both the pre- and the post-test out of an original group of 95 persons who took the pre-test. The testing period for each test lasted three days (four days for the pilot tests because of the number of questions). Thus a number of students were lost because of incomplete tests. They may have been present only one day of the three, for example. This held true despite the fact that I allowed an additional day of testing for those students in the pilot group who may have been absent during part of the regular testing period.

Table 5 lists the item difficulties, standard errors, and infit measures for each question on the pilot pre-test and the pilot post-test. They are listed according to the reading category being tested by each question. Separate calibrations of the pilot pre- and the pilot post-tests were done. It is clear that

Table 5
Summary of Rasch Model Statistics
Pilot Pre- and Pilot Post-Tests (N=19)

Item Type	Item Calibration			Stand. Error			Infit	
	Pre-	Post-		Pre-	Post-		Pre-	Post-
BSI	-3.67	-3.67		0.62	0.67		0.50	-0.50
KD	-1.73	-2.06		0.41	0.42		-0.80	-0.10
SR	-1.58	-0.55		0.40	0.36		-0.10	1.00
SIR	-0.08	-0.20		0.36	0.36		-1.60	-1.60
AG	1.05	1.73		0.44	0.52		-1.40	-1.50
APP	1.05	2.06		0.44	0.58		-1.40	-0.20
SG	3.21	1.25		0.85	0.45		-2.20	-0.70
CIR	4.21	3.21		1.24	0.96		-0.40	0.00
MEAN	0.31	0.22		0.60	0.54			

Mean Difference	Joint Standard Error	S. D.		T
		Pre-	Post-	
0.09	0.80	2.37	2.07	0.1125 Critical T 1.74 (D. F. =14)

Key: BSI–Basic Stated Information, KD–Key Detail, SR–Stated Relationship, SIR–Simple Implied Relationship, AG–Author's Generalization, APP–-Application, CIR–Complex Implied Relationship the mean item difficulties of the two tests for the pilot group are comparable. The difference in the means for item difficulty between the two tests is .09. With a joint standard error of .80, there is no difference in the overall difficulty of the items on these two tests.

The items range in a hierarchical order beginning with literal questions where the answers are not only directly stated in the text, but are also localized in one sentence or paragraph (i.e., Basic Stated Information, Key Detail, and Stated Relationship). These categories of questions have negative logit measures which indicate they are inherently easier questions. The next category in the scale is that of Simple Implied Relationship which has a borderline negative logit measure. Although this category is inferential, rather than literal, the details needed to make the inference are (like the literal questions) localized, usually in several sentences or a single paragraph. The remaining categories are inferential. They all have positive logit measures, increasing in difficulty. They represent the most difficult questions in the sequence because their answers are nowhere directly stated in the text, the details available to support an answer are spread across the text, and finally, they require generalizing about the text as a whole.

However, despite the fact that the overall difficulty of the two tests is the same, the difficulty of the items according to the variables they are purported to measure is not comparable across all eight categories. In order to determine which reading categories were statistically different, the mean item difficulty for each pair was plotted against the z statistic for each pair (Wright and Stone

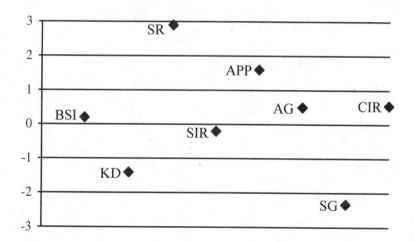

Figure 3. Plot of Pilot Mean Item Difficulty Against Z Statistic for Reading Pairs on Pilot Tests.

1979, 1990). Figure 3 is the plot of mean item difficulty for each pair of questions against the z statistic for each pair. This plot serves as a measure of the stability of the item calibrations. The z statistic is the standardized difference between the two item calibrations presumed to measure a single item difficulty. (See Wright and Stone [1979, 1990] for instructions on computing z statistic and detecting bias in item calibrations.) The plot shows that six of the eight reading categories are statistically comparable, but Stated Relationship and Structural Generalization differ in item difficulty from the pilot pre-test to the pilot post-tests by more than two standard errors in either direction.

Because the questions which measure Structural Generalization and Stated Relationship differ by more than two standard errors, the person measures of future groups, namely those students tested during the actual field conditions, were based on or anchored to the actual item difficulties for each question on the pilot pre-test and the pilot post-test. These allow calculations for measuring person abilities to take into account the differences in difficulty for these pairs. Remember the person measures are the result of a pattern of responses determined by the likelihood that this person would get a question of this difficulty right or wrong.

Although it would be simpler to calculate gain or loss between the two groups by equating the pre-test and post-test based on the fact that the overall difficulty between the two tests is comparable, such an analysis would only allow for comparisons of overall mean gain or loss. It would not allow for the more insightful analysis of gain and loss by reading category.

Why the Two Misfitting Pairs?

The z statistic greater than 2 indicates that the difference between two item calibrations is greater than two standard errors. It does not, however, explain why there is a difference. Wright and Stone (1979, 1990) acknowledge that both a qualitative as well as a quantitative analysis are required to explain item bias. Hillocks has acknowledged in personal communication that it is possible to have layers of difficulty within a given category of the hierarchy. The questions in the Stated Relationship category and the Structural Generalization category meet the qualitative criteria set out by Hillocks (1980; Hillocks and Ludlow 1984). The degree of difference in difficulty of the pairs of questions is an interaction of the structure and conventions of the stories themselves and the knowledge of particular narrative conventions which the readers bring to these texts.

The stated relationship question on the pre-test is "How was Maureen treated at school? Describe at least two examples to support your answer." The

pre-test story is taken from "Winter," from *The Bluest Eye* by Toni Morrison
(1970). It is easier for this population than the post-test question. How
Maureen Peal is treated at school is directly stated in one paragraph of the
story. However, it is also a big idea in the text that perseveres as an implied
idea throughout the story. The post-test question is "What old ideal and what
new ideal did the movies bring to Pauline?" The post-test story is taken from
"seemothermotherisverynice," also from *The Bluest Eye.* Although the answer
is directly stated in the story, this question involves a more subtle idea. The
answer appears in one place in the text and does not persevere as an implied
idea to the extent that the intended comparable item does. There was a greater
range of partial credit responses to this question. This is because raters gave
partial credit when a student identified or described either the new or the old
ideal. Often, when students were unable to locate the sentence that specifically
identified the new and old ideals that Pauline found in the movies, they
broadly interpreted the new ideal of physical beauty by describing Pauline's
idealization of Jean Harlow and Pauline's attempt to apply that ideal of beauty
to herself. This is clearly a more complex concept, even though the fact that
the old ideal of romantic love and the new ideal of physical beauty are directly
stated in the story.

There is a clear difference in the difficulty in the questions of the structural
generalization category. The post-test question is "Why is it important that
Pauline tell her own story as well as have an omniscient (all knowing) narrator
also tell the story? Support your answer with examples from the story." This
question may be easier because more students have a general notion of a
narrator. The pre-test question is "How does the description in the first paragraph relate to events that take place in the story?" Students found this
question more difficult. This is probably because the novice reader does not
presume unity in the text (Culler 1975; Rabinowitz 1987). Even if a relationship between sections in a text is not obvious, a literary stance assumes there
is a relationship which the author wishes the reader to uncover.

These observations do not either cast shadows on Hillocks's notion of an
inferential hierarchy, nor do they suggest that these questions do not fit the
Hillocks's categories. Rather, in the two categories which differ significantly,
I argue, the questions represent levels of difficulty within a single category.
With these differences, however, there is still an excellent spread of difficulty
across the eight questions of both exams. This spread of difficulty clearly
distinguishes literal-level questions (basic stated information, key detail,
stated relationships) from inferential-level questions (simple implied relationships, application, author's generalization, complex implied relationships and
structural generalization). As I expected, the structural generalization and
complex implied relationship questions consistently proved most difficult for
this population. This finding is consistent with the Hillocks model. Author's

generalization and application questions proved easier than indicated by the Hillocks taxonomy (1971, 1980). However, I believe this difference is due, in part, to the greater familiarity these students had with the social issues of these texts.

Scoring the Tests

The pilot tests, as well as the field tests, were scored by the same raters. Two independent raters scored each test. One rater is a former English teacher who now works in the publishing industry as an editor and has Master's degrees in both English and education. The other rater is a high school English teacher who has taught for over twenty-five years and who has a Master's degree through the Paideia training program at St. John's University in New Mexico.

All reading questions on the pre- and post-tests were answered in essay form. The purpose of the essay or short answer format as opposed to the multiple choice format was to both allow and promote a range of student responses and to determine the extent to which students were able to back up their points reasonably with examples from the text. Results on the two most recent NAEP assessments clearly show that skill in providing evidence to support one's point of view is seriously lacking among American students (Mullis, Owens, and Phillips 1990). It was important to see if students demonstrated evidence of an ability to generate reasonable interpretations to subtle questions regarding structural relationships between parts of the text, instances of ironic generalizations made by the author or narrator as well as themes and symbols within the text.

The questions in the first half of the pre- and post-tests were relatively literal types of questions. The second half of the questions was difficult and involved constructing generalizations that are nowhere directly stated within the text. Independent raters were instructed not to use issues of spelling and usage as criteria in scoring. Answering the question asked, being coherent, having an answer that was justifiable from the text (from the point of view of the two readers) and supporting answers, where appropriate, with examples from the text and/or one's prior social knowledge were the main criteria for rating an answer 0 (off target), 1 (on target, but incomplete or partially correct), and 2 (insightful, complete and supported).

For example, question 4 on the pre-test asked, "To what characteristics of winter is the father compared? Because of these comparisons, what do we learn about the father's personality?" This question was intended to test students' ability to answer questions about simple implied relationships. Questions in this category ask students to generalize a relationship that must be inferred from information that is localized in one section of the text, but is nowhere directly stated. In this instance, the father is not a significant character in the story. He is referred to only in one other paragraph later in the story. The reference to him at that point offers no evidence that would help interpret his character as represented in the opening paragraph of the story:

> My daddy's face is a study. Winter moves into it and presides there. His eyes become a cliff of snow threatening to avalanche; his eyebrows bend like black limbs of leafless trees. His skin takes on the pale, cheerless yellow of winter sun; for a jaw he has the edges of a snow-bound field dotted with stubble; his high forehead is the frozen sweep of the Erie, hiding currents of gelid thoughts that eddy in darkness. Wolf killer turned hawk fighter, he worked night and day to keep one from the door and the other from under the windowsills. A Vulcan guarding the flames, he gives us instructions about which doors to keep closed or opened for proper distribution of heat, lays kindling by, discusses qualities of coal, and teaches us how to rake, feed, and bank the fire. And he will not unrazor his lips until spring. (Morrison 1970, 47)

Students who enumerated details of the physical scene of winter such as a cliff of snow or leafless trees received no credit because they did not generalize characteristics of winter nor perceive the description as symbolic. The listing of details of the winter scene is merely a literal enumeration. Students who inferred characteristics of winter such as harshness or inflexibility were given full credit if they also attributed comparable attributes to the father and partial credit if they associated the characteristics with activities of the father. Partial credit was given because it was concluded that to make such generalizations about winter in and of itself was a difficult and localized inference. The appendix includes all test measures as well as samples of student's responses rated correct, partially correct, and wrong.

In order to establish consensus around appropriate responses, the researcher met with the raters. The criteria used for question 4 on the pre-test was established through the pre-scoring conversations between the researcher and the independent raters. Appropriate responses were discussed and a set of ten student papers were scored together. Then each rater independently read each of the remaining papers. Each rater would read all of the questions at a given level together. For example, all question 1's were read first, then all question 2's, etc. After each independent rater read all the tests (i.e., all the pilot pre-tests or the pilot post-tests, etc.), the two raters went back over the responses for which they had different ratings and reached consensus on each score. These were the scores used for the analysis. The rates of agreement between readers represent the level of agreement before consensus was reached over their differences. Percentages of rater agreement were calculated as the proportion of student responses on which raters assigned the same scores out of the total number of student responses. The following inter-rater agreements were obtained: pilot pre—89 percent; pilot post—92 percent; field pre—88 percent; field post—90 percent.

Measures of Skill in Signifying and Prior Social Knowledge

In addition to the tests of skill in interpreting literature, two additional measures were used: a test of skill in signifying and a test of prior social knowledge. The test of skill in signifying was taken from a prior study by Marsha Taylor-DeLain (Taylor 1982) on the effects that skill in a particular form of signifying called sounding had on the ability to interpret figurative language. The test used in this study is included in Appendix C. Taylor-DeLain used seventh-grade white and black students as the cohort. In the Taylor-DeLain study, the criteria for correct answers were similar to the criteria used in this study. However, she used the ratings of the seventh-grade cohort about the signifying skill of their peers as one of the criteria in grading responses.

Because the cohort in this study was high school seniors, I attempted to impose a more stringent ceiling on the range of appropriate responses by using the responses of five adult experts as the gauge by which the student responses would be evaluated. These five adults were experts in African American literature, experts in signifying and its use in African American literature as well as signifiers themselves. They included three professional poets whose writings are characterized by use of Black English and signifying, one literary critic who is also a full professor at a large midwestern state university, and a journalist who is very "street wise." Each expert completed the signifying test completely independently of other experts or the researcher. The signifying test was scored independently by one of the five experts and the researcher. A set of ten tests was scored together by the independent rater and the researcher, using the responses of the experts as the gauge for assigning full, partial, or no credit to responses. After scoring each test separately, consensus was reached on those answers for which scores did not match. The inter-rater agreement of 94 percent represents the degree of agreement before any attempts to reach consensus. The percentage of rater agreement was calculated as the proportion of student responses on which raters assigned the same scores out of the total number of student responses. Full credit for an answer received 2 points, partial credit received 1 point, and an incorrect answer was scored 0.

Section 1 of the signifying test had six sentences. Each sentence represented a figurative insult with the tenor of the comparison left out. The student was to fill in a word which appropriately describes the basis of the comparison. An example is "You so _____ the sun refuses to shine on your face!" An answer which refers to how black or ugly the person is received full credit. An answer which referred to light received partial credit and one which referred to bright received no credit. The full range of appropriate responses was provided by the experts. Responses which all five experts listed were full-credit answers. Those criteria which at least 60 percent of the experts listed were partial-credit answers.

Section 2 of the signifying test had six sentences. Each was a sound or a playful insult based on figurative language or comparisons. An example is "If brains were money, you'd be on welfare." The student was to write what the sentence means so that a visitor from another world hearing the insult would understand. The same process of determining full credit and partial credit was used.

The third section of the signifying test had ten questions. The directions for this section were as follows (Taylor 1982):

> If the first person says something insulting to you, what would be a good response? Keep in mind that you want to get the best of your opponent. Write down the first thing that comes to your mind.

These responses were judged by two criteria: first, whether the comparison made in the student's response held together as a simile or metaphor; and second, by the pithiness of the response. Because signifying is so widespread in the African American community, many sounding slurs are almost ritualized. Therefore, creativity and originality were taken into consideration in scoring. Responses which were repeated often were given partial credit, while responses which were original were given full credit.

In section 4, students were given an insulting remark or sound and were asked to rate four responses that were given on a scale from 1 (the best) to 4 (the worst).

> If the first person says: Yo momma so old she got cobwebs under her arms! Then the second person should respond by saying:
> a. Your momma so old she can't fit all the candles on her birthday cake!
> b. Your momma so old her wrinkles got wrinkles!
> c. Your momma so old she shook hands with Abraham Lincoln!
> d. The cobwebs under your momma's arms got cobwebs because she so old!

Because there was insufficient agreement among the experts who responded on the order of these responses, this section of the test was dropped. It was felt that the reliability on this section would be questionable.

The purpose of the prior-knowledge test was to determine whether there was a body of knowledge about social values and social relationships which these students held about the world that had some relationship to the social values and social relationships addressed in the two novels used. This was a very difficult test to develop.

The test is divided into three sections. The first section contains nine vocabulary words which students are asked to match with another list of words. The match is based on associations rather than definitions per se.

Questions 5 through 9 are words which have several "right" answers. There-fore, students were asked to tell why they chose an answer. This was done in order to tap the students' reasoning as well as allow for the possibility that a student could come up with an association which was culturally sound but not anticipated in the design of the test. Two of those questions were misfits under the Rasch scaling. These two questions included the vocabulary words "pressed" and "the devil's music." Pressed may have posed problems since pressing the hair straight with a hot comb is a dated form of hair care and it is possible that adolescents used to perms and chemical curls may not be familiar with pressing. This may especially be true for young men. "The devil's music" may have misfit because some students associated the phrase with the term "kinky." The definition of kinky as sexually perverse or eccen-tric is a more recent phenomenon and is not traditional within the African American community. However, young people who are involved with "rock" may associate kinky with sexual extremes or perversion more than with nappy or tightly curled hair. The root of this association with "the devil's music" results from the claim of some that devil worshipers put subliminal messages in some forms of rock music. This association with devil's music was given no credit. Perhaps, had it received at least partial credit, this item would not have misfit. Because the vocabulary section was a matching test with pre-identified appropriate answers, this section was scored by the re-searcher.

The second section of the prior-knowledge test consisted of seven prov-erbs. Proverbs were chosen for two reasons. First, using proverbs in order to socialize is both common in the African American community (Daniel, Smitherman-Donaldson, and Jeremiah 1987) and is also a strategy used in both novels by key characters who make a point by telling a proverb. Second, a major thesis of this research is that African American students process figurative language as part of normal discourse which arises out of Black English and that speakerly texts within the African American literary tradition also make extensive use of figurative language in order to convey themes, create symbols and represent characterization. The proverbs and their inter-pretations were taken directly from Geneva Smitherman's *Talkin and Testifyin* (1977). Further reliability was given to the accepted interpretations as the five experts who independently took the prior knowledge test all gave the same interpretations to each proverb. The students were asked to interpret the proverbs by restating them in their own words. Four of the proverbs were very familiar and known to be used, especially by grandmothers, to socialize children:

The Lord don't like ugly.

A hard head make a soft behind.

> If you make yo bed hard, you gon have to lie in it.
>
> You don't believe fat meat is greasy.

All of these proverbs had negative item calibrations, which indicates the students were familiar with them. Two of the proverbs were more obtuse and in less frequent use and therefore ended up with the highest item calibration for difficulty on the entire test.

> Grits ain't groceries, eggs ain't poultry, and Mona Lisa was a man.
>
> If I tell you a hen dip snuff, look under its wing and find a whole box.

The "grits ain't groceries" proverb was the most difficult because there is an unstated preface or premise which precedes it which is 'If I'm not telling the truth, then. . . .'

The third section of the prior-knowledge test consisted of nine passages taken from the two novels read during the unit of instruction. For each passage, 1 to 4 questions were asked. The answers to these questions were not stated anywhere in the passage. Rather, students had to rely on their own prior social knowledge in order to answer the question. In order to mask passages from *The Color Purple* which might be familiar to students who saw the film version of the book, the names of characters in each passage were changed. Below is an example of questions in this section:

> Jesse tell me all his love business now. His mind on Carol Butler day and night.
>
> "She pretty," he tell me. "Bright."
>
> "Smart?" I ask.
>
> "Naw. Bright skin."
>
> What does Jesse mean by bright skin?

The core ideas about what social knowledge might be relevant to the novels in question were generated by many long conversations with critic Joyce Joyce. The key ideas which were distilled into the questions included issues related to self-esteem and color, hair, childrearing, Black English, and the effects of racism on social relations both within the black community and between Whites and Blacks.

The questions on the prior-knowledge test were piloted among a group of five young people (ages 18–25) who worked at a publishing company which specializes in African American literature, a class of average high school seniors at one of the participating high schools, and an integrated class of college freshmen enrolled in an African American literature class at a midwest state university. As a result of the piloting, four of the vocabulary words and one of the passages were eliminated from the actual field test. They were

Table 6

Summary of Rasch Model Statistics
Signifying Test (N=71), Prior Knowledge (N=56)

	Mean	S. E.	S. D.	Per. Sep.*	Item Sep.**
Signifying	0.97	0.43	0.82	0.78	0.97
Prior knowledge	0.39	0.30	0.58	0.78	0.93

Note: Mean, Standard Error, and Standard Deviation are measures of person ability in logits. * Person separation reliability . ** Item separation reliability.

eliminated because, based on the pilot-test responses, there was too great a range of plausible answers for these questions.

As with the other measurement instruments, the test of skill in signifying and the test of prior social knowledge were both subjected to Rasch scaling. This was done in order to create a single linear measure which could then be used to establish reliability and statistical significance. Also, the Rasch scaling allows one to determine how easy or difficult each question was for this population and to determine the order and range of item difficulty. As indicated by Table 6, the item separation reliabilities of 0.97 for the signifying test and 0.93 for the test of prior social knowledge indicate that there is an excellent range of difficulty across the items on these tests for this population. Also, the person-separation reliabilities for each test, listed in Table 6, suggest a good range of abilities which these students brought to these tests. The person-separation reliability for both the signifying test and the prior-social-knowledge test was 0.78.

For both the signifying test and the prior-social-knowledge test, there were four misfitting items for each test. Misfitting items are those which were either easy for students which the model predicted would get the questions wrong or difficult for students which the model predicted would get the questions right. These items were dropped from the test. The items dropped as misfits (i.e., infit score of 2+) from the prior-knowledge test were all from the vocabulary section of the test. This may be because vocabulary changes from generation to generation.

7 Observations of the Instructional Process

My Role as Participant Observer

Perhaps because of my twenty-one years of classroom teaching experience, I experienced some tensions in trying to disentangle the two roles of teacher/participant and objective researcher. There were moments when I felt that time needed for teaching-related responsibilities was shifted to tasks I required as a researcher. After I would talk with one of the participating teachers as a peer, I would feel awkward stealing time as quickly as possible to record the salient details of our talk. When I broached the issue of keeping personal journals to one of the teachers of an experimental class, she quickly refused!

Still, as a researcher, I felt there was no more effective way to understand intimately what the implementation of this project involved. The project was controversial for many reasons. The debates concerning Black English in classrooms are emotional and deep seated (Delpit 1990; Rist 1970; Smitherman-Donaldson 1988a). Initiating the instructional strategies employed in the teaching unit has been difficult at best (Hillocks 1986; Mullis, Owens, and Phillips 1990). Both of the experimental-group teachers had flatly warned me in advance that their students would not read two novels in six weeks, especially if they were expected to read at home. Finally, I had nightmares about irate parents accusing me of teaching an obscene book in the form of *The Color Purple*. Because of these controversies and tensions, I am glad I taught. I believe my teaching under similar conditions helped to establish a bond with all of the participating teachers and served to validate my role as a researcher and observer in a school district that is daily maligned in the public media. One of the control-group teachers told me that her daughter had warned her not to serve as a control in the study. The daughter, who was about to begin student teaching, told her that the purpose of the control teacher was to "have somebody to bash." Although I fear I may have met the daughter's expectations, I have certainly tried to present the practices I observed within the framework that produced them, understanding not only the difficult circumstances under which these teachers worked, but also the assumptions and objectives which informed their practice, many of which I share. The fundamental disagreement I have, however, is that the teaching practices, on the whole, which I observed do not achieve the lofty goals these teachers have for their students.

One class in particular seemed to exemplify what were both my worst fears about teaching and my greatest hope for the project. Mrs. Hayden, who normally taught this class and who served as one of the teachers of an experimental group, had warned me of a bumpy ride. The experimental class called "Topics in World Literature" proved most difficult for me personally. I taught this class along with one other experimental class. It became quite evident by the third week that these students were simply not going to do any homework. One student asked me when I was going to leave. I had to put several students out of the classroom at one point in order to maintain order. Many of these students had deep-seated problems. One young man was twenty years old and still in high school. Another fell asleep almost every day. I came to find out that he was leaving school and getting home by 2:30 PM, going to night school at 5 PM in order to make up a failure of a prior English class, and finally going to work by 8 PM, and returning home from work by 1 AM. The pace eventually affected his health and he nearly passed out in class one day. Homework was virtually an impossible task for this young man, despite his good intentions. Eventually, I compromised, and we read *Their Eyes Were Watching God* out loud in class.

These were also students who had learned to live with violence. On one of the days the post-test was being given, some of the students were not in class in order to attend the funeral of a friend, a student who died as a result of being beaten with a lead pipe. When faced with a challenging question on the day of the funeral, one young man who had made great strides during the instruction simply refused to attack the question. Jim, another young man in the class, was out for four days during the period of post-testing because he had been hit in the head with a glass bottle while riding in a car and required nineteen stitches. Despite the immense problems I had with this class, the experience of working with them was both rewarding and enlightening, and they achieved mean gain beyond both control classes.

Unfortunately, this climate of violence was not limited to the one class. Although violence appeared to be a reality in the lives of many of the students, particularly the young men, the school was not beset with violence. Uniformed police were on duty and always visible. I was told that the school administration had worked hard to keep gangs out. In the second high school, there were at least five acts of violence over the course of the six weeks I was there. The administration was new and was faced with many problems, each requiring immediate attention. Although there were uniformed police assigned to the school, they were not as visible as the police in the first school. Three acts of violence occurred in one day—one in a class taught by the teacher of one of the control groups (although not one of the participating classes). All involved female students: in one case a girl was stabbed, in another a girl was hit in the head with a metal lock, and in the third a girl's head was slammed against a locker door.

The second incident occurred in one of Mrs. Hemingway's classes, although not the control class in the study. I visited her control class that same day. She was visibly shaken, with blood stains still on her foot and traces of blood on the floor near the door. In amazement, Mrs. Hemingway recounted the gruesome details of the scene, wondering how girls, in particular, could be so violent. She rightly asserted that she had not been trained to serve as a policeman, but as a teacher, and that she was not sure how long she could continue. Interestingly, on the teacher questionnaire given at the end of the project, the instructional objectives listed by Mrs. Hemingway all related to values promoting human understanding. As noted in the chapter on "Talk in the Classroom," when I observed discussions in her classroom, they were always exchanges of personal opinions about value-related themes. I believe that Mrs. Hemingway's instructional strategies, as I observed them, were sometimes an accommodation on her part that involved no challenges, no discomfort for students, and created, therefore, a safe and calm atmosphere in which she could work. Without adequate support for skills she already possessed at some level (for example, Mrs. Hemingway had been trained in teaching Socratic seminars), I can certainly empathize with the stance she has chosen.

In both schools, elaborate precautions were taken to identify nonstudents and to prevent their entry into the schools because of the very real danger of violence. I share these frightening stories only because they underscore the importance of the academic gains evidenced by this research. It is difficult to teach in urban schools such as these. It is also difficult to carry out educational research in dangerous environments. Yet, clearly one of the major crises in American education today is present in classrooms of such schools. Whatever answers educational research can offer will demand that researchers take up the struggle too. I also offer these personal observations to acknowledge that entering the fray is not an easy matter.

Implementation Issues

Teachers

I will not attempt to describe in any detail the range of unanticipated variables which influenced instruction; however, I think it important to at least mention some of them. The two teachers participating in the experimental unit were very different. Mrs. Payne was used to working with small, peer-discussion groups. It seemed part of her teaching style to allow students the time and opportunity to venture tentative answers and to work collectively to construct meanings. Mrs. Hayden, the other teacher, was used to whole-class instruction entirely, and tended in her teaching style to want to tell students what they should know. In a teacher questionnaire given at the end of the project, Mrs. Hayden acknowledged that small-group work was different from her normal instructional strategies. In the opening discussion of the first story in the unit, "My Man Bovanne" by Toni Cade Bambara, 43 percent of student responses to Mrs. Hayden's questions were 1–3 words in length. Twenty-eight percent of the student responses were 1 line in length when transcribed. Mrs. Hayden's responses, on the other hand, averaged 3.7 lines. No student made a response longer than 5 lines—Mrs. Hayden's talk sometimes ran from 10 to 16 lines.

However, we established early-on a friendly rapport, and because she recognized her own teaching style and the limitations it placed on this kind of a unit, she adopted, over the course of the six weeks, a less controlling stance in the classroom. I met daily with Mrs. Hayden and we discussed the progress of instruction, including her instructional style. We discussed her class as well as the class of hers which I taught. On one occasion during the third week of instruction, when students were just beginning to work in small discussion groups, Mrs. Hayden rose from her desk with official green district notebook and pencil in hand, and towered over the first discussion group. She looked down at the group and said in her authoritative voice, "All right, what's your answer to the question?" Because we had a friendly rapport, I felt it was appropriate to whisper in her ear, "Let's step outside for a moment." We laughed in the hall as I mimicked her controlling stance with the group and suggested that she instead listen to the group talk and intercede only if she felt they needed prodding. She knew I respected her talents as a teacher and because she was a professional who understood that learning is a lifetime vocation, she listened, and returned to the classroom as a listener and a prodder rather than as an authoritative dispenser of information and the final evaluator of right and wrong.

I believe that the major impetus for this teacher to modify the teaching style with which she was most comfortable was that I continued on almost a daily basis to hammer home that her students would not be given a test of factual questions or even inferential essay questions on the novels read in class and taught by her. Rather, they would have to develop skills that they could apply independently to a short story that neither they nor the teacher had laid eyes on before the final exam. The fact that the class taught by Mrs. Hayden achieved the greatest gain of all participating classes is a testimony to her skill as a teacher and her willingness to incorporate different teaching strategies. I believe it also provides evidence of the benefits which may derive from content-specific support services for experienced teachers.

Table 7

Attendance Rates, Drops, and Students Available

Class	Total	Drops		Chr. Abs. *		Sts. Avail.**	
N (%)	N	N	%	N	%	N	%
E–1***	23	1	4	9	39	13	57
E–2	29	5	17	3	3	21	72
E–3	28	1	1	7	7	20	71
E–4	30	2	2	12	12	16	53
C–1	28	0	0	0	0	28	100
C–2	22	3	14	8	36	11	50
Total	160	12	8	39	24	109	68

* Chronic absences
** Students available
*** E–Experimental class #1, #2, etc., C–Control Class #1, #2, etc.

Thus, teachers' instructional style, their belief systems (Freeman and Porter 1988; Stodolsky 1989; Zancanella 1991), and the nature of support given to the teachers for implementing new instructional strategies and curriculum content were crucial considerations for the effectiveness of this unit. Specific recommendations for teacher training are given in the final chapter.

Students

Absenteeism was a problem in several of the classes. The second control class had an absenteeism rate of 36 percent. I did not realize this until after the implementation phase of the project. One of the experimental classes also had a high rate of absenteeism. Again, I did not realize this was a problem until after implementation. However, it was clear that the absenteeism for this class was due to its being the first period of the day, beginning at 8:00 AM. For whatever reason, absenteeism seems highest in this school for most classes at the first and last periods. The pre- and post-test scores for students who were chronically absent (10 days or more) were not used in the analysis. Table 7 shows that 24 percent of the students across all classes were chronically absent. I reasoned that if students missed two weeks of instruction out of six

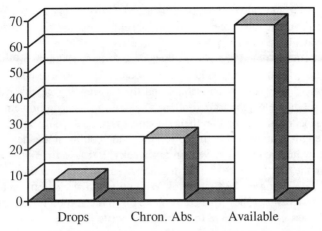

Figure 4. Summary Data of Drops, Chronic
Absences, and Available Cohort for All Students.

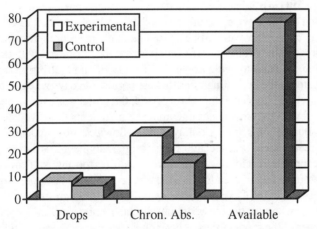

Figure 5. Summary Data of Drops, Chronic
Absences, and Available Cohort by Treatment.

weeks, one third of the instructional time, it was reasonable to assume that
they had missed too much to provide a meaningful contribution to the study.
Table 7 and Figure 4 represent the attendance rates, drop-out rates, and the
students available for participation in the project. These figures are given in
both raw numbers and percentages.

Figure 5 graphically contrasts all students by treatment along the dimensions of drop-out rate, rate of chronic absenteeism, and the percentage of students available to participate in the project.

As previously noted, the classes themselves were each quite different. The prior school history of the students, the social climate of the classroom, the environment provided by the school and the surrounding neighborhood (including the home neighborhood of each student) influenced implementation. Both teachers had warned that their students in the past would not read works of any length at home and both showed much incredulity at the idea that these students would read two novels in six weeks. Because time was always a problem, the first four weeks of instruction used up the instructional scaffolding and the reading of the first novel. With only two weeks left, each teacher asked the students if they wished to move on to the second novel, indicating that the class could continue to discuss and write about the first novel. The condition under which the students could move to the second novel was that they would have to read the entire second novel over what was then the upcoming four-day weekend. Three of the four classes readily agreed and did in fact read two novels in six weeks.

The fourth class, identified as underachievers and posing many challenges, behavioral and otherwise, for this researcher, read only the first novel and read it aloud in class. However, only by listening to the tapes of their reading could one appreciate the drama and the involvement they achieved with that novel.

Getting the class to settle down was a daily ritual requiring an average of five minutes at the beginning of each class period. On days when an assembly or long division[1] preceded this class period, the group was even more difficult to quiet down since it was not uncommon for students to arrive late to class. Had I followed the school's policy of not allowing tardy students into class and redirected them to a special office designed to record tardies and administer appropriate discipline, I felt there would be too few students to teach. However, once the oral reading started, the room would become silent except for the voices of Tea Cake and Janie coming alive through student readers. At first, Larry, who was twenty years old, literally grunted strange noises in the back corner of the room as part of his strategy to disrupt the class and maintain what he thought was power over a coterie of young men who surrounded him. When we first began to read, Larry asked to read the part of the narrator, a role he fulfilled faithfully and dramatically for four weeks. Jim, who saw himself as a lover and a sweet talker, volunteered for the role of Tea Cake. Because he empathized with the character of Tea Cake, he read with sophistication and verve. You may remember that Jim was the young man who was out of school during the post-test because of the stitches he received as a result of being hit in the head with a bottle while riding in his friend's car. Jim missed several other days during the project because, he said, he had been arrested for shooting at some young men who he said had been shooting at him. On the very first day they read, I felt compelled to tell the group how their reading reminded me of my days as a child, before the massive popularity of television, listening attentively to "The Romances of Helen Trent" on the radio. I was indeed entranced by their dramatization of the novel. I would have to consciously make myself step back and interrupt the reading to pose questions to the class. When the group came to the dramatic scene in *Their Eyes Were Watching God* where the impending hurricane ominously looms in the distance, two other young men, without being asked, assumed the parts of several characters whom I had forgotten to assign. In the midst of Tea Cake and Janie's dialogue, Joe and Mike just stepped in and started reading. Joe had been suspended from school because of discipline problems (not in my class, although he'd been no angel) for one week during the instructional period. Mike had blossomed over the course of the instruction from a young man who spoke little and wrote little to a student whose response to the question "How was Tea Cake and Janie's relationship like that of a bee to a blossom?" was poetic. This observation about his writing was one he preferred that I not share with anyone else in the room.

The point of this discussion is twofold. First, these young men specifically were touched by *Their Eyes Were Watching God*. They approached what Rosenblatt (1978) would call an aesthetic reading, and what Vipond, Hunt, and Wheeler (1987) would describe as literary engagement. Second, it is significant that the mean gain of this very difficult class was greater than that of either of the control classes.

Instruction

Although the instructional unit progressed generally as planned, several problems emerged. Some of these problems were due to time restrictions. There were more activities planned than could be carried out, considering the time required to acclimate the students to the pace of instruction, the amount of homework, and the overarching motif characterized by the following guidelines: prove your point, more than one answer is possible, and there's no direct answer stated in the text. In addition, time schedules changed often. This meant that either classes were shortened or canceled due to some senior class activity. The worksheets on which the students were to keep records of their observations about characters and images proved too cumbersome to keep up. There were too many sheets; students would lose them; and, above all, too much unnecessary time was taken up either reviewing how or whether they were being kept up. After the opening chapter of the Hurston novel, we simply stopped referring to them.

The students never wrote their own signifying dialogue, in large part because of time restraints, but also because after further thought we decided that signifying occurs best under conditions that are spontaneous rather than contrived. Also, we did not believe the students' insights into their processing of signifying dialogue would actually be enhanced by their own writing.

The Mitchell-Kernan (1981) article on signifying proved too technical for the students to handle on their own. Although teacher-directed lessons were conducted to assist students in accumulating information about the formal categories of signifying, except for the student-generated examples of each category, the discussion of Mitchell-Kernan did not happen quite as planned. Because of the pressure that reading the technical prose of Mitchell-Kernan imposed, students were not asked to read the article on Black English by June Jordan (1988), even though the Jordan article is easier for the general public to read than Mitchell-Kernan.

At the beginning of the instructional unit, students were given three dialogues of extended signifying taken from Mitchell-Kernan (1981). Then they were asked in whole and small groups to interpret what each speaker actually intended, since in signifying—and in these dialogues in particular—the words never mean what they seem to mean. The interpretation was relatively easy for the students. The more challenging issue which they addressed was how they knew what they thought they knew about the text. From this discussion, the students generated a set of criteria that signaled to them that the words meant more than they seemed to on the surface. (The criteria are listed in Table 21 in the chapter "Talk in the Classroom.") The students were then able to articulate the strategies they used to construct what the inferred meaning was. As expected, those clues and strategies were comparable to those Booth (1974) and Smith (1987) suggest expert readers use to recognize and construct interpretations of irony in literature.

Those strategies were first applied to the process of constructing answers to a plethora of intense, difficult inferential questions about a short story by Toni Cade Bambara, "My Man Bovanne," and each of two novels. The students then read Zora Neale Hurston's *Their Eyes Were Watching God* and Alice Walker's *The Color Purple*. Samples of the kinds of questions with which the students grappled in both whole-group and small-group discussions are included in Appendix B. Students also regularly wrote answers to these kinds of questions. They were constantly admonished that the teacher would not automatically believe anything they said and that they would have to back up any claims they made with evidence.

As noted earlier, the experimental classes were characterized by small-group discussions of teacher- and student-generated questions, close textual analysis—particularly of figurative passages—application of student-generated interpretive strategies, and great attention to students' justification of their answers. Both observations and discussions with teachers of the control classes indicate that none of these strategies could be said to characterize instruction in the control classes. No small-group work was observed in the control classes, although a circle discussion intended as a Socratic seminar was held on the last day in one of them. Part of the discussion is analyzed in the chapter "Talk in the Classroom." Mrs. Hemingway, one of the control-group teachers, visited a discussion group in one of the experimental classes. She revealed that she had training in conducting Socratic seminars, but had never tried the approach with her students because she didn't feel they would respond.

The only time student-generated questions were indirectly incorporated in instruction was in one control group through logs or dialogue journals of student responses while reading *Hamlet*. The kind of student-generated questions to which I am referring are open-ended questions for which there are no explicit answers in the text. Certainly students in the control classes asked both literal questions and questions based on localized inferences. Students in the experimental classes, on the other hand, asked a number of open-ended questions about *The Color Purple:*

1. Why is Mr. _____ referred to as "Mr. _____"?
2. Why did Shug marry Grady if she loved Celie?
3. Why did it take Celie so long to leave Mr. _____ ?
4. Why did Mr. _____ have so much love for Shug?
5. Why did Alice Walker use this title, *The Color Purple?*

In terms of close textual analysis by the students themselves, the control and experimental classes differed greatly. In Mrs. Hemingway's control class, students did no close textual analysis that I observed because she did all of the interpreting for her students. Dr. Johnson's control class attended to the dialogue in *Hamlet,* but Dr. Johnson routinely elaborated at great length, shifting the weight of critical analysis to his own shoulders. For example, the class watched on video the scene where Hamlet, in soliloquy, contemplates suicide and then criticizes Ophelia with the stinging attack, "Get thee to a nunnery" (Act 3, Scene 1). Dr. Johnson asked students what Hamlet was trying to communicate. When a student responded that Hamlet was telling Ophelia that he didn't love her anymore, Dr. Johnson gave a mini-lecture about the fact that the king and others in the court heard Hamlet's attack on Ophelia. He offered a comprehensive interpretation of the scene, telling the students that Hamlet was being clever, trying to convince Claudius that he, Hamlet, was insane. The only questions which Dr. Johnson asked after his mini-lecture were literal ones like "With whom did Hamlet share his plan" and "With whom did the king share the fact that despite Hamlet's pretense before

Ophelia, he did not trust Hamlet?" Although the students seemed to enjoy the video and the discussion about *Hamlet,* they did not independently interpret the text.

In the experimental classes, the shift of the burden of interpretation to the students was not easily accepted. They often commented and complained that they were not used to thinking this much on their own. One commented that the three-day final exam was more taxing than the ACT exam. They explicitly complained that they were used to having questions for which there was only one right answer and the teacher should be the one to verify an answer's correctness. At one point during the discussion of why the book was called *The Color Purple,* one student looked at me in frustration and said "Do you know?" When I would not offer a quick solution, the students looked at Mrs. Payne (who was their usual classroom teacher), and another student said, "Mrs. Payne, do you know the answer?"

It is noteworthy that the students did not feel that a focus on this form of talk, signifying, was appropriate for school. When they began reading Hurston's speakerly text *Their Eyes Were Watching God,* they claimed they could not read the so-called "dialect" and saw no relationship between the speech of the characters and their own speech. Once the teachers encouraged the students to read out loud to themselves, this distance disappeared. This initial distance is one reason why the epiphany achieved by the more difficult class through reading the novel out loud was so important. In order to compensate for the slower pace at which the class moved, at the end of each period the students would be given a "difficult" inferential question about which they had to write while in class. A testimony to the power of this culturally sensitive instructional scaffolding is the fact that this group, the lowest-achieving class of the four experimental classes (in terms of accumulated grade-point averages, a possible indicator of how hard they have traditionally worked in school), made a greater gain than even the high-achieving control class.

Note

1. A division period in this district is normally a short period in which a homeroom teacher takes attendance for the group of students for which she/he is administratively responsible. Once a week, the homeroom teacher meets with the group for an extended period known as "long division."

8 Results

The analyses of the results of this study revolve around three foci: the overall
gain in the skill of interpreting fiction achieved by students in the experimental group and the control group; the reading categories in which each group
made the most change; and how skill in signifying and the level of prior social
knowledge related to achievement.[1]

Overall Gain

Table 8 summarizes the achievement of each group on the pre- and post-test.
The group means alone indicate that the experimental group had greater gain
than the control group. The control group outscored the experimental at the
pre-test by 0.4 of a logit, although this edge is not statistically significant,
considering the standard errors. In order to determine whether the gain of the
experimental group over the control group was statistically significant, that is,
greater than one would expect by chance, a T-test of statistical significance
was carried out. The T-test (independent samples) indicates statistical significance at the $p < 0.004$ level; that is, the probability that the difference in means

Table 8

Summary of Pre- to Post- Means by Group

	Experimental			Control		
	Pre-Test	Post-Test	Change	Pre-Test	Post-Test	Change
Mean	-0.70	0.83	1.53	-0.37	0.30	0.67
S. E.	0.75	0.70		0.73	0.69	
S. D.	1.02	0.99		0.86	0.71	
Per. sep.*	0.65	0.66		0.58	0.52	

* Person separation reliablity

Table 9

T-Test–Significance of Change Score by
Treatment (Independent Samples)

Group	N	Mean	S. D.	S. E.
Experimental	52	1.5279	1.230	0.171
Control	25	0.6736	1.036	0.207
T Value	*D. F.*	*2-Tail Problem*		
3	75	0.004		

Pooled variance estimate

Table 10

Class Mean Gains by Treatment, Experimental and Control

Group	N	Mean	S. D.	S. E.
Experimental				
Group 1	15	1.4460	1.3963	0.3605
Group 2	9	1.8200	0.9976	0.3325
Group 3	17	1.3935	1.3175	0.3195
Group 4	11	1.6082	1.1383	0.3432
Control				
Group 5	20	0.754	1.0675	0.2387
Group 6	5	0.352	0.9333	0.4174

is by chance is 4 out of 1,000. The gain by the experimental group is substantial and significant. Table 9 summarizes the results of the T-test.

This first test of statistical significance uses the individual student as the unit of analysis. This approach, although valid, allows greater room for variability because of the number of degrees of freedom it affords. A more

Table 11

T-Test–Significance of Change Score by
Treatment, Class Means (Independent Sample)

Group	N	Mean	S. D.	S. E.
Experimental	4	1.5625	0.194	0.097
Control	2	0.5500	0.283	0.200
T Value	D. F.	2-Tail Prob.		
5.33	4	0.006		

Pooled variance estimate

stringent analysis uses the class as the unit of observation. This reduces the degrees of freedom allowable and represents, therefore, a more conservative approach to the data. Hillocks (1979) notes,

> Bock (1975) argues that because the mean gains for students within a particular class are correlated by virtue of their having the same teacher or method, the teacher or method should be the unit of analysis. (29)

A second T-test (independent samples) was calculated using the experimental groups' means and the control groups' means, this time using the class mean as the unit of observation. Table 10 lists the class means for each experimental and control class. Table 11 summarizes the results of the T-test using the class as the unit of analysis. The difference in means between the two groups is one logit. With four degrees of freedom, this difference is significant at the 0.006 level. Thus, whether one uses the more liberal or the more stringent method

Table 12

T-Test–IS Change for Experimental and Control
Different from 0 (1 Sample)

	T Value	D. F.	2-Tail Problem
Experimental	8.95	51	0.0005
Control	3.25	24	0.0030

of analysis, the gain of the experimental group over the control group is substantial and statistically significant.

Although the gain of the experimental group is significantly greater than that of the control, the control group also made gains. A T-test was conducted to measure the significance of each group's change against a mean of 0 (indicating no change). Table 12 summarizes the results of these T-tests. Both the control group and the experimental group experienced change that was statistically different from no change.

Change by Reading Category

Once the significance of mean gain had been established by treatment, the second major question was how these gains played out by reading category. A hypothesis of the research was that the most significant gains would be made in the inferential categories as opposed to the literal categories, and in particular, greater change would be observed in the category of complex implied relationships.[2]

Table 13 lists the difference in item calibrations by category and z statistics computed for that difference. The z statistic is the number of standard errors represented by the difference in calibrations and is computed by dividing the difference in calibrations by the joint standard error of the two items. In Table 13, any reading category with a z statistic above 2 is significant at the 0.05 level. A positive z (expressed in logits) represents a loss from pre- to post-test and a negative z (expressed in logits) represents a gain from pre- to post-test. Table 13 shows significant differences from pre- to post-test within a treatment group. Although the comparison across the groups is informative for the overall hypothesis of the research, a look at the gain of each group in and of itself is both interesting and useful. Of the eight reading categories, the experimental group made significant gains in five: key detail, simple implied relationships, application, structural generalization, and complex implied relationships. The control group made significant improvement in three of the reading categories: key detail, simple implied relationships, and structural generalizations. It is clear from this table, however, that in looking at each group by itself, the experimental gains within each category are greater than the gains within each category by the control group. That is to say, as a group the experimental students made greater overall change from pre- to post-test.[3]

The most important question regarding change by reading category is which gains are the greatest and most significant across both tests when comparing treatments. In order to calculate this, the differences in the item

Table 13

Pre- and Post- Item Calibrations and Z Statistic

| | Experimental (N = 52) | | | | | Control (N = 25) | | | | |
	Pre-	Post-	SE12*	Diff.	Z	Pre-	Post-	SE12*	Diff.	Z
BSI	-2.44	-2.97	0.5185	-0.53	-1.02	-2.99	-4.43	1.1090	-1.44	-1.30
KD	-1.18	-4.29	0.7589	-3.11	-4.10**	-1.72	-4.43	1.0620	-2.71	-2.55**
SR	-1.30	-0.49	0.3189	0.91	2.54	-3.82	-1.41	0.6842	2.41	3.52
SIR	1.81	-0.63	0.3560	-2.44	-6.85**	0.91	-0.39	0.4841	-1.30	-2.69**
APP	1.34	-0.18	0.3189	-1.52	-4.77**	-0.01	-0.57	0.4313	-0.56	-1.30
AG	1.17	0.90	0.3255	-0.27	-0.83	0.52	0.91	0.5099	0.39	0.76
SG	2.94	0.52	0.4695	-2.42	-5.15**	3.31	1.06	1.0826	-2.25	-2.08**
CIR	3.13	1.67	0.5333	-1.46	-2.74**	1.61	2.60	0.8653	0.99	1.14

Key: BSI– Basic stated information; KD– Key detail; SR– Stated relationship; SIR– Simple implied relationship; APP– Application; AG– Author's generalization; SG– Structural generalization; CIR– Complex implied relationship.

* SE12 = Joint standard error of pre- and post-item calibrations.

** Significant at or above .05.

Note: Measures are expressed in logits. A positive logit indicates a more difficult question and a negative logit indicates an easier one. A positive z (in logits) represents a pre- to post- loss. A negative z (in logits) represents a pre- to post- gain.

Table 14

Significance of Change by Reading Category

	Control Gain	Exp. Gain	Diff. in Gain	Joint S.E.	t	p
BSI	-1.40	-0.50	-0.90	1.23	-0.73	n.s.
KD	-2.70	-3.10	0.40	0.72	0.55	n.s.
SR	2.40	0.80	1.60	0.21	7.61	<.0005
SIR	-1.30	-2.40	1.14	0.60	1.90	<.05
APP	-0.60	-1.50	0.90	0.54	1.77	<.05
AG	0.39	-0.27	0.66	0.60	1.11	n.s.
SG	-2.30	-2.40	0.10	0.97	0.17	n.s.
CIR	1.00	-1.50	2.50	1.01	2.42	<.01

Note: Change scores expressed in logits, rounded to the nearest tenth.
Key: n.s. = not significant.   DF= 75.

calibration from pre- to post-test for the experimental and the control groups were listed in Table 14. The fourth column in that table contains the difference between the mean change for each. Those differences in mean change of one or more logits were subjected to a T-test for significance. This was done by dividing the difference in mean change by the joint standard error of the four pairs of items. The t statistic and the p value are listed if the t statistic is significant at 0.05 or above.

The greatest overall differences in gain by reading category for the experimental group over the control group were in the categories of complex implied relationships (2.5), stated relationships (1.6), and in simple implied relationships (1.1). The smaller the logit measure (as with negative scores), the easier the question was for the group. Conversely, the larger the logit measure (as with positive scores), the more difficult the question was for the group. So for example, in the most difficult reading category of complex implied relationships, the questions in that category became more difficult for the control group by one logit. For the experimental group, the questions in that category were easier by 1.5 logits.

Greater gain by the experimental group in complex implied relationships and simple implied relationships confirms the hypotheses. Although stated relationships require literal interpretation, such questions are the most difficult of the literal categories and represent the necessary threshold for interpreting inferential questions. Examining the differences in stated relationship calibrations without taking into account the differences in the difficulty of the questions reveals that both groups' scores went down, except that the experimental group showed less loss.[4]

The lack of significant differences in gain in the categories of application and author's generalization may be partially because the questions were answerable from prior knowledge. In the category of structural generalizations, the experimental group made phenomenal gain when compared to its performance on the pre-test. When compared to the gain of the control group, however, that experimental gain is not statistically significant.

The fact that the gain of the experimental group over the control group within reading categories was not consistent across each and every inferential category poses some reservations to the hypothesis. However, the fact that the experimental group made greater significant gains in the most difficult inferential category, complex implied relationships, lends critical support to the hypothesis. This evidence, when marshalled with the overall mean gain of the experimental group over the control group, makes a strong case in support of the hypothesis that the instructional strategy would result in the experimental group achieving greater gains in inferential questions.

The Relationship of Signifying and Prior Knowledge to Achievement

Two fundamental tenets of the hypothesis of this research are that skill in signifying and prior social knowledge of themes, values, and social conventions relevant to the texts in question would be significant variables in achievement. Originally, within the framework of quantitative analysis, it proved difficult to establish this principle. In the early regressions which were run using change as the dependent variable, the independent variables of prior knowledge and signifying were not statistically significant. That observation led me to an important conclusion. The tests of signifying and prior knowledge were measures of knowledge which the students brought before instruction. They did not test how and if students used that knowledge in the process of constructing literary interpretation. The post-test presumes this knowledge was either directly used or transformed in some way, but it does not provide any direct measure of such use or transformation. I then decided from the data I had accumulated that the transcripts would be the most direct way of tapping into the significance of the variables of prior knowledge and signifying. Even though I have since found statistical significance for these variables, that decision has informed my analysis of the transcripts of classroom talk.

I recalculated the regressions with the pre-test and the post-test as separate dependent variables. This proved useful. Using both a simple regression with one independent variable and a stepwise multiple regression using all three variables—treatment, signifying, and prior knowledge—as independent variables, some interesting relationships emerged.

Table 15 is a matrix which lists correlations among all the variables and their significance across both groups. Table 16 and Table 17 are matrices which list correlations among the variables by treatment. All the following discussion of Pearson Correlation Coefficients (r) is based on this data.

Across all the regression analyses in which pre-test and post-test were used as the dependent variables, prior knowledge consistently proved significant. When all three independent variables were loaded into a stepwise regression, signifying did not prove significant but prior knowledge did. What became evident, however, was that prior knowledge and signifying themselves are significantly correlated (Pearson correlation coefficient = 0.36, p = 0.004, 1-tailed significance, see Table 15). Therefore, when both prior knowledge and signifying were loaded along with treatment in a stepwise regression, prior knowledge took up part of the variance it shared with signifying. On the other hand, when signifying was loaded by itself, it also consistently proved significant as a predictor of achievement on the pre-test (r = 0.32) and the post-test (r = 0.38).

Table 15

Correlation Matrix–Prior Knowledge, Signifying,
Pre-Test, Post-Test, and Change

	Significance	Pre-Test	Post-Test	Change
Prior knowledge	0.3631 p = .004	0.5165 p = .000	0.4187 p = .001	-0.1872 p = .090
Signifying		0.3240 p = .009	0.3861 p = .002	-0.0057 p = .484
Pre-test			0.5137 p = .000	-0.6309 p = .000
Post-test				0.3416 p = .006

Note: 1-tailed significance; N = 53 (includes students with all four measures).

Table 16

Correlation Matrix–Prior Knowledge, Signifying,
Pre-Test, Post-Test, and Change–Experimental (N=34)

	Significance	Pre-Test	Post-Test	Change
Prior knowledge	0.3632 p = .017	0.6432 p = .000	0.4276 p = .006	-0.3174 p = .034
Signifying		0.2920 p = .047	0.3579 p = .014	0.0267 p = .440
Pre-test			0.5394 p = .000	-0.6113 p = .000
Post-test				0.3367 p = .026

Table 17

Correlation Matrix–Prior Knowledge, Signifying,
Pre-Test, Post-Test, and Change–Control (N=19)

	Significance	Pre-Test	Post-Test	Change
Prior knowledge	0.3365 p = .079	0.3320 p = .089	0.4761 p = .020	0.0731 p = .383
Signifying		0.3103 p = .098	0.6359 p = .002	0.2339 p = .168
Pre-test			0.5462 p = .008	-0.6339 p = .002
Post-test				0.3016 p = .105

Although signifying and prior knowledge were significant predictors of both the pre- and the post-tests, the amount of variance predicted by each is less at the post-test. I presumed this could be attributed to the powerful effects of the treatment. However, in the stepwise regression on the post-test, prior knowledge predicted the greatest amount of the variance (Multiple R 0.43, R Square 0.18, $p < 0.00013$), signifying was on the verge of significance ($p < 0.0662$), and treatment was not significant. On the other hand, when change is used as the dependent variable, only treatment proves significant (Multiple R $= 0.32$, R Square $= 0.10$, $p < 0.00037$).

Even though the experimental group gained significantly more from the pre- to the post-test, it ended up at the same level on the post-test as the control. Because the control group started out higher than the experimental, the experimental group had to make greater gain in order to catch up (see Table 8). Therefore, because the experimental group gained more, treatment predicts change. It does not predict achievement on the post-test because the experimental and control groups ended up at the same point.

In terms of the effects of prior knowledge, interesting differences emerged between the experimental and control groups. First, prior knowledge accounted for almost twice the variance for the experimental group as it did for the control group on the pre-test (Experimental, $r = 0.64$; Control, $r = 0.33$). Second, the change was greatest for students in the experimental group with low prior-knowledge scores. The correlation between prior knowledge and gain is negative in the experimental group (Experimental, $r = -0.31$; Control, $r = 0.07$). Thus, students with low prior knowledge gained the most. This observation is important because it suggests that although prior knowledge was a significant predictor for all students at both the pre- and post-tests, the treatment may have helped to overcome the expected limitations that low prior knowledge would have on achievement.

Again, I emphasize that prior social knowledge, in and of itself, does not assure the kind of interpretation of texts sought in this instructional unit. I argue that the missing link here is knowledge of signifying as a code or framework on which to map a literary stance toward the interpretation of figurative language. In the transcripts there is evidence of this mapping process in the direct teaching as well as in the appropriation strategies of the students. Analysis beyond that offered in this study would be required to refine the frequency of this appropriation by students, but clear evidence is presented that such appropriation occurs.

These correlations indicate that signifying and prior knowledge are meaningful variables and are positively related to the students' skill in interpreting such "speakerly" texts. These relationships are evident both before and after instruction. These measures do not, however, tap directly into how this knowledge, especially that of signifying, is transformed. They test knowledge students had before instruction.

Summary of Results

The experimental group achieved a gain from pre- to post-test over the control group by one logit or a broad ratio of three to one. In order to test the statistical significance of this gain, that is, in order to ascertain the probability that one would find such a difference by chance, two tests of significance were conducted: first, a T-test using the mean obtained for each treatment group by averaging the individual scores or person measures in logits; and then a second T-test using the mean for each treatment group obtained by averaging the overall mean of each class. The second T-test (using class means) was used because it imposed stricter demands on the data in order to prove significance. Both tests showed the experimental gain was statistically significant.

A second level of analysis looked at the gain or loss by each treatment group according to each of the seven reading categories tested. The experimental group by itself achieved pre- to post-test gains that were greater than two standard errors in five categories: key detail, simple implied relationships, application, structural generalization, and complex implied relationships. The control group by itself achieved gains in three categories: key detail, simple implied relationships, and structural generalization. A gain that is greater than two standard errors has the probability of occurring by chance only in 5 out of 100 random instances when there is no underlying difference. When comparing the pre- to post-test gain of the experimental group over the control group by reading category, the experimental group achieved statistically significant gains in the following categories: stated relationship ($p = 0.0005$), simple implied relationships ($p = 0.05$), application ($p = 0.05$), and complex implied relationships ($p = 0.01$).

In order to determine the extent to which prior social knowledge and skill in signifying predicted the variance or distribution of scores on the pre- and post-tests, a series of simple and stepwise regressions were calculated. Also a correlation matrix of all of the variables (pre-test, post-test, change from pre- to post-tests, signifying and prior social knowledge) was generated. These analyses indicate statistically significant correlations between prior knowledge and scores on the pre- and post-tests; between signifying and scores on the pre- and post-tests. For the experimental group, prior knowledge predicted twice the amount of variance for the pre-test than it did for the control group. Also, for the experimental group, students with the lowest prior knowledge scores before instruction had the highest change scores.

Thus, on the level of statistical analysis, the hypotheses articulated for the effects of instruction have been supported.

Notes

1. All analyses of the gain from pre- to post-test are based on person measures expressed in logits and are calculated on pilot tests item calibrations. Pilot tests item calibrations are based on the difficulty of each question for the pilot group. All analyses of reading categories and how groups of students improved within the categories are based on local calibrations and include separate calibrations of the tests by treatment (experimental versus control). "Local calibrations" means that item difficulties were generated by the field group rather than the pilot group and that the field group's response patterns to questions from the pre- and post-tests were pooled into individual analyses by treatment. All measures include only the person measures of those who took both tests.

2. The analysis of change by reading category looks at changes in locally calculated item calibrations for each reading category by treatment: pre-experimental against post-experimental and pre-control against post-control.

3. An interesting caveat, however, is in the categories of stated relationships and structural generalization. These are the two categories for which the pre- and post-test item calibrations differed by more than two standard errors. Thus, any comparisons even within a group for these items should take into account the difference in difficulty. One might look at this in the same light as one looks at the role of a handicap in bowling or golf. In order to balance the difference in difficulty for these pairs of items, I used the pilot item calibrations for a baseline from which to extrapolate the difference in difficulty.

   To make such an adjustment for the structural generalization category makes no difference in the analysis because the distinction in the difference for the experimental and the control groups is only 0.2 of a logit. This is confirmed in the later analysis of the significance of differences between the experimental and control groups by reading category. For structural generalization, there was no critical difference in the change. To make the adjustment for the category of stated relationship renders the significant z for the experimental group insignificant. (On the pilot pre- post- anchors, there is a 1.03 logit difference in the pairs of stated relationship questions.) That is, adjusting for a more difficult question on the post-test, the experimental group remained roughly at the same level. The control group, on the other hand, goes from a z of 3.52 to a z of 2.07, just on the verge of significance. This means they did not get better, but actually did worse in this category. In a roundabout way, then, the experimental group did better at least at maintaining their level of skill in this area while the control did not.

4. In the original analysis, stated relationship (SR) and structural generalization (SG) were the categories which were not of comparable difficulty from the pre- to post-test. However, even if one adjusts for the difference in difficulty, the difference in pre- post- gain for the two groups remains the same. If we adjust the item calibration of the post-test stated relationship (SR) question by one logit (the original difference), the experimental group gets better by 0.19 logits (not significant) and instead of the control getting worse by 2.41 logits, they get worse by only 1.41 logits. The difference in the mean gain for the two groups, however, remains 1.6.

9 Talk in the Classrooms: The Transformation of Signifying

The research design was originally planned to include quantitative as well as qualitative methods. The instruments used in this research attempt to measure students' interpretive ability before and after instruction. Conclusions are based on statistical inferences about variables. As such, that phase of the design fits within a traditional process-product paradigm. What these instruments do not provide is insight into how the existing skills and knowledge that the students brought—skill in interpreting complex inferential questions about fiction, skill in signifying, and prior social knowledge about values and social conventions within the African American community—were transformed and applied within the social context of the classroom. The discourse within these classrooms is the most immediate source of insight into this question. The analysis that follows is not intended as a thorough explication or representation of the dynamics of this discourse. Rather, it is intended as a glimpse at critical junctures in the progress of the unit of instruction and to provide a contrast with the discourse within the control classes. I also offer a tentative typology for looking at the transactions in the discourse. The transcripts are many and rich. A thorough qualitative and quantitative analysis of the transcripts is the subject of a future research agenda.

Audiotapes were recorded for each class session of each experimental class and weekly class sessions of the control classes. I made the decision to record all experimental classroom discussions in order to have as full a representation of the experience as possible. The instruction covered a six-week period (not including pre- and post-testing), with four experimental classes and two control classes. I took field notes in all classes except those in which I taught (where the regular teacher whose classroom I had taken took them). Field notes included logs with the distribution of speaking turns in whole-class discussion; the time length and content of instructional segments; the mode of instruction as lecture, whole- or small-group discussion; materials used; and any personal observations I had about the progress of instruction. I also maintained a journal in which I recorded salient features of my discussions with participating teachers as well as important events happening in the school which impacted instruction in any of the participating classes on a given day.

The purpose then of this truncated discussion of the talk in these six classrooms is to shed some light on how this knowledge about signifying, in particular, changed over the course of the instructional unit and what role the teacher played in helping students to transform the cultural and linguistic knowledge base which they brought to the classroom. I have reported elsewhere (Lee 1991) that the framework for this transformation was a *form-function* shift as described by Geoffrey Saxe (1991):

> The problem of the interplay between knowledge forms across practices is, in traditional terms, a problem of learning transfer—children's application of learning in one context to solve a problem in another.... In order for transfer to be adequate, an individual must transform and specialize prior learning to the new problem context. Such a process would suggest that transfer itself may not occur in an instant, but may be best conceptualized as a constructive process that occurs over time with repeated encounters, false starts, and efforts to come to terms with problems encountered over and over again. (140)

Over the course of the instructional scaffolding by the teachers, the form and function of signifying slowly changed for these students. Because signifying is primarily figurative talk, as students' knowledge of its form and function evolved the new characteristics associated with signifying within the context of literature also came to include literary uses of figurative language.

In the chapter entitled "Rationale," I described a variety of categories of signifying, including sounding, playing the dozens, marking, loud talking, rapping, and testifying. Each of these categories shares broad common features with the overall genre of signifying: indirection; use of metaphor, irony, and rhythm; and plays on words (Mitchell-Kernan 1981; Smitherman 1977). At the same time, each category is discernible from the others by its formal properties of structure and purpose (see Mitchell-Kernan 1981). At the beginning of the instructional unit, students' knowledge about signifying was generally limited to two related forms of signifying, sounding and playing the dozens. Sounding and playing the dozens are forms of ritual insult. The popularity of these forms is evident in contemporary television programs which feature African American humor such as "In Living Color" and "The Prince of Bel-Air." It is also evident in the programming of a Black radio station which hosts a weekly "disin'" contest in which the audience, primarily adolescents and young adults, call in to the program and proclaim ritual insults at unnamed targets.

I propose that the instruction engendered two transformations or shifts in the students' understanding of signifying. In the first, the students expand their knowledge about the formal properties as well as the functions of other categories or forms of signifying. This first transformation is important because it provides a meta-linguistic perspective on language in general and their own language in particular. Meta-linguistic knowledge can help a person to think about language as an object, subject to manipulation and possessing formal properties. An aesthetic stance toward literature, responding to the structure of the text and the subtle layers of meaning which the words afford, requires that the reader see the language of the text as an object, also subject to manipulation and possessing formal properties.

In the second transformation of knowledge about signifying, there is first a dramatic shift in the context and function of signifying as the students come to experience it as functioning symbolically within the literary text. In some instances, the form of signifying remains the same—its function changes. For example, one could lift the scene from *The Color Purple* where Celie stands up to Mr. _____ or the scene from *Their Eyes Were Watching God* where Janie stands up to Joe Starks and identify these scenes as examples of signifying. In these instances, the essential form of the sounding remains very similar to the form in the oral discourse. The many examples of signifying in literature described by Smitherman (1977) demonstrate changes in context, but not changes in form.

On the other hand, we can look to the example in the story "seemother-motherisverynice," from Morrison's *The Bluest Eye* (1970) which was used for the post-test in this study. When the narrator, representing Morrison, criticizes the protagonist, Pauline, near the end of the story, she is signifying in a form that is not immediately recognizable using the criteria of the oral discourse alone. One could not simply lift the passage in isolation from the story and recognize it as signifying. In fact, one can only recognize the passage as an act of signifying within the structure of the story. It is also important to know that Morrison sees herself as a writer in the speakerly tradition (Morrison 1989). I have analyzed this passage in detail in the chapter entitled "Signifying in African American Fiction."

> . . . her children, her man . . . were . . . the dark edges that made the daily
> life with the Fishers lighter, more delicate, more lovely. (109)

I propose that this passage is an example of signifying because it is an insult that cuts deep, is metaphoric, is "teachy but not preachy" to the reader, is indirect, includes images "rooted in the everyday world," plays on words, and introduces "the semantically or logically unexpected" (Smitherman 1977, 121). Thus, in this example not only has the context and function of signifying changed, but so has the form. From the perspective of African American language use, one could also characterize Hamlet's biting but subtle insults to Ophelia, his mother, the king, and Polonius as signifying. Consider the following scene:

> *King:*   . . . But now, my cousin Hamlet, and my son—
> *Hamlet:* (Aside) A little more than kin, and less than kind.
> *King:*   How is it that the clouds still hang on you?

Hamlet: Not so, my lord; I am too much i'the sun.

Queen: . . . Thou know'st tis common: all that live must die, Passing through nature to eternity.

Hamlet: Ay, madam, it is—"common." (Act 1, Scene 2)

Table 18 summarizes the nature of the shift. This *form function shift* is directed by the explicit scaffolding of the teacher and the affective cooperation of the student. A key issue in this perspective is why does the student cooperate? Does the cultural context of the text and the discourse form influence the level of affective cooperation? I would argue, yes!

This scaffolding can be viewed as an apprenticeship, comparable in many respects to the Vygotskian framework of semiotic mediation in a zone of proximal development (Vygotsky 1978; Wertsch 1984). Vygotsky believed that optimal school learning occurred when the novice had sufficiently developed spontaneous concepts that were related to scientific concepts. From Vygotsky's perspective, spontaneous concepts are learned in practical community contexts, while scientific concepts are learned in school contexts. The learner, having demonstrated an independent level of problem solving within the realm of a spontaneous concept, would then be placed in a social context with a more expert teacher, who through prodding, modeling, and questioning would bring the novice closer to a more adult, a more scientific, representation of the task at hand. The learning context was considered social in that the learner does not acquire scientific concepts by herself in isolation. Vygotsky (1978) called this learning context "the zone of proximal development," and defined it as "the distance between the actual developmental level as determined by independent problem solving and the level of potential development as determined through problem solving under adult guidance in collaboration with more capable peers" (86).

Werstch (1984) acknowledges that Vygotsky did not adequately and explicitly define ". . . what constitutes problem solving under adult guidance or in collaboration with more capable peers" (8). Drawing his conclusions from Vygotsky's writings, Wertsch states there are three minimal constraints that define what constitutes a zone of proximal development. The first is *situation definition.* Initially, the learner and the teacher may have different representations of the task to be completed. As the learning interaction progresses, the learner's representation of the task should evolve to a representation closer to that of the teacher. The second constraint is *intersubjectivity.* Wertsch defined intersubjectivity as the extent to which the learner and the teacher agree upon what the task is. According to Wertsch, intersubjectivity may exist on a very minimal level. For example, they may initially agree only on the tools to be used to complete the task. Through the process of *semiotic mediation*—the third critical variable to any zone of proximal development—the

teacher may temporarily give up her representation of the task to accommodate the level of understanding of the student, while the student progressively
comes closer to the representation of the task which the teacher/expert holds.
In Wertsch's analysis of Vygotsky's concept of a zone of proximal development, the way in which the novice understands the task to be mastered
changes over the course of the instructional period. These changes, according
to Wertsch, do not necessarily mean that the novice has mastered more
knowledge in a quantitative sense. Rather, he argues, the changes in the
novice's understanding of the task may involve qualitative differences. For
example, in the present study, the novice readers did not necessarily come to
master another form of discourse, but rather to understand in more depth the
variable and scope of signifying in both oral discourse and in literary texts.
Through the process of semiotic mediation, then, the level on which intersubjectivity exists (i.e., common understandings between the novice and the
teacher about the cognitive task to be mastered) spirals in complexity.
Wertsch's observations concerning defining the context of learning within a
zone of proximal development are important because it is crucial to recognize
that not just any interaction between student and teacher, between novice and
expert, represents the social context of learning advocated by Vygotsky. The
shift in students' understanding of signifying and the scaffolding strategies of
the teachers in this study exemplify the process of semiotic mediation in a
Vygotskian zone of proximal development.

In analyzing the transcripts of class sessions, I have attempted to trace the
shifts in students' conceptions of the task of literary analysis. I have also
attempted to trace the teachers' moves to draw upon the students' existing
prior knowledge (i.e., cultural and linguistic knowledge) in order to bring the
student closer to formal strategies that can be used to construct interpretations
of themes and symbols in fictional texts. I offer the scheme in Table 19 to
represent how the novice's notion of both signifying and literary interpretation
shift and eventually merge across the instructional unit. I will offer analyses
of selected transcripts from the instructional unit in order to illustrate the
phases.

In the analysis of the transcripts, I coded the talk of the teachers and the
students in order to discern (1) how the students' understanding of signifying
was being expanded to include its metaphoric, ironic, and symbolic functions
in literature, (2) how they learned to appropriate strategies for identifying a
passage of fiction as worthy of continuing reflection, (3) how they appropriated and used strategies for generalizing across figurative passages and disparate events in the plot in order to construct their own representation of themes
and symbols in the texts, and (4) how the teachers supported these changes in
the students' understanding. An analysis of the content of discussion in lesson
segments provided evidence for questions 1–3. The content of student talk

Table 18

Form/Function Shift in Students'
Concept of Signifying

Form	Function
1. Mostly sounding–Example: Yo mama so skinny she can walk through the cracks in the door.	1. Embarrass, tease, verbal competition, for street use (not home, school, or church).
2. Expands conscious understanding of a variety of forms of signifying and meta-labels for each form.	2. Exaggeration, comparisons, double meanings, innuendo; has cross- generational historical function with political overtones.
3. Embedded in literature (fiction).	3. Psychological function for characters, symbolic function within the text, structural tool, identity and class affiliation.

about signifying was categorized according to the form-function shift already described in Table 18. The content of student-student and student-teacher dialogue was categorized according to the phases described in Table 19, "Shifts in Conceptions of the Task." The phases are not always clear cut, however. Looking at the process from the framework of a zone of proximal development (Vygotsky 1978; Wertsch 1984), one expects that the teacher would often operate at a phase above the student's independent level of ability while at the same time being sensitive to the fact that the student cannot yet operate independently at the level to which the teacher is attempting to draw the student. It is important to remember that a zone of proximal development represents the distance between where the student or novice is at any given point and where the teacher wishes him or her to go.

The more subtle and challenging analysis, however, was to infer how teachers helped to support the changes in the students' understandings. In order to investigate this question, I developed six categories for analyzing the transcripts:

1. *mode of interaction*—whether the teacher assumes the role of deliverer of information (recitative mode), or of prodder seeking to help students construct their own understandings (inquiry mode), or of director giving procedures for classroom tasks;

Table 19

Shifts in Conceptions of the Task

Phase One	
Novice–right or wrong answers; superficial; literal; signifying only applicable to the street; unconscious processing.	Teacher–conception of the task is the opposite of the student's, but must appreciate what the student knows and believes, and must figure out how to map the new association onto the student's existing conceptions.

Phase Two	
Novice–begins to adjust concepts and view of the task.	Teacher–begins to draw on what the student knows and raise to a conscious level the strategies used by students to process signifying dialogue.

Phase Three	
Novice–begins to apply existing knowledge to a new domain.	Teacher–provides student with "speakerly" texts of fiction which expand signifying to include its uses as a literary tool with metaphoric functions.

Phase Four	
Novice–through application to a new domain, begins to adjust his conceptual framework to accommodate new variables.	Teacher–raises critical questions to force student to consolidate the new concept. these questions challenge students to look at connections and relationships, and to consider disconfirming data; watches carefully in order to learn how the student's concepts are changing and to inform the teacher's own scope of knowledge about the concept or task.

Phase Five	
Novice–begins more independent applications.	Teacher–begins to remove levels of support to observe independent applications from the student.

2. *participant structures*—the kinds of discourse interactions between students and between teacher and students;

3. *segments of a lesson*—the thematic patterns of the content;

4. *teacher scaffolding moves*—the kinds of questions posed by the teacher in an inquiry mode;

5. *student interactive moves*—ways in which students influence one another's thinking during whole-class discussions but primarily in small-group discussions;

6. *categories of student responses*—kinds of responses students make to questions posed by either the teacher or a peer.

The purpose of these categories is to describe the kinds of questions teachers pose, to look at how understandings are negotiated through recitative modes of student-teacher interaction that may be followed by an inquiry mode of interaction, how students support one another, and, finally, the differences between what happens in whole-group versus small-group discussions. Table 20 explains these categories in more detail.

In summary, there are, broadly, two perspectives reflected in the analysis of the transcripts. The first perspective looks at what new understandings of signifying and literary interpretation that the students reach. The categories used in this perspective are represented in Table 18 and Table 19. The second perspective looks at how the teachers themselves and the organization of instruction work to shape those understandings. The analysis which follows includes samples of classroom talk offered to represent both perspectives.

Phases 1–2

In these first two phases, the teacher attempts to draw on the students' existing knowledge of signifying and to expand the scope of that knowledge. The excerpts of dialogue in this section demonstrate students' appropriation of two crucial tools that will form the foundation of the instructional unit.

The first tool is a conception of signifying as double-edged, figurative, and full of innuendo. The second tool is a set of strategies that alert the readers that they should consider the significance and unstated meaning of a passage of fiction.

In this first dialogue, students analyze a signifying dialogue. It is clear that they understand the intended meaning of the words. They do not, however, understand what strategies they use to reconstruct either the ironic or metaphoric meaning intended by the speaker. The purpose of the teacher's questions is to get them to articulate the strategies by analyzing the signifying dialogue that here serves as a data base.

Table 20

Typology of Classroom Talk During Literature Discussion

Modes of Instruction
1. Recitative Mode–teacher assumes the role of deliverer of information
2. Procedural Mode–teacher gives directions for classroom tasks
3. Inquiry Mode–teacher asks as a prodder seeking to help students construct their own understandings

Participant Structures
1. Teacher directs whole-class recitation
2. Whole-class, student-centered discussion
3. Small-group peer discussion

Teacher Scaffolding Moves–(within an inquiry mode)
1. Constitutive–poses questions which ask student to consider bits of evidence which the student will have to piece together to generate a relevant generalization
2. Relational–poses questions which ask student to consider the relationship between pieces of information within a conceptual framework
3. Connective–poses questions which ask student to consider connections between conceptual frameworks
4. Disconfirming–poses questions which focus on pieces of information that would stand in contradiction or direct contrast to a generalization or point of view which the student is beginning to consolidate

Student Interactive Moves–ways in which students influence one another's thinking during whole-class and small-group talk
1. Refine–places another's point of view or generalization in a more narrow or clearer focus
2. Extend–adds to or broadens the scope of another's point of view or generalization
3. Help–gives or asks for support
4. Challenge
5. Raise Questions–not necessarily in challenge to another's ideas or examples
6. Support–supports point of view by reference to text and/or prior social, discourse, or genre knowledge
7. Direct–tells others what to do, but not in response to off-task behavior
8. Redirect–attempts to get others back on task

Both signifying dialogues are from Mitchell-Kernan (1981). In the first signifying dialogue, Mitchell-Kernan is conducting field-work research on signifying in a park. A young man comes up to her, rapping (or flirting), and she signifies in her response. In the part of the conversation under discussion, the young man has said,

> "Baby, you a real scholar. I can tell you want to learn. Now if you'll just cooperate a li'l bit, I'll show you what a good teacher I am. But first we got to get into my area of expertise." (323)

Class discussion follows:

T: Now if you keep on looking at that . . . go down to "first we got to get into my area of expertise." Now what is his area of expertise?

Allen: His house. House patrol.

T: What is his purpose for telling her this?

Bob: [amidst laughter and chatter] He wants to teach her how to live well.

T: So what he really means is what?

Ann: [amidst laughter and chatter] He wants to show her how to let go. Ms. Payne maybe he really don't mean that. Maybe he means he might teach her something really.

T: If somebody came up to you like this, they sure wouldn't be talking about no books.

Ann: But see, after you keep reading on, it don't sound like that. 'Cause this is the old days and they don't know nothin' about that then. Boys weren't aggressive as they are now. Times have changed. My grandfather . . . I couldn't see my grandfather asking nobody this.

T: Okay, so what you are saying is that it has a double meaning.

Ann: Yes.

T: Okay, now let's look at this conversation, the signifying dialogue. We said the husband in this conversation works on a city garbage truck. The wife says, "Where are you going?" and what did he say?

Bob: "I am going to work."

T: The wife says, "You are wearing a suit, tie and white shirt, you didn't tell me that you got a promotion?"

Group: [laughter amidst unintelligible chatter]

T: He doesn't have a job?

Bob: [amidst laughter] No. He wants to get a job.

T: Carl, what were you going to say?

Carl: I was going to say the same thing that she said. It did seem to read where he found out information before so he would be on his defense, guard against it.

T:	Okay, so wearing this tie and white shirt, right. So what is it you already know about his job?
Carl:	That he would be wearing overalls and dirty boots.
T:	Okay, Carl?
Carl:	She had an ulterior motive so she could find out where he was going.
T:	Okay, so she was trying to find out where he was going.
Allen:	And he was trying to keep it away from her.
T:	How do you know that?
Bob:	Because he said he was going to work.
T:	So how did you know that?
Bob:	I knew it because they told us what kind of job he had and then you knew from the clothing he had on.
T:	Okay, this would mean that a—would a garbageman wear a suit and tie?
Barbara:	No.
T:	So he does or says something that is out of character, right?
Barbara:	Yes. In other words, he's lying.
T:	Okay, so he is obviously lying. But the main thing is that he does and says something that is unusual or out of character.

The students' understanding of the unstated, but implied, meanings in these dialogues is punctuated by their own signifying responses. For example, in response to the teacher's question about the young man's area of expertise, Allen and Bob signify when they say "house patrol" and "he wants to teach her how to live well." They are signifying because their responses are also figurative and double-edged, not literal responses to the teacher's questions. The context of classroom talk has become, at this point, much more informal, and one notices that the teacher becomes a willing participant in the Black language interactive context. She switches register and says, "If somebody came up to you like this, they sure wouldn't be talking about no books." The double negative in Black English syntax is an emphatic form. I believe this interactive context supports students' willingness to participate and to extend themselves. A similar context is reported in a discussion in control class one and is reported near the end of this chapter. The focus of the discussion on signifying calls forth prior knowledge and encourages meta-linguistic talk. This is evident when Ann reports that her grandfather would not talk like the young man in the park. Perhaps unconsciously, Ann is addressing the question of what register of talk and discourse form is appropriate for whom. Her comments also suggest that she is not aware of the historical continuity of signifying within the African American community.

The acquisition of meta-linguistic labels, descriptive and/or categorical labels that generalize across specific instances, is an important part of the instructional unit. The students clearly know that the signifying dialogue is full of words that have intended meanings that are either in opposition to or in addition to the literal meaning. After generating specific instances, the teacher provides the students with the meta-label "double meaning," which offers a more generalizable concept and can then be applied to other relevant instances. This meta-label can represent a viable concept or construct for the students because they have generated the examples which instantiate it themselves, before the meta-label is offered by the teacher. It is in this sense that the talk about these signifying dialogues serves as an analysis of a data set that replicates the problem the students will encounter later when they are asked to interpret the figurative and signifying passages in the fictional texts. This conceptual framework is at the core of Hillocks's model of inquiry (Hillocks 1982, 1986; Hillocks et al. 1983; Smith and Hillocks 1988). Later those strategies are restated as in Table 21.

Table 21

Rules That Signify a Passage Is Important
and Should Be Interpreted Figuratively

When is a passage worth underlining and monitoring?

1. A character says or does something that seems unusual for what the reader has come to expect; when a character makes a significant change in personality, attitude, or values.

2. A comparison is made. Often the comparison will be in the form of metaphor or simile or some other form of figurative language.

3. A statement or passage presents an apparent contradiction or oxymoron.

4. Images, colors, textures, smells, etc. are repeated throughout the course of the novel or story; images, colors, textures, smells, etc. appear to bear some possible relationship to the title of the novel, short story, or chapter.

When you underline such passages in the text, jot down your reactions in your journal or in the margins of the page and offer a possible interpretation of what it might mean. Keep that question and tentative answer in mind while you read. Adjust your interpretation as you go.

In this second discussion, students expand their knowledge of signifying to include other categories than sounding and the dozens (i.e., ritual insults) and to include other functions than to embarrass or tease. This expansion involves increasing their knowledge about language and includes meta-linguistic talk about talk.

The class has been assigned Mitchell-Kernan's "Signifying, Loud Talking and Marking" (1981) which offers a comprehensive, albeit technical, overview of the characteristics, functions, and categories of signifying. Students have been assigned a series of questions intended to ascertain that they have read and understood the article.

T:	When we talk about characteristics of signifying, what are some of the characteristics of signifying?
Ann:	Smart aleck.
T:	Okay, trying to be smart alecky.
Ann:	Trying to get a message across.
T:	Trying to get a message across. Now see, those are characteristics, right?
Allen:	And trying to get people to laugh.
T:	Trying to get people to laugh, okay.
Bob:	Back talk.
T:	Okay, good. Back talk. Can anybody think of anything that we haven't said?
Bob:	To embarrass someone.
T:	To embarrass someone, okay. Those are all good. But do you have the idea now of how you should have answered that question?
Carl:	Yes.
T:	All right, good. Now let's go on now to question 2. It says, "List and define five different terms used to name different forms of signifying and provide one example either from the article or from your own knowledge for each term." So, let me see that sheet. Let's look at your story there on page 332. What examples did you find? This time you have an idea of exactly what we are looking for. Before I give you one, what examples did you find there? It says five different terms. What terms did you find?
T:	Okay, who can give me an example of "loud talking"? That's when a person deliberately says something so that. . . .
Bob:	Like at a city hall meeting when somebody is saying something that you don't like and they holler over somebody so somebody else can't hear them?
T:	Now it might occur at a city hall meeting, but I want specific examples of loud talking. Maybe something you've seen your friends do or something you might have seen on television, or something you might have done.

Carl:	When people are arguing, right?
T:	They wouldn't always have to be arguing when you're doing loud talking, right?
Bob:	Like at a stock market or so when everybody is trying to talk over one another to get their bids in?
T:	Well, they are talking loud.
Carl:	Right.
T:	But they are not signifying, right?
Carl:	Right.
T:	Okay, Barbara?
Barbara:	What is your question?
T:	We are looking for an example of loud talking. Something from your own experience. [unintelligible] What did you have in mind?
Barbara:	If everybody was trying to find something and then he may be kicking in the back of my chair. So, I turn around and say real loud "stop" instead of turning around and saying "Will you please stop kicking my chair?"
T:	Okay, that's getting there, right. Okay, let's see what . . .
Bob:	Like at a political debate.
T:	They do have to talk loud sometimes.
Bob:	They dis [signifying insult] each other, try to down one another to get the votes in.
T:	It's kind of understood in a debate that they would be kind of going back and forth like that, right. Carl?
Carl:	Let's say that someone is getting ready to fight and then they try to draw attention by speaking loud and they say "Okay let me go." Then they get into an argument that's loud?
T:	Okay, but remember we are thinking in terms of signifying. Okay, let me give you an example of what happened with the ninth-period class. Now you remember when we talked about characteristics and Mrs. Lee used me as an example. What are Ms. Payne's characteristics? What do you think some of the things were that they said?
Bob:	[amidst laughter] Too much weight.

In the first six turns between teacher and a student, the characteristics of signifying offered by the students are limited to those which characterize sounding and the dozens. Many students had not read the entire article because most classes found its technical nature and the vocabulary difficult. Therefore, it is reasonable to assume that the source of their responses is largely their own prior knowledge. The limited nature of their meta-linguistic knowledge about signifying is demonstrated in the second half of the class discussion about loud talking. Loud talking is defined by Mitchell-Kernan (1981) as

> a speaker's utterance which by virtue of its volume permits hearers other than the addressee, and is objectionable because of this. Loud-talking requires an audience and can only occur in a situation where there are potential hearers other than the interlocutors . . . Loud-talking . . . assures that intent will be imputed beyond the surface function of the utterance, which might be to seek information, make a request, make an observation, or furnish a reply to any of these. . . . An accusation of loud-talking carries the implication that the speaker (loud-talker) has, by his remarks, trod on some taboo area. (329–30)

Clearly, these students themselves loud-talk (defined here as a specific category of signifying), but are unable to either articulate a descriptive definition of it or provide examples, even from their own experiences. This distance— between intuitive language practice and meta-linguistic knowledge about the structure, functions, and processing of discourse forms they already use—had to be reduced in order for the students to apply the strategies outlined in Table 21 to works of fiction.

The following excerpt is from the close of the discussion of the Mitchell-Kernan (1981) article. What the students now say about signifying suggests the scope of their knowledge has expanded.

T:	Did you hear what Tom said?
Carrie:	Too much weight. I don't want it to affect my grade so I ain't going to say nothing.
T:	Now, is he signifying?
Carrie:	Yes.
T:	Is he talking out loud?
Carrie:	Yes.
T:	. . . So from what we've talked about or what we've tried to talk about so far, what do you think signifying is?
Bob:	A funny way of talking about somebody.
T:	That's his thought. What do you think signifying is?
Barbara:	Trying to embarrass somebody.
T:	Trying to embarrass somebody. Okay, but what is signifying?
Carl:	Verbally abusing someone.
T:	Okay, verbally abusing someone.
Bob:	It could be a type of entertainment, over-exaggerating.
T:	Exaggeration, okay. A type of entertainment. What did you say, Carrie?
Carrie:	I said trying to talk about somebody, but in a funny way.
T:	Trying to talk about somebody in a funny way.

Carrie:	Without hurting their feelings.
T:	Without hurting their feelings? Without coming out with it directly? Okay, all of those are good thoughts that you have. Now that leaves us to this other term that you probably need to put down, and that is "innuendo." You are going to get some information on this too, but add this to. . . . Does anyone know what it means? Okay, this is an implied meaning. And this is where you would suggest something just as the idea that you said. Suggest something but you don't come out and say it, right? And you can write this down for your information and when you see it again you just have to reinforce it.

The students' references to "verbally abusing someone," exaggerating and not hurting someone's feelings are aspects of signifying which they had not considered earlier. The teacher again provides a categorical term, "innuendo," that captures the many examples provided by the students through the discussion. These new associations with signifying, including those of innuendo and figuration, are essential to the perspective on the fiction which this unit supports.

In this third discussion, the students are attempting to apply these strategies to the opening chapter of *Their Eyes Were Watching God.* This is a class taught by the researcher. The initial concern is how as a reader you determine what the author may signal is important in a passage. Rabinowitz (1987) refers to these processes as recognizing rules of signification. Rabinowitz identifies openings as structurally important, points where authors may plant signposts to guide future interpretations. Within an apprenticeship framework, the teacher models how she underlines in her own copy of the book in order to highlight passages or words that may be important. She also reinforces the understandings the students have reached by confirming that she has reached similar conclusions herself. The clues referred to are the strategies extrapolated from the students' analysis of the signifying dialogue and outlined in Table 21.

T:	I want you to see if you can find some sentences in there that fit these clues that stand out. Because the character does something that's odd or that there's a statement made that doesn't seem to make sense. Things are put together that don't seem to fit, or unusual kinds of comparisons are made. And when you find those things on the page, underline them. I'll give you around four minutes to do that. Does everybody understand what you're doing?
Group:	Yes.
T:	You're looking for statements on that first page and the top of the second page where statements are made that seem to be contradictory and that the author's making some comparisons that don't seem to fit and underline them.

[Long pause while students read and underline. Students offer examples.]

T: What did you underline?

Allen: "She had come back from the sodden and bloated and sudden dead. Their eyes flew wide open in judgement."

T: All right, she had come back. Does everyone see where that is? The third paragraph. "She had come back from the sodden and bloated and sudden dead. Their eyes flown wide open in judgement." Why did you underline that?

Bob: Because it's unusual. Because no one can come back from the dead.

T: Does this idea of her coming back from the sodden and the bloated? What does "sodden" mean?

Allen: Swollen up, I guess.

T: Sodden, swollen up, so that the idea that she's come back from something that's all wet and bloated up is unusual and it's one of the things when you read it—did it go through your mind to say, "What is she talking about?"

Group: Mmm Mmm.

T: Let me show you my book based on . . . . I'm not sure if you can see this in terms of the idea of writing in books. That's one good thing that good readers do with books that they own. And if you could glance through my book which I'm just walking around here showing you, you can see that it is full of underlines and question marks and circled words all the way through.

Group: [Talk about closing the window]

T: Okay. So coming back from the bloated is an unusual statement and I think that it would also deserve underlining. What will happen, I think, in most cases with the things that you underline—there'll be things that you're asking yourself about while you're reading—you're wondering as you're reading, "Why'd she say this?" or "Why'd she say it in this way?" Anybody underline anything else?

        [Discussion continues, clarifying the sentences about every man's wishes sailing on the horizon from the opening paragraph of the book.]

T: Did anybody find anything else that they underlined? Everything that you told me you underlined are things that I've underlined in my book as well. What did you choose?

Bob: The people saw her coming because it was sundown. They were trying to say that she was so light-skinned that she glowed in the dark.

T: But is there something unusual in that statement though? To see somebody come because of the sundown. Is seeing someone come because of the sundown unusual?

Bob: Yeah.

T: What's unusual about it?

Bob: When it's sundown, it's dark.

T: What does sundown look like? Is sundown actually dark?

Carrie: No.

T: What does sundown look like?

Group: Dusk.

Group: Orange, Red [various replies]. . .

T: So is it dark at that time?

Carrie: No.

T: So is that in itself an unusual statement?

Carrie: No.

T: Is there anything in that section, however, that is?

Carrie: Yeah.

T: What?

Carrie: The sun was gone, but he had left his footprints in the sky?

T: And the "he" in that sentence is referring to what?

Allen: God.

T: Why do you say God?

Allen: I don't know, I just heard somebody else say it.

T: One of the things we're trying to do here is to get very close to
             the words on the page, to become very sensitive to the words
             and what they mean. In the context of that sentence what does
             "he" refer to? Look at the sentence carefully. "The people all
             saw her come because of the sundown. The sun was gone, but
             he had left his footprints in the sky." The word "he" is referring
             back to what?

Group: The sun.

T: Is referring back to the sun. In referring back to the sun, it's
             making the sun seem like it is a . . .

Bob: Real . . .

Bob: It's a person.

T: Like it's a person. Who has done what?

Group: Left footprints in the sky.

T: Left his footprints in the sky.

Carl: Like it was the earth, right?

T: Exactly. Anything else in that paragraph? Did anybody else find
             anything in the paragraph?

Bob: Yeah, where it says these students had been tongueless, earless,
             and eyeless conveniences all day long.

T: These students had been tongueless, earless, and eyeless
             conveniences all day long. Why did you choose that?

Bob: Because, nobody could be all that.

Although there are instances where the students misread sentences, on the
whole they identify every passage on the first pages of the opening chapter of

Their Eyes Were Watching God that a careful reader would notice. This discussion represents their first successful application of the newly appropriated strategies to a "speakerly" text of fiction. The discussion occurs at the level of the whole class in order to provide supported practice. In later phases, students will work semi-independently in small groups, interpreting passages such as those they've identified above, except that in later phases, specifically phases 4 and 5, students will be asked to generalize across such passages which on the surface (i.e., from a purely literal perspective) appear unrelated. At this present phase, however, students are simply concerned with recognizing that such passages are significant and worthy of further reflection.

It is important to note that the teacher, on the whole, does not offer answers or interpretations to students. Even when students misread a sentence in terms of the referent of the pronouns in the sentence about the sun, the teacher redirects the students to text. Close textual analysis was emphasized throughout the instructional unit.

Phases 2–3

After the lessons in the unit where signifying was the direct content of instruction, attempts to help students interpret key figurative passages in the texts would link the task to aspects of interpreting signifying. One important passage was the opening pages of *Their Eyes Were Watching God,* where Zora Neale Hurston describes the talk of the people who sit on the porch as "crayon enlargements of life" and "thought pictures." The question concerned how these two ideas related to signifying. The task demanded three days of discussion. Reading and understanding what the question was asking was a major hurdle: students tended to interpret the question as "What do the phrases 'crayon enlargements of life' and 'thought pictures' mean?" rather than to interpret the question as a relational one requiring comparisons between the text and the discourse form. The confusion in the discussion is because the students are interpreting the first question ("In terms of signifying, what do you think Zora Neale Hurston means by thought pictures and crayon enlargements of life?") as "What does 'crayon enlargements of life' mean?" The teacher, on the other hand, anticipates that the original question may be misinterpreted and so asks a second procedural question, hoping to get the students to articulate for themselves what precisely the first question is asking them to do. The students' answers tend to be short, often just a few words. Longer turns are almost always about personal experience rather than the text. The teacher in this excerpt is operating at phase 3 (providing students with "speakerly" texts of fiction which expand signifying) while trying to connect with students who are hovering somewhere between phase 1 and phase 2. The students are still quite literal in their interpretations, except that there are

simple right and wrong answers, and are being confronted with questions that
require a new conception of the task of interpretation.

> *T:* Look at the question. "In terms of signifying, what do you
> think Zora Neale Hurston means by thought pictures and
> crayon enlargements of life?" So you're being asked to make
> a comparison between signifying and what?
>
> *Harry:* Exaggerating real life?
>
> *T:* Well, you're giving me an answer. I want to know—looking at
> the question, what's the question asking you? This sign here
> means parallel [pointing to a ‖ sign on the board]. Signifying
> is like what?
>
> *Mary:* Talking about you.
> [some confusion about which question is being addressed]
>
> *Mary:* Teaching through proverbs.
>
> *T:* See, you're trying to give me an answer. And I'm not asking
> you for an answer yet. I want to know what is the question
> asking you. . . .
>
> *Ann:* They asking you how do Black people talk?
>
> *Charles:* The thoughts in the back of they mind.

This kind of interchange goes on for ten more exchanges between students
and the teacher until one student says, "It's asking you to compare . . . signifying with enlargements . . . [and] signifying with crayon enlargements of
life." The teacher then asks the students to make associations they have with
"crayon enlargements of life" and "thought pictures." Again, the responses are
one- or two-word answers: "images," "real life," "reality," "dreams," etc. The
teacher, trying to help the students put pieces of the picture together in order
to generalize, asks, "Do any of these things have anything to do with signifying?"

> *S:* Yeah.
> *T:* All of them or some of them?
> *S:* Some.
> *T:* Do images relate to signifying?
> *S:* No.
> *S:* Yes.
> *T:* How?
> *S:* How people look.
> *S:* Imagine it.
> *S:* 'Cause like if somebody say you was fat as a cow, you would see a
> cow in your head.
> *T:* Exactly.

The last student's response is the longest made by any student during that
class segment. To some extent the terseness of the students' responses may

relate to the syntax of the original question. A more direct statement of the question would have helped, i.e., "How is signifying like 'crayon enlargements of life' and 'thought pictures?'" or "Compare signifying to 'crayon enlargements of life' and 'thought pictures.'" However, more importantly I think, at that point the students had not adopted the text as their own and felt no stake in the question. This was not because they were not interested in signifying; prior discussions of signifying dialogue reported in the description of phases 1 and 2 demonstrate their interest and adeptness. It was because at this point they saw no connection between signifying and metaphor in fiction.

In these three days of transcripts, you do not see students paraphrasing the text, referring to examples from the text, or debating narrative conventions relative to the text. The closest the classes came to any lively discussion at that stage of the instruction was conversation around a humorous passage where the men who sit outside of Joe Starks's front porch signify about Matt's stinginess with his mule. They laughed, paraphrased the text, and provided examples from the text to support their claims.

T:	Can you find any examples of anything that these characters have said where their words are like pictures?
Pat:	When he was talking about that mule. They said he was scrubbing by his [unintelligible] bones [laughing]. If you picture that, it was just too funny.
T:	While they were signifying about that mule, if you heard somebody say that, if you closed your eyes, could you see that mule? Could you see it just like it was a little movie or cartoon, just from the way they described it?
Students:	[groups of students respond] Can I read? Can I read?
T:	No. Let's read it out loud together to get a good feel for the language.
	[Students read conversation on page 49 out loud. Students laugh at section about mule and women.]
Mary:	He said they was using his ribs for a washboard. Can you imagine someone doing that to your mule or dog or something?
T:	What's she saying?
Charles:	He feed him out of a regular tea cup every morning instead of a measuring cup.
Mary:	A tea cup about that big.
	[Students continue reading out loud.]
T:	What do you think the writer Zora Neale Hurston means when she describes the way these people talk as thought pictures and crayon enlargements of life?
Mary:	They talk about a person so bad that you could picture it.
T:	That you could picture it from their words. If they are crayon enlargements of life—crayons are what?

Harry:	Then you could actually see it.
T:	It's almost like you could see the what of it?
Charles:	The entire thing, like what he say, the color, everything.
T:	Every aspect of what this picture might look like. And if what they are saying is enlargements of life, how is their talk enlargements of life?
Pat:	Things that happen are for real, but it's just a little exaggerated.

This excerpt is from the same day's discussion as the previous excerpt. This excerpt suggests that the students recognized signifying in the mule scene and yet at this phase had difficulty articulating a relationship between signifying and Hurston's references to "crayon enlargements of life" and "big picture talkers." To articulate such a relationship first requires meta-linguistic language and a stance which allows them to see language as an object. Consistent with the findings of DeLain et al. (1985), the students were able to or perhaps willing to offer interpretations of that passage because the passage most directly replicated the experience of signifying in their community environments. There is a sense in which the level of abstraction of the question asking them to relate signifying to "crayon enlargements" and "thought pictures" approaches the level of abstraction implicit in the final question of the instructional unit about the meaning of the title of Alice Walker's novel. The complexity of these kinds of inferential questions (certainly questions of complex implied relationships within the Hillocks model) is based in part on their nested quality: questions implicit within questions.

Phases 4–5

In order best to dramatize the overall transformation in these students, I will analyze sections of three transcripts of discussions which occurred on the last day of formal instruction. In phases 4 and 5, the questions posed by the teacher and the focus of interpretive tasks become more complex. The students tackle questions which not only ask them to offer and justify interpretations of implied relationships that are localized in a passage (Hillocks's simple implied relationships); but, more importantly, students are asked to tackle questions and justify interpretations of complex implied relationships (Hillocks 1980; Hillocks and Ludlow 1984). Questions of this latter type require generalizing across passages that may cover the breadth of the entire novel and that on the surface have no apparent or directly stated relationship. The teacher's support comes through the kind of questions posed at critical junctures of whole- or small-group discussions. The questions cannot simply be categorized by cognitive levels or by their degree of open-endedness. Rather the questions are aimed at focusing the attention of students on the following: (1) making connections among the bits and pieces of textual evidence that focus on a given theme, character, or relationship, and (2) seeking relationships across themes, characters, and images. The teacher's questions at this phase challenge the bounds of students' thinking by posing challenges in the form of textual evidence that may disconfirm generalizations which they are developing. These kinds of teacher questions are reflected in Table 20. These discussions represent a blend of phases 4 and 5 from the shift in students' conception of the task.

The teachers in these discussions are operating more often than not in an inquiry mode. Like a mosquito buzzing in their students' ears, they are trying to prod the students to think figuratively across bodies of data which on the surface appear to be unrelated, but which together constitute a major conceptual theme of the novel *The Color Purple* by Alice Walker.

The students in these discussions have begun to accept as a matter of course that novels contain language where the surface meaning of the text and possible intended meanings by the author may not be the same, that themes and symbols may be constructed by the author through figurative language, and that signifying may be a tool used by the author to demonstrate an important aspect of a character's development or transformation. In two of the discussions, the researcher is the teacher, and, in the other, Mrs. Payne, one of the teachers participating in the project, leads the discussion. The first discussion is led by the researcher. However, the researcher led this discussion only because Mrs. Hayden, the regular teacher, was absent on that day. Thus, the fact that the students talked as they did is a tribute to the regular teacher who had taught them for the full six weeks, rather than to the researcher who only stepped in that one day. The topic of discussion across the three class sessions is why the book is called *The Color Purple*. Of particular concern is how the title of the book relates to the presentation of God and the transformation of the protagonist Celie. This was a complex question, a complex concept, and, although generated by the teachers, had also been raised independently by at least one of the classes before it was formally introduced by the teachers.

The first discussion occurred in the first-period class. This class had the teacher for whom the changes in instructional mode were the most dramatic, the class which was the weakest of the six classes (experimental and control) at the pre-test, and the class which eventually achieved the greatest gain across the six classes. On this day, the class had been divided into small groups for discussion. The discussion starts off in a small group with five students, three females and two males. I will not take time to cite examples, but this transcript, like most of the others of small-group discussions, includes off-task behavior where students, even though being tape recorded, venture into short-lived discussions that have nothing to do with the topic but are often quite humorous and even on rare occasions tangentially related (one example will be cited from Period 6). This discussion, like all small-group discussions, is replete with student references to pages in the text which contain passages to support claims they are making. This very clearly became a motif for all experimental classes. All teachers continuously made comments to the effect that they would not believe any claim a student made unless she could cite in her own words support for the position. In fact, to my dismay in some respects, this unit was clearly dominated by textual referents as support for generalizations in response to inferential questions. At the same time, I believe such a focus was necessary for the close rhetorical analysis intended in this unit.

The first segment of this small-group discussion revolves around Celie and God, a complex network of associations. Ultimately, the students were trying to figure out why Alice Walker named the book *The Color Purple*. In piecing together their response, they had to think about how God was represented in the novel and what that representation of God might have to do with the significance of the book's title.

T:	Give your names and then start off with the first part of the question.
S:	Yvonne, Willard, Janet, Leonard, Lana.
Willard:	Now we gonna bust a good rap upon this funky microphone. What is the question? Let me see the questions. Come on, we can't talk about that. We got to answer these questions.
	[intervening background noise]
Willard:	Come on, let's do this work. "What did we learn about what Celie and Shug think about God?" Come on, that is a hard question. Come on, Yvonne, let's do our work. Do you know the answer? "What did we learn about what Celie and Shug think about God, in terms of 1? What does God look like?" She described God; what God looked like. Oh yes, they did describe Him.
Laverne:	Page 18.
Yvonne:	Hey, look in that bag and give me *The Color Purple*.
Leonard:	I was gonna get it. I know what you are talking about.
Yvonne:	You better had.
Laverne:	Boy, shut up.
Janet:	Willard said knock you out. Mamma said knock you out. What up, Solid?
Willard:	I know the answer.
Janet:	Yvonne, what does this do?
Yvonne:	Not a thing. John Haynes, pass this up to her. We got division today.

Willard:	Sheneka writing the answer, but she not telling it to us. We got to answer those questions on pieces of paper. The homework from last night is what we are talking about now.
Yvonne:	What's that writing on your paper?
Willard:	We talking about it now.
Laverne:	You were suppose to have read the whole book. What is image of God?
Willard:	I did read the whole book.
Laverne:	Then what was the image of God?
Willard:	He looked like me.
Laverne:	Stupid. How ghetto can you be? Notice he didn't come to class.
Willard:	You all better get off my brother, Jack Hamilton. He smart. He even has a smart name.
Leonard:	You all want to know what God looked like. I think it's on 252.
Janet:	It's on 252.
Yvonne:	What are all of these page numbers?
Laverne:	If you did your homework last night you would know.
Willard:	Did you do yours?
Laverne:	No.
T:	You might want to split the pages up, some people looking at the beginning. Don't write the questions. The question is not important. The answer is important.
Leonard:	It's on 264.
T:	Can you speak loud?
Laverne:	She said, "God all white too, looking like some stout white man work at the bank. God blow out a big breath of fire and suddenly Sofia free."
Willard:	I don't know what page it's on?
Laverne:	On page 96.
Willard:	No, when her and Shug was talking. They both described what God looked like. I just don't know where.
Laverne:	Didn't you say on page 252 they got one on there?
Willard:	Page 264.
Laverne:	Here's one on page 164.
Leonard:	Read it. . . .[off-task talk follows]

The first move of the group is to establish a data bank. Much time is spent with group members locating pages that contain references to the topic. The conversation is dotted with restatements of the question, some off-task forays, and many references to portions of the text.

This next section is from the same move to establish a data bank. It demonstrates how students refined each other's ideas and raised questions about each other's assertions. It also demonstrates one scaffolding role of the teacher. During small-group discussions, the teacher would move across groups, listening, and asking questions or making comments only when she felt the direction of the group needed to be adjusted in some way.

Janet: I think that this is it. It says, "God is different to us now. After all of these years in Africa, more spirit than ever before and more internal. Most people think that he has to look like something or someone [unintelligible] for Christ, but we don't and not being tied to what God looks like frees us."

Willard: That's Nettie discussing what God is to her. What does Celie think He looks like? This question is about Celie and Shug.

T: Their ideas are very similar so you need to take that into consideration.

Willard: Like you knew that.

Laverne: What page is that anyway?

Willard: Page 264.

Laverne: Wasn't it another one of 267?

Leonard: I don't know. I didn't look at that page. I think it is one on page 267 too.

Janet: Do you see it?

Laverne: I don't know. I'm trying to see who is saying it, who is talking. [off-task talk]

T: That's a very important step and that is the one we are talking about. Shug and Celie are having this conversation about God.

Willard: That is what I was looking for. I know I remember reading that. See people who read the book can recall it. At the beginning, Celie was talking about God.

Janet: She said what God is to me?

S: What page is that?

S: Page 199.

Group: "She said that he gave me a lynched daddy, a crazy mother, a low down stepfather."

Willard: She said all of my life I never cared what people thought about nothin I did, but deep in my heart I care about God.

Janet: She said anyhow, "I say the God I've been praying to and writing to is a man. And act just like all of the other mens that I know. Trifling, forgetful and lowdown" (199).

Willard: She was talking about churches. She said, "Celie tell the truth. Have you ever found God in church? I never did. I just found a bunch of folks hoping for him to show" (200). Will you read? I can't spell your name, you old boot-head girl.

The data bank of examples emerging from the discussion has grown significantly. This is obvious in part because the descriptions by the students of their examples are longer than before, when one-liners about page references were the norm. From the beginning of the group's move to assemble references to pages that contain information relevant to the question, only one on-task statement by a student has been more than two lines in length until this episode. It is important to note that the textual references made by the students are not concentrated in any one section of the book. This breadth of references is further testimony of the extent to which these students came to own these novels, able to recapture information from them at will. The teacher recognizes that data is accumulating, but there is not sufficient focus on the relationships between the examples the students are locating and the larger conceptual issue. That is, the students have located information about Celie and God in different parts of the text, but they have put forward no generalization which connects the examples. She implicitly asks a *relational* question by suggesting that the group consider the relationship between Nettie's ideas about God and Celie's ideas.

Midway through the conversation, a transition occurs. The group is now making a move from establishing a data bank to solidifying their ideas. Student responses become longer.

T: What are you coming up with?

Laverne: We are looking at the conversation between Celie and Shug and we found on some pages about the way that Celie thinks about God.

T: Okay.

Willard: She believes in Him and she really cares about what He thinks, but on one page she was talking about Him, blasting Him. She was signifying.

T: Why?

Janet: Because she thought that God wasn't helping her. She was praying to Him and He wasn't answering her prayers.

In this segment of the discussion, the students' responses are longer than statements by the teacher. Students refine one another's ideas. Of special interest is the comment that Celie was signifying about God. This student has appropriated a broader concept of signifying beyond the limited idea of teasing within the familial context of family and friends. The student has applied signifying within a literary context and seen it as an index of a character's transformation.

Recognizing that the group has reached a critical point in their discussion of Celie and God, the teacher initiates another move with a series of pointed *constitutive* questions. These questions are aimed at focusing the students' discussion on any possible parallels between God as represented in the novel, God as transformed in Celie's mind, and Celie's transformation as symbolized through the title and the images associated with the color purple in the novel. *Constitutive* questions ask students to consider bits of evidence which the student will have to piece together to create a relevant generalization. The questions initiated by the teacher are reformulated (Cazden 1988) and recycled until the students begin to generate some relationships between the disparate bits of information.

> *T:* At that point God to her was like any other what?
> *Laverne:* Man, I thought that was Shug that felt He was like every other man. No, that was Celie.
> *T:* Did she view God as a man before then?
> *S:* No.
> *T:* On page 96 what [unintelligible]
> *Laverne:* She wasn't looking at Him as a man, but she [unintelligible]
> *T:* Not that she believed that God was a man, but this image was like—close your eyes and figure it out.
> *Willard:* She still think of man as being God.
> *T:* What did He look like at the beginning? What did this God look like early to her?
> *Laverne:* An old white man. She said He was white and looked like some stout white man that worked at the bank.
> *T:* Okay, by the time that you come to the end of the book is her idea about God the same that it was at that point?
> *Group:* No.
> *T:* How is it changing?
> *Laverne:* She is saying now that He is just another trifling, low-down man like all the rest of them.

The students have appropriated the text to the point where they can paraphrase key passages at will, picking up the signifying tenor as in Laverne's last statement about a trifling God. Although the participant structure of this portion of the transcript is clearly recitative (Mehan 1979), this segment is embedded in a larger episode that is within the inquiry mode. Carlsen (1991) correctly observes that "utterances are interpreted in terms of nested frames of reference" (162). He argues that a thorough analysis of classroom discourse must consider what came before.

When the question of why the book is called *The Color Purple* first arose, one student said it was because purple was Celie's favorite color. In order for students to piece together a more complex response, they had to be forced to consider a wider spectrum of data than Celie's favorite color. A more sophisticated and sensitive response generalizes across a number of contexts: references to purple in the novel, conceptions of God across the novel, Celie's perception of herself and her relationship to God across the novel, to name a few. When the teachers would ask what I have labeled constitutive questions, they were asking students to explore, and establish for themselves, a network of associations about each of those contexts. Later, the teachers will move to ask what I have called relational questions that will ask students to articulate what relationships they see across these contexts; that is, what does what you know about purple in the novel and how the ideas about God change across the novel and how Celie sees herself, etc.—what do all of these networks of associations together have to do with why Alice Walker called the book *The Color Purple?* I have given some focus to the kinds of questions which teachers raised because it is impossible to understand the growth of the students' understanding of each novel without considering how the kinds of questions influenced how the students began to think (which was to think analogically), not simply what they began to think about. These moves on the part of the teachers, from helping students to constitute or build ideas, to helping them consider relationships across ideas which on the surface appear unrelated, cannot be specifically preprogrammed. A good inquiry-oriented teacher must sense where students are at any given moment and determine on the spot when it is appropriate to change the direction of the questions. This sense of the teachable moment is at the heart of scaffolding, especially as it is viewed within the Vygotskian framework of semiotic mediation.

The discussion which follows is between the teacher and one student, Willard, although the larger context is that of a small-group discussion. Some of Willard's comments are uptakes from data previously generated in the talk of this group. The purpose of this excerpt is not so much to share the level of Willard's insights (which are in part a result of his prior interactions with the whole group), but rather to focus on the kinds of questions which the teacher poses in order to respond to Willard's thinking. The column on the right categorizes each turn according to the typology outlined in Table 20.

T: Keep looking through that section and find out now 'cause you are running out of time.

Teacher Scaffolding Move (TSM)

What is God like now? What does He look like? Where do you find God? What does God have to do with people? What does God expect of people?

Relational Question

Willard: Shug made her see God differently 'cause she was talking at the end after Shug told her what God looked like and she said, "Let's talk and talk about God, but I'm still adrift trying to chase that old white man out of my head. I've been so busy thinking him I never notice nothing God make, not a blade of corn, not the color purple, not the little wildflower, nothing. Now that my eyes are open I feel like a fool." [Some references to page numbers and some off-task exchanges follow.]

Willard: She is talking about how Shug changed Celie's opinion about God.

T: How?

Willard: She made her think, uh, rethink about how God look.

T: How did God look then? What did she see?

Willard: She said that she was trying to get the vision of the old white man out of her head.

T: But where does she see God now? If you want to see God, where do you look?

Willard: Everywhere. The things you make and does. She was seeing Him like in the food, in the flowers, the color purple.

Student Generates Example from Text to Answer a Difficult Question; the passage selected by the student offers criteria by which one can define what God has to do with the book's title (that is, the white image of God has kept her from noticing what God has made).

Student Interactive Move (SIM); Restates/Refines his own prior comment. Although Willard is refining and clarifying his thoughts through the talk, it is important to remember that the reference to God as a white man had been initiated earlier by Laverne.

TSM—Constitutive Question

SIM—Restates/Supports his own comment

TSM—Still within the same meta-script,[1] teacher reformulates the question.

SIM—Support/Refine; This student is still reworking, reconceptualizing this same data set and its relevance to the metascript.

TSM—Constitutive Question; Reformulates and recycles earlier question of "Where do you find God?"

The student has put the pieces together. He has appropriated the data which the group has been generating throughout most of this discussion and extrapolated a meaningful generalization that also connects to the larger question of why this book is called *The Color Purple*.

T: All right, what about God's expectations for men and women at this point?

TSM—Connective Question; Teacher appropriates the "teachable moment" and does not put the analysis to rest, but rather pushes the group to consider a possible relationship between the generalization they have come to so far and the behavior of people, i.e., the author's generalization (Hillocks and Ludlow 1984).

[short intervening dialogue in which question is repeated]

T: The most important parts are going to be like 203, 204, 202. You have to find out. I'm not telling anybody anything. I'm here to listen. What does God expect out of people?

The final statement by the teacher loomed as a primary motif and metascript throughout the unit of instruction and across experimental classes.

The other motif or metascript for the unit was signifying as figuration. I have argued that part of what happened during this instructional period was that students broadened the scope of their knowledge about signifying to include its application to literature. The following conversation occurred during small-group work in the experimental class taught by Mrs. Payne. This conversation occurred also on the last day of instruction and represents the maturity of phase 5. Some background knowledge is necessary in order to interpret this portion of the transcript. Mrs. Payne has been trying to get the students to address the question of why the book is called *The Color Purple*. In this segment of the lesson, she has reformulated the question in terms of the message Alice Walker may be trying to communicate through the title of the novel. The small discussion group of three males and two females has been arguing over the question of what role any knowledge about the personal life of Alice Walker may play or any specific statements she may have made on the back cover of the book. The students have assumed that the copy on the back cover of the paperback book represents Alice Walker's words as author (rather than through any fictional character). In addition, a few days earlier, a whole-class discussion occurred on the intimate relationship between Celie and Shug in the novel. There had been very lively discussion over the passage where Celie describes how Shug taught her and awakened Celie to her own sensuality:

> Why Miss Celie, she say, you still a virgin.
>
> What? I ast.
>
> Listen, she say, right down there in your pussy is a little button that gits real hot when you do you know what with somebody . . . I look at her and touch it with my finger. A little shiver go through me. Nothing much. But just enough to tell me this the right button to mash. Maybe. (Walker, 82)

In this section of the group's conversation, the first student is responding not so much to the teacher's question as to an idea introduced a few lines earlier by another student, "God. She had God in her."

T: So thinking about the author, what message is she trying to communicate?

Tom: She is trying to say that everybody should have a God in their life. At least somehow associate some parts of their life with God because as long as you have God in your life, you should have a little happiness in your life even if you have hard times. Or he could be your best friend if you don't have none. Remember when her father told her not to write to nobody but God. She was writing to God and telling him what was happening and it was like even though you are down, God would always be there to help you up. It will be your friend even if you don't have any. He will be like your brother or sister. He will be there if you need him.

Verdell: When she was talking to Shug, she was saying that she was trying to forget God because he hadn't did anything. It's like he took her sister away and she was the only person that loved her.

Anthony: But she was thinking of God as a person. She thought that he would send her messages through letters and stuff like that and Shug had to tell her that he was everything so that everything that happened God had some part to play with it in some indefinite way.

Tom: Anyone else?

Donald: You pressed the button kid.

Anthony: That's all I got.

Sharon: Is there anything in the Bible that says something about purple?

Donald: I don't think so. I don't study the Bible that much.

Verdell: That's cause it ain't on the back of the book.

The students challenge and extend each other's thinking. When the young man talks about the button, he is signifying both with the other student as well as upon the text itself. When the student responds to the reference to the Bible as a possible source of support, he is signifying both on the speaker as well as the group's idea that the information on the back cover of the paperback is some kind of authoritative text in itself. These two brief examples demonstrate one way in which the students' knowledge of signifying has been both expanded and transferred to a literary domain.

Another indication of the literary sophistication of the group's discussion of the question regarding the significance of the title *The Color Purple* is the intense debate of what constituted an appropriate criterion for evidence. This was not an issue introduced by the teacher. Rather the students' dedication to logic and their intense involvement with the text seemed to spur this argument along. Some members of the group have been offering examples of images and actions associated with purple in the novel. One young man, Anthony, is not satisfied with the examples.

Anthony: So why do you think she called the book *The Color Purple?* Not examples, but why you think she called the book that?

Donald: Who me? I told you my examples of it.

Anthony: No you didn't. We didn't hear you. You all keep referring to examples of how they use the word.

Tom: I said that because she called it *The Color Purple* because it was. . .

Anthony: You keep referring to everything in the book that refers to the color purple instead of why she named the book. Why do you think she said I think I'm going to name this book *The Color Purple?*

Donald: That was the color that she thought.

Verdell: Because she was revealing the truth about God, men, women, Blacks and Whites and love through using the color purple.

Anthony: But why did she pick the color purple? She could have used blue.

Donald: That was the color she thought best represented pain and all of that.

Anthony: Red could symbolize pain.

Verdell: It is certain things that represents the color purple. You know like the bruise, say it was purple.

Anthony: Red could symbolize a bruise.

Donald: The flowers were purple.

Anthony: I've seen red roses.

Verdell: But she doesn't say red roses in the book.

Donald: That is what I'm saying: we got to relate to the book. Everything goes back to the book.

Anthony:	Ask the question that you asked again.
Tom:	Why? Cause the teacher is here?
Sharon:	He said tell him why the book is called *The Color Purple* without referring back to the book.
Anthony:	I didn't say all of that. You all are referring to it as a coincidence.
Verdell:	It is.
Tom:	You said I think it was because she said a flower or she said a eggplant.
Anthony:	I didn't say it like that.
Tom:	I know, but you talking about he trying to say we answered it indirectly. We were asking around the question.
Verdell:	We have to answer around it to get to the [unintelligible]
T:	That is the purpose of discussing.

The conclusion of this segment of the group's discussion does not settle finally the question of appropriate criteria. They have, however, raised an essential question of literary interpretation: how do you know what you think you know when interpreting? The conclusion of this segment, namely that you must take an indirect route around such a question, and that that route must relate back to the text is not only important, but is analogous to the meta-linguistic knowledge the students have gained about signifying. Signifying is an indirect route to communication, and interpretation of signifying talk must relate back to the text, which in this instance would include what you know about the speakers, the situation, and the genre of talk. It is as if we have come full circle, from the early discussions of the signifying dialogues to the literary text of *The Color Purple*.

The Contrast of the Control

The experimental classes were characterized by an on-going focus on difficult, inferential questions, by an on-going expectation that students would consistently refer to the text as an initial source of explication, and by a concern with the figurative or metaphoric aspects of the texts. The contrast with the control classes is stark.

The teacher of control class two, Mrs. Hemingway, was active in school activities and took pride in her positive relationships with students. She volunteers her time to help put on a Shakespeare festival at the school each year and her rapport with students is excellent.

All teachers completed a survey at the end of the instructional period. The two control teachers were asked to describe the instructional unit which I had observed weekly and to discuss their instructional plans for the remainder of the school year and the factors which most influence their teaching. Mrs. Hemingway identified the content of her instruction during the prior six weeks as poems on "Meeting Adventure," "Doing the World's Work," "Finding Love and Friendship," "Seeking Wisdom," "Discovering Beauty," "Understanding Others," "Developing a Personal Philosophy," and "Building a Better World." Mrs. Hemingway wanted her students to appreciate how ideas in poems are applicable to the students' own lives. Although her goals are laudatory and important, they differ in significant ways from the goals of the experimental instructional unit. The experimental instructional unit presumes that students can construct their own alliances and engagement with the fiction as they learn strategies to analyze the rhetoric of the text.

Mrs. Hemingway's goals, in practice, meant that she would pick out poems under those headings from any one of three anthologies which she regularly used. These anthologies included two on British literature even though this was a class in world literature. She indicated in a final interview that in the next marking period the students would read Shaw's *Pygmalion* and Sophocles' *Oedipus the King*. Considering the fact that the final marking period for seniors is hectic with the rush of pre-graduation activities, reading these two plays closely would be challenging indeed. On the final day of my observations of that class, the teacher assigned the next day's reading. She told the students to read the first act of *Oedipus the King*. There was absolutely no preparation of any kind for the assignment. This class consistently had at least 50 percent of the enrolled student population absent on a daily basis.

In the normal class population of eight to ten people, the three males who dutifully came never spoke and the remaining females participated in exchanges of personal opinion. The pattern, as I observed, was that the teacher would read or have one of the students read directly from the anthology. This reading would include any editorial comment about the work as well as the work itself. The teacher would render her interpretation of the work, section by section. She would then engage the students in a discussion of whatever the theme of the work was. The discussion, without exception, consisted of the students' personal opinions about the theme. For example, one day after the teacher read and interpreted a Tolstoy poem on work, she asked the students if they had thought about how they would prepare for their eventual retirement so that they could avoid the sense of frustration which the teacher said the narrator of the poem experienced. The students were in no way required to engage the words, the images, or the ironies of the texts themselves. This class made the least gain of all six participating classes.

To place this teacher in an appropriate context, let me share two topics of concern at the one meeting of the English department which I attended during my stay at the school: (1) a vocabulary list of words for each grade level which the department chairman felt was important, and (2) how the staff could get the students to come to take the district- and state-mandated achievement tests (not how they could help the students do better on such tests, but simply how they could get the students there to take the tests). The vocabulary list included such words as "satire" and "irony." I chided Mrs. Payne and asked if they planned for the students to look up satire and irony in the dictionary and write the definition three times. She laughed in sympathy. Mrs. Payne had commented on several occasions about how difficult she felt it was to influence the rest of the English department staff to make any significant changes in instruction.

A more appropriate contrast was control class one. As mentioned before, this class was taught by the department chairperson, a Ph.D. in English, and had been kept together as a group across their four years of high school because they had been identified as a highly motivated group, even though their test scores in reading were average as defined by the range of test scores in that school. This class intensively read *Hamlet* for six weeks. A significant portion of instructional time was spent watching and analyzing, scene by scene, a video of *Hamlet*. This is not to suggest that the class did not attend to the text itself. Rather, they read quite closely, usually moving from a scene in the text to that same scene in the video. The teacher had very high expectations for the group and placed stringent academic demands on the group.

I believe several factors influenced the fact that this class did not achieve the same high pre-post gain as the experimental classes. Booth (1974) talks about five "crippling handicaps" (222) which impede a reader's ability to understand irony appropriately. Although Booth employs a somewhat tongue-in-cheek tenor, below his satiric voice is a crisp and serious representation of factors which any good literature curriculum should address. Three of these handicaps indicate an important line of demarcation between the experimental and control classes. The three handicaps are ignorance, inability to pay attention, and lack of practice. Although Booth intends these as handicaps to an accurate comprehension of irony, I would argue that metaphor and irony are reverse sides of the same coin and that the process of reconstructing the intended meaning of such tropes may often be similar. Of this relationship, Booth says,

> There are many verbal devices that "say" one thing and "intend" another and thus invite the reader to reconstruct unspoken meanings. Metaphor and simile, allegory and apologue . . . have all been discussed in terms similar to those employed for irony. . . . (7)

In defining ignorance as a handicap, Booth says, "the more remote a work is from my home province (my century, my country, my family, my profession, my church, my club, my generation), the more mistakes I will make in a given reading period" (223). Such distance may be defined by what Scholes

(1985) calls the "cultural codes" of the text. The teacher in control-class one saw as one of his responsibilities in teaching *Hamlet* to overcome the handicap of ignorance, to use Booth's term. The dramatic conventions of the Elizabethan theater, the vocabulary which was archaic, the vocabulary words which although still used today the students simply didn't know definitions for, the familial conventions of a European royal household in the Middle Ages, the emotional incongruence of Hamlet's character for an American adolescent in 1991—these are just a few of the conventions that stand between the text and a novice African American adolescent reader in 1991 (or for that matter almost any novice adolescent reader in 1991).

Dr. Johnson, the teacher of control class one, saw part of his responsibility to render the text more comprehensible by providing his class with the necessary experiences and information to tackle those factors which distanced them from *Hamlet*. Thus, the level of discussion about *Hamlet* hovered between a literal rendition of the plot, just what was happening from one scene to the next, to an interpretive discussion about the motives and intentions of characters. They did not take apart Shakespeare's metaphors to discern what multiple layers of meaning might reasonably rest under the surface.

There are other approaches intended to help students think beforehand about the kinds of thematic problems which a difficult or distant text might pose (Curry 1987; Smagorinsky, McCann, and Kern 1987). These approaches, however, also tend to focus on themes, or on the motivation of characters, but rarely on the rhetoric of the text. Dr. Johnson's goal was for the students to "know" *Hamlet*. Proof that they came to "know" *Hamlet* was how well they did on a one-hundred item multiple-choice exam on *Hamlet*.

The second crippling handicap is the inability to pay attention. By this, Booth means an inability to pay attention to the words themselves, to the rhetoric of the text. Many of the battles fought in discussions in the experimental classes were precisely over the issue of paying close attention to the words on the page. The transcripts of discussions in the control classes do not show a consistent attention to helping students become independent close readers. Dr. Johnson was clearly concerned about a close reading of *Hamlet*, but *he* did the close reading and the students attentively listened as he would explicate delicate points in the text for them.

The third crippling handicap is simply lack of practice. Concerned with demands of reading narrative, Booth (1974), Hillocks (Hillocks et al. 1971) and Rabinowitz (1987) stress that reading widely by author, by genre, by historical period, and by theme leads to a wide and subtle body of knowledge which the expert reader brings to bear in the act of interpretation. Smith and Hillocks (1988), (Hillocks et al. 1971) rightly argue that the literature curriculum should be sequenced in such a way as to give students multiple opportunities, both within a school year and across school years, to practice reading for particular conventions, for instance interpreting irony and satire or recognizing unreliable narrators, well-defined genres as well as motifs which recur in literature. The practice of jumping around from theme to theme in the second control class meant that those students did not receive any consistent instruction that would be transferable to comparable texts. I question whether the approach for teaching *Hamlet* that was used in control class one would help the students to read *Othello, Julius Caesar,* or *King Lear* any better. A clear intention of the instructional unit in which the experimental classes participated was for the short story they read to prepare them for the first novel, and for the first novel to prepare them for the second novel, and finally for the second novel to prepare them to apply their skills independently to a new story, one they had never read. Such a principle of organization helps to overcome the handicap of lack of practice, defined as lack of consistent close reading of particular kinds of texts (in Booth's case, consistent close reading of texts in which irony plays a major role).

The following excerpt is offered as an example of the discourse in control class one. This discussion occurred after the students had completed their study of *Hamlet*. It was intended by Dr. Johnson as a Socratic seminar on some of the great ideas in *Hamlet* and as preparation for an essay which the students were going to write in which they would distinguish between related pairs of ideas and discuss how these ideas played out in *Hamlet*. These pairs included free will and freedom, evil and badness, forgiveness and pardon. In the discussion, the examples which distinguished one from the other came from Dr. Johnson's personal experience, personal experiences of the students, or from *Hamlet*:

> *T:* What does the king ask when he gets down on his knees?
> *S:* Forgiveness.
> *T:* Forgiveness for his foul what?
> *S:* Play.
> *T:* Murder. Forgive me. Whom is he asking in the video when he got down? What was he looking up towards?
> *S:* The sky.
> *T:* That is right. He was asking for forgiveness. It wasn't pardon. . . .

I do not believe that simple counts of turn-taking and the number of words per turn or T Units per turn is sufficient to characterize classroom discourse (Carlsen 1991). A round of recitation within a lesson or unit segment that prepares students for more open-ended inquiry and dialogue about a literary text, for example, takes on a different significance from a round of recitation that is the dominant mode of instruction for either the entire or the majority of the series of lessons or the unit. The following and the previous excerpt are embedded in a larger framework which aims at preparing the students to think about the "great ideas" in *Hamlet*. The following excerpt, however, demonstrates how the overarching goal is thwarted by the continuing dominance of the discussion by Dr. Johnson.

T: ... All right, fate and fortune. What does fate mean, Willy? What does fate mean? It was your fate to be here on this date looking at me trying to respond to a question that I gave you and you looking all around trying to get an idea from Maria and she just can't be loud enough to tell it, to help you out. It is your fate not to be able to hear what she is saying so you can respond. And it was your fate to get ordained long ago before you ever thought at this moment, at this time you would be here at my mercy trying to respond to the question. Now what does fate mean?

S: Is it like a destiny?

T: It is your destiny. It is all of your destinies to be here with me. That is right. You had no choice in this.

S: I'm the one signed my name.

T: What choice did you have? It is your fate to get a grade too. You better watch yourself. All right, let's apply it to *Hamlet*. Where is the first instance that this term applies to *Hamlet?* Where or how? How was it used? Where is the first time it is used in the play?

S: When the ghost appears.

T: All right. What do you mean? You tell that.

S: The ghost came two or three times, so when his friends or whatever came and told him that it was his fate that he was going to go and talk to the ghost of his father.

T: All right. When they are all around and the ghost comes, what do they try to do to Hamlet? Hold it. What does he say?

S: He says let me go.

T: He says let me go because he says that my fate cries out. What does he mean by that?

S: He wanted to know what he longed to do.

T: He wanted to know what he longed to do.

S: When his best friend tells him not to fight [unintelligible] he said no. If it is meant for me to die, I will die.

T: That is beautiful. That is right. That is wonderful. Turn to page 801. Fate has played a big part throughout the whole play. It is full of chance and circumstances and things of that nature. It was, what was his name, Horatio's fate to [unintelligible]. It was just his fate to have to have this hurt and have to be there. It is a whole lot of fate going on here. This is dealing with a situation when Osric has left, right, and Osric is told about how these two are going to get together and have a duel and Horatio says you will lose this wager and Hamlet says, "I do not think so. Since he went into France I have been in continual practice." I will win. But he says, "Thou wouldst not think how ill all's here about my heart." What does that mean to you?

S: That he feels something is wrong.

(I included the opening turns of the teacher because Dr. Johnson is signifying; as the kids would say, he is cracking on Willy. Signifying in the classroom by black teachers and black students alike is not an uncommon practice.) All of Dr. Johnson's questions either ask for reference to some literal event in the play or to paraphrase a statement from the play which only requires that one know the meaning of the words themselves. The students who respond to Dr. Johnson's question obviously "know" the play in terms of who does what, when, where and why. However, even the brunt of paraphrase is carried by Dr. Johnson. In the experimental transcripts, the only time one would find a teacher taking so long a turn as Dr. Johnson's final turn would be when the teacher was clarifying a question, not giving an answer.

In the one segment of this transcript in which Dr. Johnson asks the students to interpret a passage from *Hamlet* which is both figurative and symbolic, Dr. Johnson continues to take on the burden of interpretation. The image in question, a sparrow, is not distant in the way that Booth describes. In fact, later in the discussion, Dr. Johnson refers to an African American gospel song, "His Eye Is on the Sparrow," as a way of mapping onto the student's prior knowledge.

T: What did he mean by this statement? "There is a special providence in the fall of a sparrow"? Take a second and think about that. Your second is up. What does it mean Valora?

S: I don't know.

T: Valora is still thinking. What does it mean Diane?

S: Which section?

T: "There is a special providence in the fall of a sparrow."

S: Repeat what you said again.

T: What do you think that line means? Taking in context he is talking about what?

S: Life and death.

T: Life and what is to . . .

S: Come . . .

T: Come. Right. So, now what does that line mean in terms of what he is talking about?

S: He is going to live now and die later on or he is going to die now and live later on.

T: Deal with the sparrow. What is so important about the sparrow? Why do they use the sparrow?

S: Is it like an angel or something?

T: What is the sparrow a symbol of?

S: Freedom.

T: It is all the [unintelligible] that you have?

S: No, it's not.

    T: Symbolically. It is something that is insignificant. So, if he watches
       the sparrow he is watching something insignificant and it has no
       meaning. . . . So regardless how insignificant the sparrow seems to
       be, there is still a providence, there is still what?
    S: A future.

This discussion continues in a similar manner. Students respond to the
teacher's questions with one-line answers which show evidence that they
"know" the plot of *Hamlet* and understand the basic motivation of characters.
What the discussion does not show, however, is students who take on the poet
in the dramatist and thereby gain insights into more subtle layers of meaning
which I believe most writers intend.

Note

1. Ronald Gallimore and Roland Tharp define a metascript as "verbal instruction
   that has a general format and general guidelines suggestive of a particular
   strategy, but is not so highly prescriptive that there is no room for responsive
   teaching" (cited in Cazden 1988, 107).

10 Implications and Final Thoughts

This study investigated the implications of signifying, a form of social discourse in the African American community, as a scaffold for teaching strategies to interpret complex implied relationships in fiction. The study also investigated the relevance of prior social knowledge to novice's skill in interpreting fiction.

Quantitative analysis demonstrated positive and statistically significant correlations between skill in signifying as well as levels of relevant prior social knowledge and achievement on the pre- and post-tests. The pre- and post-tests measured skill in making localized and complex inferences about texts of African American fiction in the "speakerly" tradition. Four classes participating in the experimental unit made greater and statistically significant gain from the pre- to post-test over the two control classes.

Qualitative analysis of classroom transcripts documents the following:

1. the expansion of experimental students' understanding of signifying;

2. their extrapolation of a set of interpretative strategies applicable to identifying that a passage (of either signifying dialogue or fiction) suggests multiple layers of meaning;

3. strategies for reconstructing layers of significance that are supportable from the text and the students' prior social/cultural knowledge.

The transcript analysis also documents distinctions between the talk in experimental classes and the talk in control class.

The usefulness of this instructional model is twofold. First, it brings to the forefront of research in the teaching of literature a focus on texts of African American literature. Traditionally, research in the teaching of literature very rarely focuses on literary texts by authors who are not white and male. Second, it presents one model for bringing community-based prior knowledge into classroom instruction. Many declare that the growing diversity of the American student population demands that teachers find ways to close the gap between home/community culture and the culture of the classroom, but few offer solid examples of how this can be done. The research model adds to a growing body of research in the teaching of literature which deals with the issue of test construction and matching assessment to the specific construct being taught in the unit. Finally, it supports Hillocks's (Hillocks et al. 1971;

134

Smith and Hillocks 1988) claim that literature instruction should be organized around literary conventions, genres, and concepts that serve as tools of interpretation.

The effectiveness of this instructional model is important precisely because it enabled students who are academically marginal to interpret figuratively dense works of fiction and answer difficult inferential questions of those texts. The students who started out the weakest were the students who achieved the greatest gain. Prior social knowledge and skill in signifying both showed positive correlations with both pre- and post-test scores. This was true for students with both high and low prior social knowledge. These variables did not correlate highly for students with moderate knowledge in these two areas.

There are three areas of limitation in this study. First, there is no way to disentangle the effects of the inquiry mode of instruction from the effects of the texts themselves. The inquiry mode has been labeled and defined by Hillocks (1986):

> A treatment was coded as focusing on inquiry when it presented students with sets of data (or occasionally required them to find data) and when it initiated activities designed to help students develop skills or strategies for dealing with the data in order to say or write something about it. Ordinarily, such activities are designed to enhance particular skills or strategies such as formulating and testing explanatory generalizations, observing and reporting significant details to achieve an effect, or generating criteria for contrasting similar phenomena. (211)

Although Hillocks's description of inquiry as a mode of teaching was applied to research studies in the teaching of composition, it applies equally well to the mode of instruction used in this research. The inquiry mode of instruction used in this research included

1. a data set consisting of three signifying dialogues as well as signifying examples which the students generated,
2. a forum for students to construct the conventions for analyzing signifying talk as a springboard for applying those conventions to selected texts of African American fiction (providing a kind of rehearsal of the strategies before analyzing the actual texts of fiction),
3. open-ended inferential questions aimed at close textual analysis,
4. small-group work in order to maximize opportunities to talk extensively about these questions, and
5. multiple opportunities to write about their ideas about these questions.

It is my position that the inclusion of "relevant" texts in and of themselves is insufficient for teaching these skills of literary analysis.

The small body of research which approximates an inquiry mode of instruction with literary texts rarely uses low-achieving African American high school students as its population. If African American students are included in such studies, they are normally part of an integrated school setting. Research on the effects of integration on school achievement suggests that the climate of such settings does have a positive correlation with school achievement (Anderson 1984), although I would argue that the correlation is due to the organization and climate of instruction in these schools rather than the fact that students of different racial and/or ethnic backgrounds simply attend classes together. The strength of this study, I believe, is in its combination of inquiry-based instruction with rich texts to which the students bring significant prior knowledge. However, the research design offers no direct opportunity to disengage these two major variables.

I have some ambivalence about whether it is ultimately necessary to disengage these variables, since it is not the aim of this research agenda to suggest that other literary texts are somehow not "relevant" or useful ingredients in the high school literature curriculum for African American students. Rather, I believe the critical issue is how to recognize the prior knowledge that these and other ethnically diverse students bring to the classroom and harness that knowledge into sophisticated readings of meaningful literature. I believe that an inquiry-based mode of instruction is an effective way of tapping into the prior social, cultural, and linguistic knowledge students bring into literature classrooms. The nature of data sets examined or generated by the students themselves early in such instructional units should ideally tap the prior knowledge of students and link their existing prior knowledge to the tasks of the instructional unit.

Incorporation of prior social and cultural knowledge into literature instruction can support sophisticated and subtle interpretations of literature. For example, interpretive communities (Fish 1980) of Black Aesthetic, Feminist, Marxist, as well as Gay and Lesbian critics bring a perspective to the act of interpretation that emerges out of the prior social, cultural, and political knowledge/experiences of particular groups of people. These particular perspectives inform their interpretation of a wide variety of works. Black Aesthetic criticism is not limited to works by black authors, just as Feminist criticism is not limited to works by female authors. That point was dramatically brought home to me by Toni Morrison (1989), who offers a profoundly "Black" interpretation of Melville's *Moby Dick*.

Morrison asserts that the striking lack of consideration of the riveting effects of racism on the psyche of American life is in itself subtly revealing. How could the founding literature of the United States fail to address it? At a time when human beings were regarded and treated as chattel, it is difficult to believe that some significant, albeit small, body of white writers were not struggling to find some way through their art to explore the reverberations of such an inconceivable set of common social practices. Morrison says,

> There is a great, ornamental, prescribed absence in early American Literature and I submit it is instructive. It only seems that the canon of American literature is "naturally" or "inevitably" "white." In fact it is studiously so. In fact these absences of vital presences in Young American literature may be the insistent fruit of the scholarship rather than the text. Perhaps some of these writers, although under current house arrest, have much more to say than has been realized. Perhaps some were not so much transcending politics, or escaping blackness, as they were transforming it into intelligible, accessible, yet artistic modes of discourse. (14)

Morrison applies this point of view to an interpretation of Melville's *Moby Dick,* although she says that it can also be extended to inform interpretations of other American writers such as Poe, Cather, Hemingway, Fitzgerald, and Faulkner, to cite a few. According to Morrison,

> Melville's "truth" was his recognition of the moment in America when whiteness became ideology. And if the white whale is the ideology of race, what Ahab has lost to it is personal dismemberment and family and society and his own place as a human in the world. The trauma of racism is, for the racist and the victim, the severe fragmentation of the self, and has always seemed to me a cause (not a symptom) of psychosis— strangely of no interest to psychiatry. Ahab, then, is navigating between an idea of civilization that he renounces and an idea of savagery he must annihilate, because the two cannot co-exist. The former is based on the latter. What is terrible in its complexity is that the idea of savagery is not the missionary one: it is white racial ideology that is savage and if, indeed, a white, nineteenth-century, American male took on not abolition, not the amelioration of racist institutions or their laws, but the very concept of whiteness as an inhuman idea, he would be very alone, very desperate, and very doomed. Madness would be the only appropriate description of such audacity, and "he heaves me," the most succinct and appropriate description of that obsession. (15–16)

She does not suggest that this is the only viable interpretation of Ahab's whale as a metaphor. Rather she says,

> A complex, heaving, disorderly, profound text is *Moby Dick,* and among its several meanings it seems to me this "unspeakable" one has remained the "hidden course," the "truth in the Face of Falsehood." To this day no novelist has wrestled with its subject. To this day literary analyses of canonical texts have shied away from that perspective: the informing and determining Afro-American presence in traditional American literature. (18)

Besides disentangling the effects of the text from the effects of the instructional mode, the second limitation of the study is its inability to measure directly how signifying knowledge and skill are transformed and applied. The specific measures of signifying skill and prior social knowledge are measured before any instruction and therefore represent in one sense what the students bring to the classroom. At the small-group level, transcript analysis offers insights into how students used, transformed, and applied this knowledge. It does not, however, allow for analysis at the class level, or more importantly at the level of the individual. Post-test measures only indicate that there was transformation in the ability to answer inferential questions that are based on interpreting figurative passages in texts of fiction. They do not offer a trace of the process.

Finally, the transcripts, perhaps the richest source of insight into the process, await a fuller analysis. Some studies in classroom discourse, particularly around the topic of interpreting literature, suffer from an incomplete analysis. Nystrand and Gamoran (1989, 1990) accumulated a huge data set which was meticulously analyzed. However, this data collected across fifty-two classes only included two classroom observations in the fall and another two observations in the spring. Adler (1987) properly points out that a Socratic seminar may include recitative or declarative talk by the teacher as preparation for helping students progress to a difficult and open-ended question. He admonishes researchers that a simple counting of the proportion of declarative talk versus interrogative questions is insufficient to characterize the entire seminar as successful or unsuccessful according to the goals of inquiry which Socratic seminars aim. Nystrand and Gamoran's studies offer valuable empirical evidence of the positive correlations between the quality of teachers' questions and reading achievement. Their studies are also important in that they measure reading achievement relative to the specific texts which students studied in class. However Carlsen (1991) observes that the research on the level of teacher questions as a correlate of the levels of students' response is inconsistent. Carlsen notes,

> From a sociolinguistic perspective, the content of a question cannot be assessed without reference to a broader linguistic context and the knowledge of the speakers. It is highly unlikely that such assessment can be done during real-time observations by observers visiting classrooms for single lessons, particularly if the observers are unfamiliar with the subject-matter content, the students, and the participation structures common in those classrooms. (166)

I propose that the unit of instruction, not the daily lesson, should be the unit of analysis of classroom discourse. Such analysis yields a more complete and informed picture of how one navigates the often muddy waters of didactic and inquiry-based instruction. I believe that classroom research should provide practical and workable insights for classroom teachers. I also know that it is very difficult to maintain over time the high level of questions and levels of student responses which the research on classroom discourse and especially that on teacher questioning proposes as the ideal. The real world of classroom teaching is quite complex and often involves necessarily moving in and out of didactic or purely recitative modes in order to prepare students for rich discussions and higher-order questions. When researchers draw inferences about relationships between classroom discourse and achievement, long-term observations are required. Because of these considerations, I propose that using the unit of instruction as the unit of analysis may yield a more detailed and realistic picture of the course of effective classroom discourse as it relates to achievement. In using this unit of analysis researchers can chart

1. the structural relationships between recitative modes versus inquiry modes,
2. how the levels or categories of teachers' questions in one mode prepare or support the levels of teachers' questions in the other mode,
3. how the goals of the instructional unit and the teachers' subject matter knowledge influence the range of the discourse (Carlsen 1988; Stodolsky 1988).

To use the proportion of certain categories of questions and student-teacher or student-student verbal interactions across a series of daily lessons can only offer limited insights which likely have limited external validity. If the purpose of the analysis of the classroom talk is simply descriptive, observations of a few lessons are sufficient. If the purpose of the research is to infer from observations of classroom talk some relationship between the talk and achievement, then the unit of instruction should be observed and serve as the unit of analysis. The transcript analysis offered so far seeks only to illustrate the major leaps in the transformation of the students' knowledge and skills.

Implementation Variables

The variables influencing implementation of this model include three broad categories: cost, teacher in-service, and assessment. Cost may be the least difficult variable with which schools have to cope. The "speakerly" texts of African American literature on which this study is based are not part of the traditional storage of books that English departments have on hand. Although it would be ideal to have paperback copies available for each student so that students could underline and write in the book, this is not necessary for the successful implementation of the approach. However, at least an initial outlay of funds for book purchases is necessary and the amount of funding needed would depend on the scope of implementation.

The more challenging variable is that of teacher training and/or teacher in-service. This is, of course, the primary challenge for almost all curricular reforms in schools. The interaction I had with the participating teachers was similar to the models proposed under the rubric of peer coaching. The teachers were able to see the inquiry mode of instruction not in theory but in practice by a peer. The dialogue we had about the strengths and weaknesses in my instruction as well as theirs both allayed much of their fear and made it clear that this model was broad enough for individual differences and creativity. Ideally, I believe, such units of instruction should be developed by groups of teachers at a school site.

Any model for in-service or pre-service teacher training aimed at assisting teachers in implementing such a program must itself operate in an inquiry mode and must address the following issues:

1. developing open-ended but challenging questions that require close textual analysis;

2. organizing small-group discussions that both allow students room to hypothesize and generate tentative interpretations and at the same time stimulate students at critical junctures in their reasoning;

3. as a peer group, having teachers participate in critical discussions of the works in question so that the teachers themselves come to "own" the texts;

4. expanding teachers' knowledge base regarding the strengths of the oral language which students individually and as members of a linguistic community bring to school;

5. expanding teachers' knowledge base regarding the symbiotic relationship between talk and thinking, between oral language and literary tradition.

This final point is very sensitive, especially when it comes to the validity of Black English. Teachers, regardless of ethnicity, often have very stereotyped and negative attitudes toward Black English and may become very emotional when considering its relevance to classroom instruction. In fact, teachers tend to see the purpose of English classes as effectively erasing any demonstrations of Black English Vernacular in the classroom. This issue can become especially sensitive regarding the language of signifying because of its raunchy and competitive tone.

The third implementation variable is assessment. It is a widely accepted adage in education that assessment and textbooks drive the curriculum. The one teacher who had the greatest difficulty adjusting to the inquiry mode of instruction was ultimately most influenced by my constant reminder of the assessment tool. I often reminded her that her efforts to tell the students what the "right" answer was would be of no value to them when they took the test. The test was not about either novel, but rather was based on a short story that neither the students nor she had seen. The students had to be able to negotiate the difficult inferential questions on their own and they could only learn this independence through practice. Implementation of an inquiry-based mode of instruction such as this would at least amend, if not replace, the traditional multiple-choice departmental exam as the sole tool of assessment. Such traditional departmental exams tend to emphasize rote grammar or identification of certain rules for essay organization (i.e., the tenets of the five-paragraph theme) as opposed to writing original essays. Such exams also generally include hordes of literal-level questions about so-called "canonical" texts.

Although he did not use a departmental exam, the department chairperson who taught one of the control classes in this study prided himself on how well his students did on a 100-question multiple-choice exam on *Hamlet*. These same students did not do as well as the lowest achieving experimental class in terms of pre- to post-test gain. This departmental chairperson is, in fact, a superb teacher, but the unstated objective of his teaching was fundamentally different from the objective of this instructional approach. His goal for the students in this unit was to "master" *Hamlet*. My goal, in his place, would have been for the students to gain some level of mastery in tragedy as a genre, or have some skills that they could and would then apply to another Shakespearian tragedy, such as *Julius Caesar* or *King Lear*. In contrast, the goal of the experimental instruction was for students to acquire meaningful levels of mastery over a set of interpretative strategies which could be applied to a broad spectrum of texts which shared comparable structural and/or thematic properties. The point here is that objectives of instruction should and do influence the assessment instruments used.

Developing appropriate instruments for evaluation is a challenging implementation issue. The instruments for measuring signifying and prior social knowledge were necessary for the research focus of this unit. Schools implementing such a literature program would not need such instruments. Their challenge when using other novels would be to develop questions which fit the Hillocks taxonomy for both pre- and post-test measures. More often than not, English teachers at the secondary level do not assess what their students already know about an instructional unit before instruction begins. When they do, it is more likely to be a unit on mechanics and usage in which they use a commercial pre-test. One of the benefits of questions based on the Hillocks taxonomy given before instruction is to alert the teacher about strengths when it comes to literal versus inferential questions. Such an assessment can appropriately influence grouping patterns for small-group discussions. In addition, sometimes a teacher may be surprised. The students who seem most verbally agile may not be the best thinkers when it comes to subtle analogical reasoning.

Two criteria which the assessment measures must address are those of reliability and validity. Although it is unlikely that high school English departments will engage in the process of establishing statistical reliability and significance, the questions of reliability and validity are still relevant and necessary issues. In terms of validity, teachers must be sure that the thematic and structural demands of the stories used for pre- and post-test measures are comparable to the thematic and structural demands of the novels and/or short stories in the instructional unit. If there is no qualitative analysis of comparability, one's assessment measures may test something other than what was taught. Also, a qualitative assessment, at least, must be made of the questions themselves, to be sure they address the foci of the unit.

An example of lack of clarity on this issue occurred during the instructional phase of this project. I have pointed out elsewhere that this was a learning experience for both the students and the teachers. The written copy of the unit had more questions for each reading than were possible to discuss. The idea was that this would allow teachers and students to make choices about questions. When the first short story was discussed in one of the classes, my intention was that the more literal questions would be addressed by students writing the answers for homework as a kind of prereading activity. Instead, the teacher who was unaccustomed to conducting student-centered discussions about more open-ended questions directed the entire class discussion around the literal questions. As a result the class became a recitation.

The issue of reliability arises around the grading of the essay exams. Some training on using scales for evaluating the short-answer responses written as paragraphs or mini-essays would be necessary. Simple inter-rater reliabilities computed as percentages of agreement between readers would suffice in order to establish that there was some common standard used by the teaching staff in evaluating such exams.

In essence, these implementation variables are no different than those required by any meaningful curricular changes in language arts instruction in schools. As others have pointed out (Miller-Jones 1988; Means and Knapp 1991), as educators do what is best for America's disempowered minorities, they do what is best for all students.

Implications for Future Research

I see this work as exploratory even though the results have been positive. Replication with a larger student population and further definition of the control conditions would be useful. There are problems, of course, with implementation for a larger cohort, one of which is the problem of sufficient training and support for teachers in order to assure relative stability of implementation. This is an area where support of a university would be helpful. Replicating the study with other "speakerly" texts would broaden the applicability of the model. Eventually, a larger study in which experimental groups shared working in an inquiry mode but differed according to the kind of texts studied would help disaggregate the effects of instructional strategy and content. Great care would have to be taken to be sure that the conventions of the two texts were of comparable difficulty. This, of course, is a challenging task in itself. I would eventually like to contextualize such distinctions between the demands of different texts in a taxonomy of reading fiction, particularly African American fiction. Although Booth (1974), Rabinowitz (1987), Culler (1975), and others have developed useful frameworks through which to view the demands of reading narrative, these frameworks have been concerned with expert reading at the university level. I think a more basic taxonomy is needed for instruction at the secondary school level (see Hillocks et al. 1971).

Before any such large-scale effort, however, I believe an intimate analysis at the level of individual students would be most informative regarding the process of student change. Such a study would concentrate its analysis on one class, taping all small-group discussions as well as whole-class discussion. The purpose of taping all small-group discussions would be to follow the progress of either all or selected students in the class. In addition, use of talk-aloud protocols with students would likely offer the most insightful investigation at the individual level, in contrast to the interpersonal level within small-group discussions. Of specific interest is how students transform existing linguistic knowledge into interpretive strategies. In such a study, it would be interesting to contrast how such transformation might occur as students engage texts to which they bring differing levels of prior knowledge.

Final Thoughts

The results of this study support the following recommendations for literature instruction at the secondary level:

1. a thorough integration of multiethnic literature in the curriculum of secondary schools;

2. incorporation of practices which draw on cultural strengths as well as linguistic and prior social knowledge that students, especially diverse ethnic and linguistic populations, bring to school;

3. use of an inquiry mode of instruction incorporating the examination of data sets which emulate concepts and strategies which students are expected to acquire in an instructional unit;

4. focus of literature instruction on teaching interpretative strategies and knowledge of specific genres of literature; sequencing texts in such a

way as to provide consistent practice within genres and across strategies;

5. incorporation of multiple frames of reference for interpreting literature;
   such frames of reference should include perspectives which reflect the
   particular points of view and special interests of groups represented in
   the student body, as well as points of view of individuals within groups.

None of these recommendations is new (Hillocks et al. 1971, 1986; Smith and
Hillocks 1988; Hynds 1989; Scholes 1985; Wimmers 1988). One problem,
however, has been that too few empirical and/or ethnographic studies have
incorporated these practices with African American underachieving students.
Marshall's (1990) observational studies of inner-city English classes would
imply that such practices are not the norm in such school environments. There
is increasing national interest in making use of cultural and linguistic prior
knowledge as well as incorporating instructional practices which emphasize
critical thinking skills. The research based on pedagogical practices which
support such a perspective, unfortunately, is limited.

Two controversial issues arise from the present study. One issue is a focus
on African American literature in the curriculum, and the second is the emphasis on close textual analysis. The debate over appropriate texts in literature
classrooms is a highly emotional struggle over the issue of canon formation.
Although the debate is sharpest at the university level, the shape of that
discussion influences discussion at the secondary level. Although public pressure has influenced some state legislatures and some boards of education to
require the inclusion of African American literature in the curriculum, little
practical support has been offered to classroom teachers in how to incorporate
these texts. This problem becomes especially complex for classroom teachers.
Teachers feel torn between testing mandates (district-required achievement
tests, departmental exams, SAT and ACT exams) which do not test knowledge
of or ability to interpret such texts and, on the other hand, public bodies such
as state legislatures, boards of education, and special parent and community
interest groups. Part of what is lacking in the debate is a set of warrants that
take into account sound pedagogical principles as well as democratic political
principles.

The controversy over the emphasis on a close reading of the text emerges
in part from the popular reception of reader-response theories, especially at
the elementary and secondary levels. However, classroom observational studies suggest there is significant lag between the theory and the actual practice
of teachers (Goodlad 1984; Hillocks 1989; Marshall 1989, 1990), and that the
lag is greatest in inner-city schools (Marshall 1990; Means and Knapp 1991).
The perspective as adopted by elementary and secondary practitioners emphasizes the role of the subjective response of the reader to the text. It is not

unlikely that criticism may be raised that the emphasis on close textual analysis in the present study represents a conservative reversion to the principles of New Criticism. A thorough response to the controversies surrounding these two issues is the subject of another book. On the other hand, I believe it is imperative that I offer some brief response here.

My response to the criticism of requiring close textual reading is politically inspired. I think it is unfair to accept from novice readers, especially those from unempowered communities, simply purely subjective responses to literature. Delpit (1986, 1988) argues that unempowered minority students should be explicitly taught the rules of power concerning language use with which they will have to contend. Although Delpit's specific criticism focuses on the process approach to writing,[1] I believe that her criticisms are relevant here.

Those critics, for example, who are most commonly associated with the more subjective school of reader-response theory (Bleich 1978; Fish 1980) are themselves clearly grounded and empowered by their training and abilities in close textual analysis. Those who are trained in close textual analysis are, in my opinion, most empowered to go beyond the text, to stand critically in opposition to the text, if they so choose. Part of what influences that freedom is the confidence one feels about one's power over the text. When there is some congruence between the themes and language of a work of fiction and the life conditions of the reader, the kind of self-reflection and self-definition which Scholes (1985) describes as part of criticism is more likely to occur, especially for novice readers. A critical subjective response presumes that self-reflection is a response to the text. The reader's response to the text is best informed when it is a result of close reading.

This does not mean that such congruences are intended simply to reinforce existing perceptions. Rather the processes of self-reflection and self-definition are influenced more when a work challenges the assumptions that the reader brings to the text. The point is simply that ethnic literature offers promising possibilities for novice readers of that ethnicity. This point of view does not contradict the claim that exposing students to multi-ethnic literature expands students' understanding and perceptions of other groups. (I agree wholeheartedly with this claim.) However, it must be remembered that literature curricula of U.S. high schools, on the whole, are not multi-ethnic and that African American students in huge numbers (as well as other groups including Hispanics, Native Americans, certain Asian American populations such as the Vietnamese, the Laotian, and the children of the poor in general) do not fare well in public education. Freire (1970) argues correctly when he says that the poor and unempowered are empowered through dialogue and reflective contemplation about their own experiences, both politically, culturally, and personally. Close readings of an ethnic group's literature offer such possibilities. Freire (1970) is right to call for a pedagogy of the oppressed.

A basic assumption underlying the criticism that close textual analysis is a conservative aim of instruction is the idea that it will limit and invalidate subjective responses. In contrast, I propose that this instructional unit that emphasized close textual analysis in fact empowered students to respond more fully. As illustrated in the chapter "Talk in the Classroom," at the beginning, students' responses were terse. They did not initiate questions of their own and were generally unconcerned about anything that might appear problematic about the texts. By the time they read the second novel, *The Color Purple,* the students independently raised questions. The questions were authentic in that the students genuinely cared about them, and there were no simple right or wrong responses to them.

A vivid example of this transition occurred when a young man came into the classroom in the middle of the day, three periods before his class met with me. He wanted to know why in her letters Celie referred to her husband as "Mr. _____" instead of either using his last name or his first name. The fact that the young man asked about Celie (rather than, for example, about the author) suggests the kind of aesthetic stance which Rosenblatt describes (1978). Among the questions raised by the students was "Why is this book called *The Color Purple?*" Although the teachers had also planned to pose the question, the students beat them to the punch, and the question dominated class discussions for the final week of instruction. Another example of the students' responses driving discussion is the excerpt described in detail in the chapter "Talk in the Classroom" where, in a small-group discussion, students debated intensely about what criteria were appropriate for ascertaining why Walker used purple instead of another color. This was not an issue raised by the teacher or discussed in whole-group sessions.

Rather than constraining the breadth of their responses, their close attention to textual detail, the enduring requirement that they prove any assertions, and the challenge of difficult inferential questions broadened their responses. Examples of the quality of student responses to the text by the end of the instructional unit are the following by Charles and Diane. Charles was the young man who came to me between classes to ask about Celie's references to Mr. _____. Diane had been out of school the previous semester because she had just had a baby.

> *Charles:* God does not want people to go through life looking at the material things and the unnecessary things that make life impossible. He wants people to look at life as a gift and they should cherish that gift. *The Color Purple* is a pass way to look and realize that life is not a toy, but a gift from the earth. Alice Walker to me is the messenger through this book to tell that life is a gift or treasure
> ... The [unintelligible] is an example of life and how life [unintelligible] through a young girl's life, like saying one purple flower is an individual and are individuals like yourself. That's all I wrote.

> *Diane:* I said that *The Color Purple* was Celie's life and how she behaved all through the whole book. I came to this conclusion from what Shug had said about it pisses God off when you walk through the color purple in a field and don't notice it. On the next page, Celie says that her eyes were opened. And Sofia went through the color purple too. I think that the color purple was just like a depression or trying period and she went through when she was in jail and she was working for Miss Millie and she transformed into someone else. When Celie came out of her shell, when she signified on Mr. _____ and I think that the red, they always put red and purple together, I think that would represent a transformation from being in a depression and coming into something new.

Rather than being constrained by the requirements to read closely, the responses of these students were empowered. They have generalized across the breadth of the text and have appropriated the details of the text for their own interpretations. Diane's introduction of the significance of the image of red and purple together was not only unique, but one which I had never thought of before, an observation which I readily shared with Diane and the rest of the class.

The two major components of this research agenda revolved around an inquiry-based mode of instruction and the inclusion of cultural texts in instruction. The instructional mode has a great deal of support in research and theories of learning. As an approach, it shares much with the Socratic seminars of both the Paideia Program and the Great Books Foundation. Although it is challenging to use this family of instructional practices in classrooms, it will be much easier to gain acceptance for the inquiry mode than for the integration of such "speakerly" texts in the secondary school canon. The literature curriculum at the university level has become more diversified, but such diversification has not yet reached the secondary school in any significant proportion (Applebee 1989; Gates 1990; Spurlin 1990). The question of diversification of the literature curriculum at both levels simmers in the cauldron of the current battle over canonization. It is not my intention to enter the larger fray, but rather to limit my focus to the implications that the selection of texts may have for instruction at the secondary level.

At the core of the question of texts is the question of what ought to be the aim of literature instruction at the secondary level. I maintain that the aim of literature instruction ought to be to teach adolescents how to become more sensitive and subtle readers of literature and to be capable of carrying out such readings with relative independence. At the same time, I believe there is a kind of hermeneutical function that the teaching of literature can serve. Consider the many perils of modernity: the seeming loss of childhood under the weight of a massive media, the explosion of traditional family networks and support, the struggle for identity amidst the maze of bureaucracy and technology—along with the enduring perils of poverty, racism, sexism, and classism—these very real conditions argue for the possibility that the literature class may be an island for self-reflection and self-criticism, a place from which to view one's place in the world. Literature can serve such a function. The author Toni Morrison (1989) says, "Writing is, after all, an act of language, its practice. But *first* of all it is an effort of the will to discover" (20). Making it through readings of Western canonical texts or "speakerly" texts of African American literature that are interpreted for the student by the teacher, where the student demonstrates her competence by regurgitating facts and figures on multiple choice tests, does not serve the more fundamental functions of teaching literature which I have outlined.

The act of reading any text, literary texts in particular, places many demands on a good reader:

1. paying close attention to the words themselves (since playing around with surface meanings is one of the hallmarks of literary texts),

2. having sufficient prior social and linguistic knowledge to read between the lines of the text,

3. having sufficient prior readings in order to generate inter-textual links that can expand the array of associations a reader makes with the language of the text,

4. bringing an interest and point of view, both the possibility and the baggage which one's own personal experience brings to the act of interpretation,

5. and, finally, being knowledgeable of the narrative, dramatic and poetic conventions which authors in various literary traditions use to construct and convey meaning.

On the one hand, logic alone would argue that the closer the demands of the text are to the prior social, linguistic, and genre knowledge of the novice reader, the more likely a teacher/expert reader can effectively teach, at least in the initial stages, students to read in the manner I have outlined above. On the other hand, common sense would argue that schools do not need to provincialize the borders of reading to which students are exposed; still, the practical effects of the Eurocentric literature curriculum in American secondary schools provincializes in the profoundest sense. The practical question, then, is how these two propositions interact with one another and how they can be merged into a healthy and truthful whole.

I have acknowledged that there are those who would argue that the kind of reading I have outlined is text driven. However, I believe that reading literature is a kind of marriage, if you will, between the author, the text, and the reader. I do not believe that students who are novice readers can participate forcefully in discussions with themselves or others about the multiple meanings which good works offer as possibilities unless they themselves become close readers. One cannot dismiss a text which one cannot read and understand.

The problem with merging these opposing propositions revolves around the content of literature instruction, what texts are to be taught to whom. The question itself is not new. The question of canonization and curriculum has been an on-going debate in the history of Western schooling. The debates around Latin theological texts versus Greek and so-called "classic" texts, the viewpoint that literature in English was somehow less valuable than the "classics" in Greek, the emergence of American literature as worthy of canonization instead of the predominance of British literature, the question of whether American twentieth-century writers like Hemingway, Fitzgerald, and Faulkner were worthy of being included on the canonical pedestal, and for that matter the continuing dominance of British literature in many American university curricula, all attest to the fact that the battle over literary canon did not begin with Bloom (1987) and Hirsch (1987). Morrison (1989) aptly notes that "canon building is Empire building" (8). The process and aims of canonization are not merely questions of literary merit and tastes, but also of politics and power. Morrison (1989) also notes that the tenor of the contemporary debate is particularly virulent. She argues that the bitterness of the present debate is not over the expansion of the canon, but rather over the "miscegenation" of the canon (6). I choose to address here not the politics of the "miscegenation" of the canon, but from a pedagogical point of view the enhancements that such expansion can have on the very life of the literature curriculum.

Spurlin (1990) describes a theory of criticism which allows for dialogue between multiple frames of reference on the literary text:

> Inge Crosman Wimmers, whose theory of reading has been influenced by the aesthetics of reception and her work with Iser at the University of Konstanz, has recently written of the need to broaden the interpretive space between text and reader by paying attention to multiple frames of reference, a formulation which helps us to move away from an either/or approach of choosing one reading over another so that we can see which readings are possible within cultural, mimetic, personal, intertextual, or historical referential frames . . . articulating the various ways readers can situate themselves in relation to the texts. . . . (739)

Spurlin is arguing for an approach to reading Black texts that does not reduce acceptable interpretive frameworks to what he and others call an essentialized, singular notion of Black literature or criticism (see also Henderson 1989). However, I suggest that the notion of multiple frames of reference provides a foundation for a literature curriculum that can merge the warring propositions around culturally diverse texts and Western canonical texts. It can also provide an effective means for achieving the ends for teaching literature which I have already outlined. However, in order for such an interpretive framework to be a viable alternative for instruction, teachers and critics must come to terms with the unique characteristics of the writings of such groups as Blacks, women, and Native Americans. That does not necessarily mean a teacher must become an expert in the national literature of every ethnic group, but rather the teacher and the critic must be cognizant of the following risks:

> 1) the gathering of a culture's difference into the skirts of the Queen is a neutralization designed and constituted to elevate and maintain hegemony. 2) circumscribing and limiting the literature to a mere reaction to or denial of the Queen, judging the work solely in terms of its referents to Eurocentric criteria, or its sociological accuracy, political correctness or its pretense of having no politics at all, cripple the literature and infantilize the serious work of imaginative writing. (Morrison 1989, 10)

Morrison warns that our perspective on African American literature must not

> lead to an incipient orphanization of the work in order to issue its adoption papers. They can confine the discourse to the advocacy of diversification within the canon and/or a kind of benign co-existence near or within reach of the already sacred texts. Either of these two positions can quickly become another kind of silencing if permitted to ignore the indigenous created qualities of the writing. So many questions surface and irritate. What have these critiques made of the work's own canvas? Its paint, its frame, its framelessness, its spaces? Another list of approved subjects? Of approved treatments? More self-censoring, more exclusion of the specificity of the culture, the gender, the language? (Morrison 1989, 10)

When I approach a Chicano text, I must expect that there is a richness that might evade me and that I must actively seek to uncover. I should not expect merely that it is a sociological imitation of Chicano life.

Multiple frames of reference are applicable in a variety of interpretive contexts:

1. opposing frames of reference within a cultural perspective (for example, critics Stephen Henderson, Henry Louis Gates, and Mae Henderson) represent a spectrum of literary perspectives within the cultural frame of Black Aesthetic criticism (see Spurlin 1990; Baker and Redmond 1989);

2. a variety of cultural perspectives on the interpretation of Western canonical texts as well as texts of other traditions (for example, Morrison's [1989] interpretation of Moby Dick already described; or a Native American perspective on American frontier literature).

Such multiple perspectives empower students to become close readers of literary texts and to validate their cultural experiences and prior knowledge by incorporating these experiences and knowledge into not only the content but also the mode of instruction in literature classes. To adopt multi-ethnic literature texts, and an inquiry-based mode of instruction, and to advocate an interpretative posture based on multiple frames of reference across a wide spectrum of texts can enhance the teaching of literature for all students.

Note

1. I have some reservations about Delpit's specific comments about composition instruction within the process approach or what Hillocks (1986) identifies as the natural process mode of instruction. However, I do agree with the basic thrust of her argument about the need to empower students from disenfranchised communities by teaching strategies that will lead to mastery of particular skills and the need for the research community to listen to perspectives articulated by minority researchers.

References

Abrahams, R. D. 1970. *Deep down in the jungle: Negro narrative folklore from the streets of Philadelphia.* Chicago: Aldine.

Adler, M. 1987, May. The three columns revisited with special attention to the conduct of seminars. *The Paideia Bulletin: News and Ideas for the Paideia Network,* 1–6.

Afflerbach, P. 1990. The influence of prior knowledge on expert readers' main idea construction strategies. *Reading Research Quarterly, 25*(1), 31–46.

Anderson, J. D. 1984. The schooling and achievement of Black children: Before and after Brown vs. Topeka, 1900–1980. *Advances in Motivation and Achievement, 1,* 103–22.

Anderson, R. C., and P. Freebody. 1981. Vocabulary knowledge. In J. Guthrie (Ed.), *Comprehension and teaching: Research reviews* (77–110). Newark, DE: International Reading Association.

Anderson, R., and P. Pearson. 1984. A schema-theoretic view of basic processes in reading. In P. D. Pearson (Ed.), *Handbook of reading research* (255–92). New York: Longman Inc.

Andrews, M., and P. Owens. 1973. *Black language.* Los Angeles, CA: Seymour-Smith.

Applebee, A. N. 1989. *A study of book-length works taught in high school English courses* [Report Series 1.2]. Albany, NY: Center for the Learning and Teaching of Literature.

Baker, H. 1980. *The journey back: Issues in Black literature and criticism.* Chicago: University of Chicago Press.

Baker, H., and P. Redmond. (Eds.) 1989. *Afro-American literary study in the 1990's.* Chicago: University of Chicago Press.

Baldwin, J. 1953. *Go tell it on the mountain.* New York: Dell Publishing.

Bambara, T. C. 1972. My man Bovanne. In *Gorilla, my love* (1–10). New York: Random House.

Baratz, J. C. 1969. A bidialectical task for determining language proficiency in economically disadvantaged children. *Child Development, 40*(8), 889–901.

Barr, R. 1986. Studying classroom reading instruction. *Reading Research Quarterly Review, 21*(3), 231–36.

Bartlett, F. C. 1932. *Remembering: A study in experimental and social psychology.* Cambridge: Cambridge University Press.

Beck, I., and M. G. McKeown. 1984. Application of theories of reading to instruction. In N. Stein (Ed.), *Literacy in American schools: Learning to read and write* (63–84). Chicago: University of Chicago Press.

Bleich, D. 1978. *Subjective criticism.* Baltimore: Johns Hopkins University Press.

Bloom, A. 1987. *The closing of the American mind.* New York: Simon and Schuster.

Bloome, D. M. 1981. An ethnographic approach to the study of reading activities among Black junior high school students: A sociolinguistic ethnography [dissertation]. *DAI, 42,* 2993. Kent State University.

Booth, W. 1974. *A rhetoric of irony.* Chicago: University of Chicago Press.

Bransford, J. D., and M. K. Johnson. 1973. Visual information processing. In W. Chase (Ed.), *Consideration of some problems of comprehension.* New York: Academic Press.

Brewer, W. F. 1985. The story schema: Universal and culture specific properties. In D. R. Olson, N. Torrance and A. Hildyard (Eds.), *Literacy, language and learning: The nature and consequences of reading and writing* (167–94). New York: Cambridge University Press.

Brody, P., C. DeMilo, and A. C. Purves. 1989. *The current state of assessment in literature* [Report Series Number 3.1]. Albany, NY: Center for the Learning and Teaching of Literature.

Brown, R. 1969. *Die nigger die!* New York: Dial Press.

Bruner, J. 1986. *Actual minds, possible worlds.* Cambridge, MA: Harvard University Press.

Carlsen, W. S. 1988. *The effect of science teacher subject-matter knowledge on teacher questioning and classroom discourse* [unpublished Ph.D. dissertation]. Stanford University.

———. 1991. Questioning in classrooms: A sociolinguistic perspective. *Review of Educational Research, 61*(2), 157–78.

Carraher, T. N., D. W. Carraher, and A. D. Schliemann. 1985. Mathematics in the streets and schools. *British Journal of Developmental Psychology, 3,* 21–29.

———. 1987. Written and oral mathematics. *Journal for Research in Mathematics Education, 18,* 83–97.

Cazden, C. 1988. *Classroom discourse: The language of teaching and learning.* Portsmouth, NH: Heinemann.

Chiesi, H. L., G. J. Spilich, and J. F. Voss. 1979. Acquisition of domain-related knowledge in relation to high and low domain knowledge. *Journal of Verbal Learning and Verbal Behavior, 18,* 257–72.

Cooke, M. 1984. *Afro-American literature in the twentieth century: The achievement of intimacy.* New Haven, CT: Yale University Press.

Culler, J. 1975. *Structuralist poetics: Structuralism, linguistics, and the study of literature.* Ithaca, NY: Cornell University Press.

Curry, J. 1987. *Improving secondary school students' inferential responses to literature* [unpublished Ph.D. dissertation]. University of Chicago.

Daniel, J. L., G. Smitherman-Donaldson, and M. A. Jeremiah. 1987. Makin' a way outa no way: The proverb tradition in the Black experience. *Journal of Black Studies, 17*(4), 482–508.

Davison, M. L., P. M. King, and K. S. Kitchener. 1990. Developing reflective thinking and writing. In R. Beach and S. Hynds (Eds.), *Developing discourse practices in adolescence and adulthood* (Vol. 39, 265–86). Norwood, NJ: Ablex.

de La Rocha, O. 1985. The reorganization of the arithmetic practice in the kitchen. *Anthropology and Education Quarterly, 16,* 193–98.

Delain, M., P. Pearson, and R. Anderson. 1985. Reading comprehension and creativity in Black language use: You stand to gain by playing the sounding game. *American Educational Research Journal, 22*(2), 155–73.

Delpit, L. 1986. Skills and other dilemmas of a progressive Black educator. *Harvard Educational Review, 56*(4), 379–85.

———. 1988. The silenced dialogue: Power and pedagogy in educating other people's children. *Harvard Educational Review, 58*(3), 280–98.

———. 1990. Language diversity and learning. In S. Hynds, and D. L. Rubin (Eds.), *Perspectives on talk and learning* (247–66). Urbana, IL: National Council of Teachers of English.

DeStefano, J. S. 1977, August. A difference is a difference, not a deficiency. *Contemporary Psychology,* 600–601.

Dewey, J. 1966. *Democracy and education: An introduction to the philosophy of education.* New York: The Free Press.

Dole, J., G. G. Duffy, L. R. Roehler, and P. D. Pearson. 1991. Moving from the old to the new: Research on reading comprehension instruction. *Review of Educational Research, 61*(2), 239–64.

DuBois, W. E.B. 1903. *The souls of Black folk: Essays and sketches.* Chicago: A. C. McClurg.

Earthman, E. A. 1989. The lonely, quiet concert: Readers creating meaning from literary texts [dissertation]. *DAI, 50,* 1583. Stanford University.

Eeds, M., and D. Wells. 1989. Grand conversations: An exploration of meaning construction in literature study groups. *Research in the Teaching of English, 23*(1), 4–29.

Farr, M. 1991. Dialects, culture and teaching the English language [Sponsored by the International Reading Association and the National Council of Teachers of English]. In J. Flood, J. M. Jensen, D. Lapp, and J. R. Squire (Eds.), *Handbook of research on teaching the English language arts* (365–71). New York: Macmillan.

Fish, S. 1980. *Is there a text in this class? The authority of interpretative communities.* Cambridge, MA: Harvard University Press.

Freeman, D. J., and A. C. Porter. 1988, April. Does the content of classroom instruction match the content of textbooks? [Paper presented at the annual meeting of the American Educational Research Association]. New Orleans.

Freire, P. 1970. *Pedagogy of the oppressed.* New York: Seabury.

Fritz, M. C. 1987. The culture of the reader, the origin of the text, and how children predict as they read [dissertation]. *DAI, 49,* 66. University of Illinois at Urbana-Champaign.

Garman, N. 1986. Reflection, the heart of clinical supervision: A modern rationale for professional practice. *Journal of Curriculum and Supervision, 2*(1), 1–24.

Gates, H. L. 1984. The blackness of blackness: A critique of the sign and the signifying monkey. In H. L. Gates (Ed.), *Black literature and literary theory* (285–322). New York: Methuen.

———. 1988. *The signifying monkey: A theory of Afro-American literary criticism.* New York: Oxford University Press.

———. 1990. Introduction: "Tell me, sir, . . . What is 'Black' literature?". *PMLA, 105,* 11–22.

Gauntt, H. L. 1989. The roles of prior knowledge of text structure and prior knowledge of content in the comprehension and recall of expository text [dissertation]. *DAI, 50,* 3539. University of Delaware.

Gayle, A. (Ed.). 1971. *The Black aesthetic.* Garden City, NY: Doubleday.

Ginsburg, H., J. Posner, and R. Russell. 1981. The development of mental addition as a function of schooling and culture. *Journal of Cross-Cultural Psychology, 12,* 163–78.

Giroux, H., and P. McLaren. (Eds.). 1989. *Critical pedagogy, the state and cultural struggle.* Albany, NY: State University of New York Press.

Goldhammer, R., R. Anderson, and R. Krajewski. 1980. *Clinical supervision: Special methods for the supervision of teachers.* New York: Holt, Rinehart and Winston.

Goodlad, J. I. 1984. *A place called school: Prospects for the future.* St. Louis: McGraw-Hill Book Company.

Hall, W. S., and R. Freedle. 1975. *Culture and language.* New York: Halsted Press.

Hall, W. S., and L. F. Guthrie. 1980. On the dialect question and reading. In *Theoretical issues in reading comprehension* (439–52). Hillsdale, NJ: Erlbaum.

Harris, V. 1989, 6–7 October. Instructional materials and literacy learning: Using African-American literature in the classroom [Paper presented at the conference on "Literacy among Black Youth: Issues in Learning, Teaching, and Schooling,"]. Literary Research Center, University of Pennsylvania.

Heath, S. B. 1983. *Ways with words: Language, life, and work in communities and classrooms.* Cambridge: Cambridge University Press.

———. 1988. Protean shapes in literacy events, ever-shifting oral and literate traditions. In E. R. Kintgen, B. M. Kroll, and M. Rose (Eds.), *Perspectives on literacy* (348–70). Carbondale: Southern Illinois University Press.

———. 1989. Oral and literate traditions among Black Americans living in poverty. *American Psychologist, 44*(2), 367–73.

Helen, J. W. 1980. *Schema modification as one aspect of reading comprehension: A comparison of strategies of adult proficient and non-proficient readers* [unpublished Ph.D. dissertation]. Southern Illinois University.

Henderson, M. 1989. Response. In H. Baker and P. Redmond (Eds.), *Afro-American Literary Study in the 1990s* (155–63). Chicago: University of Chicago Press.

Hillocks, G. 1979. The effects of observational activities on student writing. *Research in the Teaching of English, 13,* 23–35.

———. 1980. Toward a hierarchy of skills in the comprehension of literature. *English Journal, 69*(3), 54–59.

———. 1982, November. Inquiry and the composing process: Theory and research. *College English, 44,* 659–73.

———. 1986. *Research on written composition: New directions for teaching.* Urbana, IL: National Council of Teachers of English.

———. 1987, April. Mode and focus of instruction: Teaching procedural and declarative knowledge for writing [Paper presented at the annual meeting of the American Educational Research Association]. Washington, DC.

———. 1989. Literary texts in classrooms [88th Yearbook of the National Society for the Study of Education]. In P. W. Jackson and S. Haroutunian-Gordon (Eds.), *From Socrates to software: The teacher as text and the text as teacher* (135–58). Chicago: University of Chicago Press.

Hillocks, G., E. Kahn, and L. Johannessen. 1983, October. Teaching defining strategies as a mode of inquiry: Some effects on student writing. *Research in the Teaching of English, 17,* 275–84.

Hillocks, G., and L. Ludlow. 1984. A taxonomy of skills in reading and interpreting fiction. *American Educational Research Journal, 21,* 7–24.

Hillocks, G., B. McCabe, and J. McCampbell. 1971. *The dynamics of English instruction: Grades 7–12.* New York: Random House.

Hirsch, E. D. 1987. *Cultural literacy: What every American needs to know.* Boston: Houghton Mifflin.

Hobson, V. L. 1987. Some effects of Black language on reading achievement in urban schools [dissertation]. *DAI, 48,* 886. Claremont Graduate School.

Hughes, L. 1926. The Negro artist and the racial mountain. In A. Gayle (1979) (Ed.), *The Black aesthetic* (167–72). Garden City, NY: Doubleday and Company.

Hurston, Z. N. 1935. *Mules and men.* New York: Harper & Row.

———. 1990. *Their eyes were watching God.* (1937). New York: Harper & Row.

Hynds, S. 1989. Bringing life to literature and literature to life: Social constructs and contexts of four adolescent readers. *Research in the Teaching of English, 23*(1), 30–61.

———. 1990. *Questions of difficulty in literary training* [Report Series Number 4.6]. Albany, NY: Center for the Learning and Teaching of Literature, State University of New York.

Johnson, J. W. 1932. Introduction. In *Southern road* [by Sterling Brown] (16–17). New York: Harper and Row. (Reprinted from *The collected poems of Sterling A. Brown* (1980)).

Johnston, P. H. 1984. Prior knowledge and reading comprehension test bias. *Reading Research Quarterly, 19,* 219–39.

Jones, G. 1991. *Liberating voices: Oral tradition in African American literature.* New York: Penguin Books.

Jordan, J. 1988. Nobody mean more to me than you and the future life of Willie Jordan. *Harvard Educational Review, 58*(3), 363–74.

Kintsch, W., and E. Greene. 1978. The role of culture-specific schemata in the comprehension and recall of stories. *Discourse Processes, 1,* 1–13.

Kochman, T. (Ed.). 1972. *Rappin' and stylin' out: Communication in urban Black America.* Urbana, IL: University of Illinois Press.

Kozol, J. 1985. *Illiterate America.* New York: Doubleday.

Labov, W. 1972. *Language in the inner city: Studies in the Black English vernacular.* Philadelphia: University of Pennsylvania Press.

Langer, J. 1984. Literacy instruction in American schools: Problems and perspectives. In N. Stein (Ed.), *Literacy in American schools, learning to read and write* (111–36). Chicago: University of Chicago Press.

———. 1989. *The process of understanding literature* [Report Series Number 2.1]. Albany, NY: Center for the Learning and Teaching of Literature, State University of New York.

Langer, J., A. Applebee, I. Mullis, and M. Foertsch. 1990. *Learning to read in our nation's schools: Instruction and achievement in 1988 at grades 4, 8, and 12.* Princeton, NJ: Educational Testing Service, U. S. Department of Education.

Lave, J. 1977. Cognitive consequences of traditional apprenticeship training in West Africa. *Anthropology and Education Quarterly, 7,* 177–80.

Lee, C. 1990. Signifying in the zone of proximal development [Unpublished manuscript]. Department of Education, University of Chicago.

———. 1991, April. Signifying as a scaffold to literary interpretation: The pedagogical implications of a form of African-American discourse [Paper presented at the annual meeting of the American Educational Research Association]. Chicago, IL.

Lemke, J. 1990. *Talking science: Language, learning, and values.* Norwood, NJ: Ablex.

Locke, A. 1925. *The new Negro.* New York: Simon and Schuster.

Lomotey, K. (Ed.). 1990. *Going to school: The African-American experience.* Albany, NY: State University of New York Press.

Louise, A. T. 1980. *Relationship between good and poor readers' awareness of reading schemata and their performance on measures of reading comprehension* [Unpublished Ph.D. dissertation]. University of Maryland.

Major, C. 1970. *Dictionary of Afro-American slang.* New York: International Publishers.

Malik, A. A. 1990. A psycholinguistic analysis of the reading behavior of EFL-proficient readers using culturally familiar and culturally nonfamiliar expository texts. *American Educational Research Journal, 27*(1), 205–23.

Mandler, J. M., and N. S. Johnson. 1977. Remembrance of things parsed: Story structure and recall. *Cognitive Psychology, 9,* 111–51.

Marshall, J. D. 1989. *Patterns of discourse in classroom discussions of literature* [Report Series Number 2.9]. Albany, NY: Center for Learning and Teaching of Literature, State University of New York.

———. 1990. *Discussions of literature in lower-track classrooms* [Report Series Number 2.10]. Albany, NY: Center for Learning and Teaching of Literature, State University of New York.

McNeil, L. M. 1988. *Contradictions of control: School structure and school knowledge.* New York: Routledge.

Means, B., and M. S. Knapp. (Eds.). 1991. *Teaching advanced skills to educationally disadvantaged students: A Final Report.* Washington, DC: U. S. Department of Education.

Mehan, H. 1979. *Learning lessons: Social organization in the classroom.* Cambridge, MA: Harvard University Press.

Miller-Jones, D. 1988. The study of African-American children's development: Contributions to reformulating developmental paradigms. In D. Slaughter (Ed.), *Black children and poverty: A developmental perspective* (75–92). San Francisco: Jossey-Bass, Inc.

Mitchell-Kernan, C. 1981. Signifying, loud-talking and marking. In A. Dundes (Ed.), *Mother wit from the laughing barrel* (310–28). Englewood Cliffs, NJ: Prentice-Hall.

Morrison, T. 1970. *The bluest eye: A Novel.* New York: Holt, Rinehart, and Winston.

———. 1989. Unspeakable things unspoken: The Afro-American presence in American literature. *Michigan Quarterly Review, 28*(2), 1–49.

Morse, L. B. 1989. A descriptive study of student-centered small-group discussion of eight short stories [dissertation]. *DAI, 50,* 890. Ohio State University.

Mullis, I. V. S., E. H. Owens, and G. W. Phillips. 1990. *Accelerating academic achievement: A summary of findings from 20 years of NAEPs.* Princeton, NJ: Educational Testing Service.

National Alliance of Business. 1987. *The fourth r: Workforce readiness.* New York.

Nelson, K. (Ed.). 1989. *Narratives from the crib.* Cambridge, MA: Harvard University Press.

Nicholas, D. W., and T. Trabasso. 1981. Toward a taxonomy of inferences. In F. Wilkening and J. Becker (Eds.), *Information integration by children* (243–65). Hillsdale, NJ: Erlbaum.

Norris, S. P., and L. Phillips. 1987. Explanations of reading comprehension: Schema theory and critical thinking theory. *Teachers College Record, 89*(2), 281–306.

Nystrand, M., and A. Gamoran. 1989. Instructional discourse, student engagement, and literature achievement [Paper presented at the Annual Meeting of the American Educational Research Association]. Boston.

Nystrand, M., and A. Gamoran. 1990. Student engagement: When recitation becomes conversation [in press]. In H. Waxman and H. Walberg (Eds.), *Contemporary research on teaching.* National Society for the Study of Education. Chicago: McCutchan Publishing.

Oakes, J. 1985. *Keeping track: How schools structure inequality.* New Haven, CT: Yale University Press.

Ohlhausen, M. M., and C. M. Roller. 1988, Winter. The operation of text structure and content schemata in isolation and interaction. *Reading Research Quarterly, 23*(1), 70–87.

Ortony, A., T. Turner, and N. Larson-Shapiro. 1985. Cultural and instructional influences on figurative language comprehension by inner-city children. *Research in Teaching of English, 19*(1), 25–35.

Parrish, B. 1974. *The effects of experimental background upon the informal reading inventory of Anglo and Mexican American ninth grade students* [unpublished Ph.D. dissertation]. Arizona State University.

Paznik, J. 1976. The artistic dimension of Black English: A disclosure model and its implications for curriculum and instruction [dissertation]. *DAI, 37,* 1377. Columbia University Teachers College.

Pearson, P. D., J. Hansen, and C. J. Gordon. 1979. The effect of background knowledge on young children's comprehension of explicit and implicit information. *Journal of Reading Behavior, 11,* 201–09.

Pearson, P. D., and D. D. Johnson. 1978. *Teaching reading comprehension.* New York: Holt, Rinehart and Winston.

Petitto, A. 1982. Practical arithmetic and transfer. *Journal of Cross-Cultural Psychology, 13,* 15–28.

Petitto, A., and H. Ginsburg. 1982. Mental arithmetic in Africa and America: Strategies, principles and explanations. *International Journal of Psychology, 17,* 81–102.

Polkinghorne, D. E. 1988. *Narrative, knowing and the human sciences.* Albany, NY: State University of New York Press.

Potts, R. 1989, April. West side stories: Children's conversational narratives in a Black community [Paper presented at the biennial meeting of the Society for Research in Child Development].

Pritchard, R. 1987. A cross-cultural study of the effects of cultural schemata on proficient readers' comprehension monitoring strategies and their comprehension of culturally familiar and unfamiliar passages (Palau, United States) [dissertation]. *DAI, 48,* 1161. Indiana University.

Purves, A. C. 1984. The potential and real achievement of U. S. students in school reading. In N. Stein (Ed.), *Literacy in American schools: Learning to read and write* (85–110). Chicago: University of Chicago Press.

Purves, A., and V. Rippere. 1968. *Elements of writing about a literary work: A study response to literature.* Urbana, IL: National Council of Teachers of English.

Rabinowitz, P. J. 1987. *Before reading: Narrative conventions and the politics of interpretation.* Ithaca: Cornell University Press.

Read, S., and M. Rossen. 1981. Rewriting history: The biasing effects of beliefs on memory. *Journal of Social Cognition.*

Reed, H., and J. Lave. 1981. Arithmetic as a tool for investigating relations between culture and cognition. In R. Casson (Ed.), *Language, culture, and cognition: Anthropological perspectives* (437–55). New York: Macmillan.

Resnick, L. B. 1990. Literacy in school and out. *Daedalus, 119*(2), 169–86.

Reynolds, R. E., M. A. Taylor, M. S. Steffensen, L. L. Shirey, and R. C. Anderson, 1982. Cultural schemata and reading comprehension. *Reading Research Quarterly, 17*(3), 353–65.

Rist, R. 1970. Student social class and teacher expectations: The self-fulfilling prophesy of ghetto education. *Harvard Educational Review, 40*, 411–51.

Robinson, J. 1988. The social context of literacy. In E. Kintgen, B. Kroll, and M. Rose (Eds.), *Perspectives on literacy* (243–53). Carbondale, IL: Southern Illinois University Press.

Rosenblatt, L. 1978. *The reader, the text, the poem: The transactional theory of the literary work.* Carbondale, IL: Southern Illinois University Press.

Rumelhart, D. E. 1975. Notes on a schema for stories. In D. Bobrow and A. Collins (Eds.), *Representation and understanding: Studies in cognitive science* (211–36). New York: Academic Press.

———. 1980. Schemata: The building blocks of cognition. In R. J. Spiro, B. C. Bruce, and W. F. Brewer (Eds.), *Theoretical issues in reading comprehension* (34–58). Hillsdale, NJ: Erlbaum.

Saxe, G. B. 1982. Culture and the development of numerical cognition: Studies among the Oksapmin of Papua New Guinea. In C. Brainerd (Ed.), *Children's logical and mathematical cognition* (157–76). New York: Springer-Verlag.

———. 1988. The mathematics of child street vendors. *Child Development, 59*, 1415–25.

———. 1991. *Culture and cognitive development: Studies in mathematical understanding.* Hillsdale, NJ: Erlbaum.

Schank, R., and R. Abelson. 1977. *Scripts, plans, goals, and understanding.* Hillsdale, NJ: Erlbaum.

Scholes, R. 1985. *Textual power, literary theory and the teaching of English.* New Haven, CT: Yale University Press.

Schon, D. 1983. *The reflective practitioner: How professionals think in action.* New York: Basic Books.

———. 1987. *Educating the reflective practitioner: Toward a new design for teaching and learning in the professions.* San Francisco: Jossey-Bass.

Schweder, R. A., and R. A. LeVine. 1984. *Culture theory: Essays on mind, self, and emotion.* Cambridge: Cambridge University Press.

Scott, S. R. 1989. A comparison of the effects of two types of short stories on literal and inferential reading comprehension of tenth-grade language arts students [dissertation]. *DAI, 50,* 1615. Memphis State University Press.

Scribner, S. 1984a. Studying working intelligence. In B. Rogoff and J. Lave (Eds.), *Everyday cognition* (9–40). Cambridge, MA: Harvard University Press.

———. 1984b. Literacy in three metaphors. In N. Stein (Ed.), *Literacy in American schools: Learning to read and write* (7–22). Chicago: University of Chicago Press.

Scribner, S., and M. Cole. 1981. *The psychology of literacy.* Cambridge, MA: Harvard University Press.

———. 1988. Unpackaging literacy. In E. Kintgen, B. Kroll, and M. Rose (Eds.), *Perspectives in literacy* (57–70). Carbondale, IL: Southern Illinois University Press.

Singer and Zaggara. 1982. Anglo and Chicano comprehension of ethnic stories. In *National Reading Conference Yearbook* (203–07). n.p.

Smagorinsky, P., and S. Gevinson. 1989. *Fostering the reader's response: Rethinking the literature curriculum, grades 7–12.* Palo Alto, CA: Dale Seymour Publications.

Smagorinsky, P., T. McCann, and S. Kern. 1987. *Explorations: Introductory activities for literature and composition, 7–12.* Urbana, IL: ERIC Clearinghouse on Reading and Communication Skills and the National Council of Teachers of English.

Smith, M. 1987. *Reading and teaching irony in poetry: Giving short people a reason to live* [unpublished Ph.D. dissertation]. University of Chicago.

———. 1989. Teaching the interpretation of irony in poetry. *Research in the Teaching of English, 23*(3), 254–72.

Smith, M., and G. Hillocks. 1988, October. Sensible sequencing: Developing knowledge about literature text by text. *English Journal, 96,* 44–49.

Smitherman-Donaldson, G. 1977. *Talkin and Testifyin: The language of Black America.* Boston: Houghton Mifflin.

———. 1988a. Discriminatory discourse on Afro-American speech. In G. Smitherman-Donaldson and T. A. van Dijk (Eds.), *Discourse and discrimination* (144–75). Detroit: Wayne State University Press.

———. 1988, January. "A new way of talkin' ": Language, social change and political theory [Presented at the Conference on "Race and Class in the Twentieth Century"]. Oxford University, Oxford, UK.

Spiro, R. 1980. Constructive processes in prose comprehension and recall. In R. Spiro, B. Bruce, and W. Brewer (Ed.), *Theoretical issues in reading comprehension* (245–78). Hillsdale, NJ: Erlbaum.

Spurlin, W. J. 1990. Theorizing signifying and the role of the reader: Possible directions for African-American literary criticism. *College English, 52*(7), 732–42.

Steffensen, M. S., and L. Colker. 1982. Intercultural misunderstandings about health care: Recall of descriptions of illness and treatments. *Social Science and Medicine, 16,* 1949–54.

Steffensen, M. S., C. Joag-Dev, and R. C. Anderson. 1979. A cross-cultural perspective on reading comprehension. *Reading Research Quarterly, 15*(1), 10–29.

Stein, N., and C. Glenn. 1979. An analysis of story comprehension in elementary school children. In R. Freedle (Ed.), *New directions in discourse processing* (Vol. 2, 53–120). Hillsdale, NJ: Erlbaum.

Stein, N., and T. Trabasso. 1982. Children's understanding of stories: A basis for moral judgement and dilemma resolution. In C. Brainerd and M. Pressley (Eds.), *Verbal processes in children: Progress in cognitive development research* (161–88). New York: Springer-Verlag.

Stewart, W. A. 1969. On the use of Negro dialect in the teaching of reading. In J. C. Baratz and R. Shuy (Eds.), *Teaching Black children to read.* Washington, DC: Center for Applied Linguistics.

Stigler, J. A., R. A. Schweder, and G. Herdt. (Eds.). 1990. *Cultural psychology: Essays on comparative human development.* Cambridge: Cambridge University Press.

Stigler, J., and R. Baranes. 1989. Culture and mathematics learning. In *Review of Research in Education* (Vol. 15, 253–307). Washington, DC: American Educational Research Association.

Stodolsky, S. 1988. *The subject matters: Classroom activity in math and social studies.* Chicago: University of Chicago Press.

———. 1989. Is teaching really by the book? In P. Jackson and S. Haroutunian-Gordon (Eds.), *From Socrates to software: The teacher as text and the text as teacher.* Chicago: University of Chicago Press.

Tannen, D. 1989. *Talking voices: Repetition, dialogue, and imagery in conversational discourse.* Cambridge: Cambridge University Press.

Tantiwong, T. 1988. Influence of cultural schemata on reading comprehension performance of EFL secondary school students in Thailand [dissertation]. *DAI, 49,* 2983. Texas Woman's University.

Taylor, M. 1982. *The use of figurative devices in aiding comprehension for speakers of Black English* [unpublished Ph.D. dissertation]. University of Illinois, Urbana, IL.

Tobin, B. J. 1989. The responses of early adolescent, White Australian readers to selected cross-cultural, folklore-based fantasy novels by Patricia Wrightson [dissertation]. *DAI, 50,* 1586. University of Georgia.

Tompkins, J. (Ed.). 1980. *Reader-response criticism: From formalism to post structuralism.* Baltimore, MD: Johns Hopkins University Press.

Trabasso, T., N. Stein, and L. Johnson. 1981. Children's knowledge of events: A causal analysis of story structure. *The Psychology of Learning and Motivation, 15,* 237–82.

Vipond, D., and R. Hunt. 1984. Point-driven understanding: Pragmatic and cognitive dimensions of literary reading. *Poetics, 13,* 261–77.

———. 1987. Shunting information or making contact? Assumptions for research on aesthetic reading. *English Quarterly, 20,* 131–36.

Vipond, D., R. A. Hunt, and L. C. Wheeler. 1987. Social reading and literary engagement. *Reading Research and Instruction, 26*(3), 151–61.

Vipond, D., R. Hunt, J. Jewett, and J. Reither. 1990. Making sense of reading. In R. Beach and S. Hynds (Eds.), *Developing discourse practices in adolescence and adulthood* (110–35). Norwood, NJ: Ablex.

Voss, J. F., G. T. Vesonder, and G. J. Spilich. 1980. Text generation and recall by high-knowledge and low-knowledge individuals. *Journal of Verbal Learning and Verbal Behavior, 19,* 651–67.

Vygotsky, L. 1978. *Mind in society: The development of higher psychological processes* (M. Cole, V. John Steiner, and S. Scribner, Eds.). Cambridge, MA: Harvard University Press.

————. 1986. *Thought and language.* Cambridge, MA: The MIT Press.

Walker, A. 1979. On refusing to be humbled by second place in a contest you did not design: A tradition by now. In A. Walker (Ed.), *I love myself when I am laughing* (1–6). New York: The Feminist Press.

————. 1982. *The color purple.* New York: Harcourt Brace Jovanovich.

————. 1983. *In search of our mothers' gardens: Womanist prose by Alice Walker.* New York: Harcourt Brace Jovanovich.

————. 1988. Coming in from the cold. In *Living by the word* (54–68). New York: Harcourt Brace Jovanovich.

Washington, M. H. 1990. Foreword. In *Their eyes were watching God* [by Zora Neale Hurston] (1937) (vii–xiv). New York: Harper and Row.

Werner, C. D. 1987. Responses of college readers with different cultural backgrounds to a short story [dissertation]. *DAI, 48,* 2266. Georgia State University.

Wertsch, J. 1984. The zone of proximal development: Some conceptual issues. In B. Rogoff and J. V. Wertsch (Eds.), *Children's learning in the zone of proximal development* (7–18). New Directions for Child Development. San Francisco: Jossey-Bass.

Wilson, W. J. 1987. *The truly disadvantaged: The inner city, the underclass, and public policy.* Chicago: University of Chicago Press.

Wimmers, I. C. 1988. *Poetics of reading: Approaches to the novel.* Princeton, NJ: Princeton University Press.

Winner, E. 1988. *The point of words: Children's understanding of metaphor and irony.* Cambridge, MA: Harvard University Press.

Woodson, C. G. 1933. *Miseducation of the Negro.* Washington, DC: Associated Publishers.

Wright, B. D., and M. H. Stone. 1979. *Best test design.* Chicago: MESA Press.

Wright, B., and G. Masters. 1982. *Rating scale analysis.* Chicago: MESA Press.

Wright, B., and M. Stone. 1990a. *Identification of item bias* [Research Primer No. 5]. University of Chicago: Mesa Psychometric Laboratory.

————. 1990b. *Control lines for item plots* [Measurement Primer No. 13]. University of Chicago: Mesa Psychometric Laboratory.

Wright, R. 1926. Blueprint for Negro writing. In A. Gayle (Ed.), *The black aesthetic* (1972) (315–26). Garden City, NY: Doubleday and Company.

Zancanella, D. 1991. Teachers reading/readers teaching: Five teachers' personal approaches to literature and their teaching of literature. *Research in the Teaching of English, 25*(1), 5–32.

Appendix A: Technical Notes

Rationale for Calculations on Misfitting Pairs

The pre- and post-tests included eight questions per test, each question representing a discrete category of reading comprehension based on the Hillocks taxonomy. Rasch analysis indicated that six of the questions or categories were of comparable difficulty from pre- to post-test. Two categories—Stated Relationship and Structural Generalization—however, represented different levels of difficulty on the pre- and post-tests. When analyzing the categories in which students made the greatest gain from pre- to post-test by group, the decision was made to use the item calibrations calculated for each question based on responses from the pilot group. The pilot group's item calibrations were used as the basis for calculating the person measures of the field group.

In order to understand this move, it is important to understand the difference between a person measure and an item difficulty in Rasch analysis. Rasch analysis "allows estimation of the person measures . . . and the item calibrations . . . independently of one another" (Wright and Masters, 15). Item difficulty is a measure of the difficulty of an item along a continuum that measures a common variable. Item calibrations represent "valid items . . . [that] define a variable," while person measures represent "valid response patterns which can be used to locate persons on this variable" (Wright and Masters, 9). Using the item calibrations from the pilot tests as the anchors for subsequent item difficulties, we can make sound predictions despite what amounts to two pairs of misfitting categories (Stated Relationship and Structural

Table 22

Comparing Populations (Person Measures)
Pilot Pre- (N=19), Experimental Pre- (N=77),
Control Pre- (N=25), and Pilot Post- (N=19)

	Pilot Pre-	Exper. Pre-	Control Pre-	Pilot Post-
Mean	-0.61	-0.60	-0.70	-0.37
S.E.	0.74	0.75	0.75	0.73
S. D.	0.88	1.36	1.02	0.86
Per. sep.*	0.59	0.76	0.65	0.58

* Person separation reliabilities–measure of the spread of person measures across the test.

Table 23

1 Sample Test–Pilot Pre- to Post- Change (N=19)

Mean	S. D.	S. E.	T Value	D. F.	2-Tail Prob.
-0.0121	1.582	0.363	-0.03	18	0.974

Generalization). Thus, person measures can be calculated based on the actual difficulty of SR at the pilot pre-test and SR at the pilot post-test rather than assuming that the difficulty of the two is the same. The pilot item difficulties, in one sense, become the standard on which the person measures for the individuals in the field group are based. The independence of the item calibrations from the person measures is demonstrated by the fact that practically all the measures of statistical significance were the same, regardless of whether they were based on the anchored person measures or person measures calibrated locally (i.e., calculated on the pattern of responses of the actual group who took the field test rather than anchored to the pattern of responses of a comparable group, in this instance the pilot group).

Another important component of the argument to anchor the field test person measures on the pilot-item difficulties is the comparability of the two groups, how the two groups of students compare before instruction. Two sources of support are offered to show these two groups of students are comparable before instruction. Table 22 lists the mean person measures, standard errors, standard deviations, and person separation reliabilities for the pilot pre-test, the pre-test for the experimental group, and the pre-test for the control group.

In addition to establishing that the groups performed comparably on the pre-test before instruction, I also tested to see if the difference in mean person measures from the pilot pre- to the pilot post-test were statistically significant. Table 23 shows the students did not change in their measured ability from the pilot pre- to the pilot post-test. One week elapsed between the pilot pre- and the pilot post- and therefore it is safe to assume that no relevant teaching occurred to influence the difference in how well the students performed on the two tests.

Thus we can conclude that the two tests are comparable in overall difficulty. However, that difficulty varies significantly within reading categories for two out of the eight reading categories being tested. All of the analyses offered in the chapter on the results of the study are based on pilot item difficulties to compute person measures for the field population. We can also conclude that in so anchoring the items that the two groups of students are comparable in ability (i.e., ability relative to the variable being measured) before instruction.

Implications for Results

As explained earlier, all results reported for change from pre- to post-test for each group are based on anchored means. Whether using in one framework the anchored means or in the other framework the local means, the results of all statistical signifi-

Table 24

Comparison of Anchored and Locally Calibrated
Means for Change from Pre- to Post-Tests

	Mean		S. D.		S.E.	
	Exp.	Control	Exp.	Control	Exp.	Control
Anchored	1.5297	0.6736	1.23	1.03	0.171	0.207
Local	1.6798	0.8244	1.26	1.08	0.175	0.217

Note: Experimental group, N=52; Control group, N=25.

cance tests except one were virtually identical down to the amount of variance predicted and the significance level. Table 24 presents the means for each group generated out of the two approaches to the data. Not only are the differences minuscule, but the standard error alone renders them virtually the same.

Appendix B: Reading Tests

Form A

Pilot Pre-Test
"The Coming of Maureen Peal"
from *THE BLUEST EYE* by Toni Morrison

Read the story completely and carefully. Answer each question below. Write your answer in the booklet provided. Put each answer on a separate page of the booklet. Number each question. You do not need to copy the question. Just answer the question as completely as possible.

1. Who is Maureen Peal? [Basic Stated Information]

2. Describe specifically what happened to Pecola that caused the girls to take up for her. [Key Detail]

3. How was Maureen Peal treated at school? Describe at least two examples to support your answer. [Stated Relationship]

4. To what *characteristics* of winter is the father compared? Because of these comparisons, what do we learn about the father's personality? [Simple Implied Relationship]

5. What *effects* does winter have on the family? Explain in your own words. Refer to at least two examples from the story to support your answer. [Simple Implied Relationship]

6. How did Maureen Peal "splinter the knot into silver threads that tangled us"? [Complex Implied Relationship]

7. On page 53, the narrator says,

   > "It was extremely important that the world not know that I fully expected Maureen to buy us some ice cream, that for the past 120 seconds I had been selecting the flavor, that I had begun to like Maureen, and that neither of us had a penny."

   Why was it important for the world not to know? Describe another incident in the story where the narrator shows a similar attitude. Explain how her attitude is similar in the two situations. [Complex Implied Relationship]

8. How does the description in the first paragraph relate to events that take place in the story? [Structural Generalization]

9. Tell us about Toni Morrison's ideas about how conceptions of beauty affect people's judgment. Explain at least two examples from the story that support your answer. [Author's Generalization]

10. Tell us about a particular problem in the black community which the story addresses. Does this story accurately represent that problem in your opinion? Choose a similar situation you know about and explain how it is similar to or different from the story. [Application]

Form B   **Pilot Pre-Test**
                              "The Coming of Maureen Peal"
                          from *THE BLUEST EYE* by Toni Morrison

Read the story completely and carefully. Answer each question below. Write your answer in the booklet provided. Put each answer on a separate page of the booklet. Number each question. You do not need to copy the question. Just answer the question as completely as possible.

1. Who is Maureen Peal? [Basic Stated Information]

2. What circumstances at school forced Claudia to talk to Maureen? [Key Detail]

3. How was Maureen treated at school? Describe at least two examples to support your answer. [Stated Relationship]

4. To what *characteristics* of winter is the father compared? Because of these comparisons, what do we learn about the father's personality? [Simple Implied Relationship]

5. At the beginning of the story, why does the narrator hate Maureen Peal? [Simple Implied Relationship]

6. Explain how Claudia and Freida's attitudes toward Maureen Peal change from *before* the incident with Pecola to *after* the incident with Pecola. Describe in detail their attitudes both before and after. Support your description with examples from the story. *Explain specifically how those attitudes have changed and why.* [Complex Implied Relationship]

7. On page 49, the narrator says,

    "It was a false spring day, which like Maureen, had pierced the shell of a deadening winter."

    Describe at least two ways in which Maureen was like a false spring day. Describe at least two examples from the story that support your answer. [Complex Implied Relationship]

8. How does the description in the first paragraph relate to events that take place in the story? [Structural Generalization]

9. Tell us about Toni Morrison's ideas concerning how conceptions of beauty affect people's judgment. Explain at least two examples from the story that support your answer. [Author's Generalization]

10. Tell us about a particular problem in the black community which the story addresses. Does this story accurately represent that problem in your opinion? Choose a similar situation you know about and explain how it is similar to or different from the story. [Application]

Form D   **Pilot Post-Test**
                          "seemothermotherisverynice"
                  from *THE BLUEST EYE* by Toni Morrison

Read the story completely and carefully. Answer each question below. Write your answer in the booklet provided. Put each answer on a separate page of the booklet. Number each question. You do not need to copy the question. Just answer the question as completely as possible.

1. What physical problem does Pauline have? [Basic Stated Information]

2. Where do Pauline and Cholly move when they leave Kentucky? [Key Detail]

3. What old ideal and what new ideal did the movies bring to Pauline? [Stated Relationship]

4. How did Pauline feel about her own homelife after she started going to the movies? [Stated Relationship]

5. On page 90, what does Pauline mean when she makes the following statement?

    "All them colors was in me."

    Be sure to identify the colors she describes and to discuss specifically what they meant to her *in your own words*. [Simple Implied Relationship]

6. The relationship between the church and Pauline's dreams is complex. Describe in detail *the apparent contradictions* in Pauline's relationship with the church *throughout the story,* not just in one part of the story. [Complex Implied Relationship]

7. The narrator states on page 87,

    "During all of her four years of going to school, she was enchanted by numbers and depressed by words. She missed—without knowing what she missed—paints and crayons."

    Think about the conditions under which Pauline lost her tooth. How might these two situations be related to one another: Pauline missing paints and crayons as a child and the conditions under which she lost her tooth? [Complex Implied Relationship]

8. Why is it important that Pauline tell her own story *as well as* have an omniscient (all-knowing) narrator also tell the story? Support your answer with examples from the story. [Structural Generalization]

9. One issue in this story is about dreams. What is one major suggestion that the author makes about dreams? Explain in your own words. [Author's Generalization]

10. Tell us about a particular problem in the black community which this story addresses. Does the story accurately represent that problem in your opinion? Choose a similar situation you know about and explain how it is similar to or different from the story. [Application]

Form E   **Pilot Post-Test**
"seemothermotherisverynice"
from *THE BLUEST EYE* by Toni Morrison

Read the story completely and carefully. Answer each question below. Write your answer in the booklet provided. Put each answer on a separate page of the booklet. Number each question. You do not need to copy the question. Just answer the question as completely as possible.

1. What physical problem does Pauline have? [Basic Stated Information]

2. What did Pauline think about how her new baby Pecola looked? [Key Detail]

3. How did Pauline's education in the movies affect how she judged people? [Stated Relationship]

4. How did Pauline feel about her own homelife after she started going to the movies? [Stated Relationship]

5. Near the end of the story, we are told that being an ideal servant filled practically all of Pauline's needs. What does this reveal about Pauline's needs? Be as complete as you can about Pauline's needs. Describe at least two examples from the story that support your answer. [Simple Implied Relationship]

6. Why does Pauline have a different attitude toward her own family than she does toward the Fisher family, the last family for whom she works? Support your answer with at least two examples from the story. [Complex Implied Relationship]

7. How does Pauline's fascination with arranging things and lining things up in rows as a child relate to later parts of the story? *How are the conditions that prompted her to focus on keeping things in order similar in both parts of the story?* Support your answer with examples from the story. [Complex Implied Relationship]

8. Why is it important that Pauline tell her own story *as well as* have an omniscient (all-knowing) narrator also tell the story? Support your answer with examples from the story. [Structural Generalization]

9. One issue in this story is about dreams. What is one major suggestion that the author makes about dreams? Explain in your own words. [Author's Generalization]

10. Tell us about a particular problem in the black community which this story addresses. Does the story accurately represent that problem in your opinion? Choose a similar situation you know about and explain how it is similar to or different from the story. [Application]

Form C   **Pre-Test**
                         "The Coming of Maureen Peal"
                    from *THE BLUEST EYE* by Toni Morrison

Read the story completely and carefully. Answer each question below. Number each question. You do not need to copy the question. Just answer the question as completely as possible. *Take time to read the question carefully* and be sure you answer all parts of the question.

1. Who is Maureen Peal? [Basic Stated Information]

2. How was Maureen Peal treated at school? Describe at least two examples to support your answer. [Key Detail]

3. Describe specifically what happened to Pecola that caused the girls to take up for her. [Stated Relationship]

4. To what *characteristics* of winter is the father compared? Because of these comparisons, what do we learn about the father's *personality?* [Simple Implied Relationship]

5. Tell us about a particular problem in the black community which the story addresses. Does this story accurately represent that problem in your opinion? Choose a similar situation you know about and explain how it is similar to or different from the story. [Application]

6. Tell us about Toni Morrison's ideas about how conceptions of beauty affect people's judgment. Explain at least two examples from the story that support your answer. [Author's Generalization]

7. How did Maureen Peal "splinter the knot into silver threads that tangled us"? [Complex Implied Relationship]

8. How does the description in the first paragraph relate to the events that take place in the story? [Structural Generalization]

Form I
                              Post-Test
"seemothermotherisverynice"
from *THE BLUEST EYE* by Toni Morrison

Read the story completely and carefully. Answer each question below. Number each question. You do not need to copy the question. Just answer the question as completely as possible. Take time to read the question completely and be sure to answer all parts of the question.

1. What physical problem does Pauline have? [Basic Stated Relationship]

2. Where do Pauline and Cholly move when they leave Kentucky? [Key Detail]

3. What old ideal and what new ideal did the movies bring to Pauline? [Stated Relationship]

4. On page 90, what does Pauline mean when she makes the following statement?

   "All them colors was in me."

   Be sure to identify the colors she describes and to discuss specifically what they mean to her *in your own words*. [Simple Implied Relationship]

5. Why is it important that Pauline tell her own story *as well as* have an omniscient (all-knowing) narrator also tell the story? Support your answer with examples from the story. [Structural Generalization]

6. Tell us about a particular problem in the black community which this story addresses. Does the story accurately represent that problem in your opinion? Choose a similar situation you know about and explain how it is similar to or different from the story. [Application]

7. One issue in this story is about dreams. What is one major suggestion that the author makes about dreams? Explain in your own words. [Author's Generalization]

8. The relationship between the church and Pauline's dreams is complex. Describe in detail *the apparent contradictions* in Pauline's relationship with the church *throughout the story*, not just in one part of the story. [Complex Implied Relationship]

Sample Pre-Test Student Responses
(Field Conditions)

Below are samples of student responses on the pre-test for which full or partial credit was given. Counts given for #7 and 8 are based on the 77 students used in the final analysis. The reason for full or partial credit is given in italics below the student's answer. Responses are given as students wrote them.

1. Who is Maureen Peal?

Full Credit   Maureen Peal is the new girl in school. She is a light skinned black girl who is considered to be rich and admired by mostly all of her school peers.

Partial Credit Maureen Peal was a rich white girl who was a new student at Claudia's and Freida's school.

(Students who misinterpreted Maureen as being white were given partial credit if they identified other accurate identifying features of Maureen.)

2. How was Maureen Peal treated at school? Describe at least two examples to support your answer.

Full Credit   She is treated with respect. examples: 1.) When teachers called on her, they smiled encouragingly. 2.) Black boys didn't trip her in the halls; white boys didn't stone her, white girls didn't suck their teeth when assigned to be her work partners; black girls stepped aside when she wanted to use the skin in the girls' toilet.

Partial Credit Maureen was treated like a saint and with Respect. She enchanted the entire school. There were 2 girls who like her and Disliked her.

(The example offered is vague. Also, only one example is offered.)

3. Describe specifically what happened to Pecola that caused the girls to take up for her.

Full Credit   A group of boys had formed a circle around her and poked fun at her by calling her black e moe and saying her father sleeps naked. The girls took up for her because of this incident.

Partial Credit A group of boys got into a circle around Pecola and started teasing her and she started crying and the girls Freida and her sister and Maureen decided to help her out.

(The student does not identify the specific reason behind the teasing and therefore why Pecola was so upset.)

4. To what *characteristics* of winter is the father compared? Because of these comparisons, what do we learn about the father's *personality?*

Full Credit   Winter moves into his face and settle's there. His eyes become a cliff of snow threatening to avalanche; (His eyes are baggey). His skin takes on the pale, cheerless yellow of winter sun (His skin is pale but fair). His high forehead is the frozen sweep of the Erie. He is a hard working, protective, concern man who cares. He working night and day, he guards his house making sure the home is well protected, and concern about his family well being as he teachers his younging on how to survive. (He give orders)

(This student attempts to give an interpretation to each of the physical images. The details about the father's personality are specific and supportable from the text.)

Partial Credit The father is compared to the cold and the snow. From the description in the story we learn the father is feared and considered mean.

(This student draws a supportable inference about the father, but does not interpret the winter description as it relates to the father.)

5. Tell us about a particular problem in the Black community which the story addresses. Does this story accurately represent that problem in your opinion? Choose a similar situation you know about and explain how it is similar to or different from the story.

Full Credit The problem this story addresses is the comparison of light skinned blacks to dark skinned blacks. I don't feel the story accurately represents the problem. Although I did run into one incident where I met a light skinned black guy who thought he was better than other blacks.

(The statement of the problem is specific and accurate. The answer describes a real life comparable situation.)

Partial Credit A problem in the story which the story addresses is the fact that there are some light-skinned blacks and some dark-skinned Blacks. Yes, it does very much. A similar situation that I know of in comparison to the story is that still today people darker than another are called Blacky, or niggers and that isn't right because of how dark someone is or how light someone is.

(The statement of the problem is more vague and general. The example is comparable and well defined.)

6. Tell us about the author, Toni Morrison's ideas about how conceptions of beauty affect people's judgment. Explain at least two examples from the story that support your answer.

Full Credit Toni Morrison seems to feel that beauty affects judgment. She demonstrates her opinion when Maureen call Freida and the Narrator ugly blacks and she also demonstrates it when she portraits the light skinned black as better looking causing Freida and the Narrator to question their own beauty.

(This student picks up Morrison's idea about questioning standards of beauty and its effect on people's judgment.)

Partial Credit Morrisons idea about how beauty affects people's judgment is never judge a book by its cover. This little girl might have the poised and beauty or even manners but do she have moral or respect for others. For example when Maureen was saying she more pretty than the other two sister's (Freida and I) and when Maureen said her mother wanted to look something like a famous movie star. So what why not be for who you are I say.

(The statement of the author's generalization is more broad and simplifies Morrison's point of view.)

7. How did Maureen Peal "splinter the knot into silver threads that tangled us?"

Full Credit   No student received full credit.

Partial Credit   Out of 95 students who took the pre-test, only 11 received partial credit. Maureen Peal splintered the knot into silver threads that tangled them by making things more confusing and hard for them.

(This student associated the image of splintering the knot and tangling with an inference that is supportable from the text, but did not offer any examples.)

8. How does the description in the first paragraph relate to the events that take place in the story?

Full Credit   No student received full credit.

Partial Credit   Like the description in the first paragraph is mean and cruel so are a lot of the events that occur in the story.

(The student has identified a relationship that is supportable from the text. He does not, however, offer any details or examples.)

Sample Post-Test Student Responses
(Field Conditions)

Below are samples of student responses on the post-test for which full or partial credit was given. Counts given for #7 and 8 are based on the 77 students used in the final analysis. The reason for full or partial credit is given in italics below the student's answer. Responses are given as students wrote them.

1. What physical problem does Pauline have?

Full Credit   Pauline's physical problems was that Pauline stuck a rail through her foot causing it to break and be crooked.

Partial Credit The physical problem Pauline has is she has a broken foot.

2. Where do Pauline and Cholly move when they leave Kentucky?

Full Credit   Pauline and Cholly move to Lorain, Ohio because they had just married and wanted to go way up north.

Partial Credit No student received partial credit.

3. What old ideal and what new ideal did the movies bring to Pauline?

Full Credit   The old ideal and the new ideal that Pauline had when she went to the movies were that the movies refreshed her and succumbed her earlier dreams. She also had an idea of romantic love and physical beauty.

(This student has located the specific answer as stated in the text.)

Partial Credit The old ideal and new ideal the movies brought to Pauline were the old ideal was on page 96 when she went to the movies she use to dress up like Jean Harlow but when her tooth fell out the new ideal she had was she was ugly.

(Although the specific answer of ideal physical beauty and romantic love are not stated directly, the new ideal of ideal physical beauty can be inferred from the examples cited.)

4. On page 90, what does Pauline mean when she makes the following statement? "All them colors was in me." Be sure to identify the colors she describes and to discuss specifically what they meant to her *in your own words.*

Full Credit   When Pauline said that all them colors was in me she meant that when she met Cholly she thought about when she was little and the berries mashed in her dress and when her mother made lemonade and Cholly made her feel like a little girl again and when he whistle it brought shivels down her skin. I believe the colors stood for beauty and it also made her feel good inside the colors just made her happy.

(The student has answered each of the parts of the question in a way that is supportable from the text.)

Partial Credit The statement means that each color represented a feeling or emotion the purple stain she got from that berry made her feel sad because the stain never got out. The yellowish color of the lemonade represented her being happy because her father would come back from the field. The green represented her being pretty because the streaks on the june bugs were very pretty to her.

(This student identifies and interprets the colors. However, the relationships between the interpretations and text are either literal [as in saying she was sad about the berry stain because it would not come out of her dress] or strained [as in green representing Pauline's beauty because she found the june bugs pretty].)

5. Why is it important that Pauline tell her own story *as well as* have an omniscient (all-knowing) narrator also tell the story? Support your answer with examples from the story.

Full Credit   Pauline tells the story best because she lived it from day to day and she knows that happen in her life. But the narrator has factual evidence to tell the story. But I believe Pauline tells the story best.

(This student implies a difference between what the narrator knows [factual evidence] and what Pauline knows [she lived it/i.e., subjective].)

Partial Credit   I feel it is important that Pauline tell her own story as well as have an omniscient narrator because it helps explain all points of the story. The narrator tell the story in general. Pauline helps you get into the story and tells you exactly how she feels. For instance she describes her feelings when she met Cholly, "When I first met Cholly, I want you to know it was like all the bits of color from that time down home when all the bits of color from that time down home when all of us chil'ren went berry picking after a funeral and I put some in the pocket of my Sunday dress, and they mased up and stained my lips."

(This student also implies a distinction between the narrator and Pauline. These differences, however, seem to serve more aesthetic functions [Narrator tells story in general while Pauline tells you how she feels and therefore gets you into the story]. He does not state or imply that the narrator knows something that Pauline does not.)

6. Tell us about a particular problem in the Black community which this story addresses. Does the story accurately represent that problem in your opinion? Choose a similar situation you know about and explain how it is similar to or different from the story.

Full Credit   One particular problem in the Black community which this story addresses is women being the bread winner of the family. There is a lot of this today in the Black community due to broken homes, death of the father, divorce, or the father (the Black male) just being a bum or a alcoholic. Pauline took up the duty of being the bread winner in her family because her husband Cholly began drinking and was lacking as the provider.

(This student answers every question fully.)

Partial Credit   I think a particular problem in black community today is that we as blacks don't stick together as one and thats why Whites try to take over. In comparing with the story Pauline said something about Northern colored folk was different and that they were no better than Whites this is some what true today. A similar problem such as what Pauline states would probably be Whites and blacks being next to each other it is causing a problem in some neighborhoods.

(The student accurately states a problem addressed in the story and provides some credible evidence to support it. However, the story does not say anything directly about Whites taking over. The answer lacks cohesion.)

7. One issue in this story is about dreams. What is one major suggestion that the author makes about dreams? Explain in your own words.

Full Credit   One major issue the author makes about dreams is when she said that to find the truth about how dreams die you can never take the word of the dreamer. The narrator meant that even though Pauline may have thought when all her dreams went away she cant really determine because it's her dreams. And she may not see the deterioration of her attitude about herself (and dream) the way the author can. And then Pauline may see only what she allows herself to see.

(This student has identified the key phrase [never take the word of a dreamer]. The interpretation is accurate. The examples highlight subtle insights into the limitations of Pauline's self-reflection.)

Partial Credit   One suggestion that the author had about dreams were that dreams die and one should never take the word of a dreamer. The author is trying to say that a person shouldn't believe in dreams because dreams are not reality it is just your subconscious mind working.

(The student has identified a key phrase [never take the word of a dreamer]. However, the interpretation offered does not relate to the opening sentence.)

8. The relationship between the church and Pauline's dreams is complex. Describe in detail *the apparent contradictions* in Pauline's relationship with the church *throughout the story,* not just in part of the story.

Full Credit   The relationship between the church and Paulines was at just in the beging of the story she went to church to feel free and rejoice She also went for security. "He was a simple presence, and all-embracing tenderness with strength and promise of rest." Thats says she felt secure at church this Presence in the curch when its around her she felt secure. To me in the second part of the story Pauline went to church to please those northern Blacks and to put down Cholly. She was try so hard to impress those other women she neglected her own family and house. She did go to church and was very active she tried her best not to sin she instaled fear in her children about lots of things that would embarrass her like don't be clumsy. she bent the toward respectibility she also gave them the fear of being like there farther If she was active in the church to feel secure like she did before in the story she wouldn't have treated Cholly as she did she would have treated him as an equal it seems she stopped loving Cholly to please everyone except her self she didn't like the image he casted on her so she was trying in her own way to get rid of him.

(This student has identified a contradiction, supported the claim with examples from different sections of the story, and offered a warrant for the claim [If she was to be secure in the church, she would have treated Cholly as an equal].)

Partial Credit   The contradictions of the church were was when on page 89 when she use to go to church she would clean house with ethusiasm but on page 95 when she got her job she use to care about her husband Cholly and her children Sammy and Pecola but when she got in (white woman) her house she would care, clean like it was her own but she didn't at her house and when your at church your suppose to care and clean for her house and her children.

(The contradiction identified by this student appears to rest more on the fact that Pauline no longer cleans her own home than on ethical issues such as how she treats her child and husband. The warrant offered in the final sentence articulates the values on which the student has based her answer and she does state a contradiction. However, this answer is more simplistic than the question demands.)

Appendix C: Tests of Prior Social and Linguistic Knowledge

Name _____ School _____
Period _____ Teacher _____ Date _____

Form I-1*

Imagine that a visitor from another world has come to Earth. You are the visitor's guide. While walking down the street, the visitor is listening to bits of conversation. At one point, he overhears people insulting each other, but he only hears parts of the sentences and is not sure what is meant.

Fill in the word that you think best fits the meaning of the sentence.

1. Your momma so _____ she can play hide and seek under a penny!

2. You so _____ the sun refuses to shine on your face!

3. Your daddy so _____ when he walks down the street, the dogs die!

4. Your momma so _____ she wears a sock for a dress.

5. You so _____ the rats and roaches in your house walk around in combat boots.

6. Your sister so _____ when she went to take a bath, the water went back down the drain.

*All I Forms taken from Taylor, 1982.

Name _____

Form I-2

The visitor is still in town, but even though now he is able to hear entire sentences, he is not always able to understand them. Below is a list of sentences.

Under the sentence, please write what you think the sentence means.

1. You can sit in the back of the bus and the front of the bus at the same time.

2. The roaches in your house walk single file.

3. Your momma got radar ears.

4. Your teeth give beavers competition.

5. Your face puts D-Con out of business.

6. If brains were money you'd be on welfare.

Name _____

Form I-3

Imagine yourself in a situation where insults are being exchanged back and forth. If the first person says something insulting to you, what would be a good response? Keep in mind that you want to get the best of your opponent. On another paper, write down the first thing that comes to your mind.

If the first person says:

1. Your momma so fat she can slide down a razor blade without getting cut!
   You might say:

2. You so ugly Raid uses your face on the roach can!

   You might say:

3. Your momma so low she can play handball against the curb.

   You might say:

4. I went to your house and wanted to sit down. A roach jumped up and said "Sorry, this seat is taken!"
   You might say:

5. Your lips so big, if you ever fell in the sea, you could use them for flippers!
   You might say:

6. Your momma is such a dog she eats Gaines-burgers!

   You might say:

7. You get your shoes from Buster Brown—brown on the top and all busted on the bottom.
   You might say:

8. Your sister's feet so big she can sit on the front porch and kill roaches in the back.
   You might say:

9. Your momma so skinny, she do the hula hoop in a Applejack!

   You might say:

10. Your shoes so thin, if you step on a dime you can tell if its heads or tails!
    You might say:

Name _____

Form I-4

Imagine that you are still in a situation where insults are being exchanged back and forth. The first person says something insulting and then the second person says something back.

Below, the first persons's insulting remark is given. Below this remark are 4 possible responses for the second person. Rate how good these responses are.

Write a number 1 beside the response you think is the very best response, a number 2 beside the next best response, a 3 beside your third choice, and a 4 beside the response you think is the worst of the four.

There are no right or wrong answers. We are simply interested in your opinion.

If the first person says:

1. Your momma so old she got cobwebs under her arms! Then the second person should respond by saying:

   a. Your momma so old she can't fit all the candles on her birthday cake.

   b. Your momma so old her wrinkles got wrinkles.

   c. Your momma so old she shook hands with Abraham Lincoln.

   d. The cobwebs under your momma's arms got cobwebs because she so old.

2. Your momma so ugly she went to the zoo and the gorilla paid to see her! Then the second person should respond by saying:

   a. Your momma so ugly that when the doctor removed one of her warts, he threw her away and kept the wart!

   b. Your momma so ugly that the gorilla ran and hid in the corner of his cage and wouldn't come out!

   c. Your momma is in a cage because she so ugly!

   d. Your momma so ugly that no one will come over to your house to visit!

3. Your momma so skinny if she stuck out her tongue and turn sideways she look like a zipper! Then the second person should respond by saying:

   a. Your momma so skinny you can't see her when she turns sideways!

   b. Your momma can go through a door without opening it because she so skinny!

   c. Your momma so skinny her clothes just hang on her!

   d. Your momma so skinny she can dance between raindrops without getting wet!

4. Your panties so raggedy when you walk they whistle!

   a. The garbage man wouldn't pick your panties up because they so raggedy!

   b. Your shirt is so raggedy you could use it for a window screen!

    c. Your panties so raggedy they're falling off!

    d. You got so many holes in your socks when you walk your shoes hum h-m-m!

5. You so poor the roaches and rats each lunch out!

    a. You so poor you gotta eat roach sandwiches for lunch!

    b. You eat dirt soup because you so poor!

    c. You so poor the rats and roaches take you out to lunch!

    d. You so poor they turned off your lights and water!

6. Your momma so big she sits around the house!

    a. Your momma uses a truck for a bed because she so big!

    b. Your momma so big she can't buy any clothes in the store!

    c. Your momma so big your daddy has to hug her on the Installment Plan!

    d. Your momma so big she lives in Tennessee and Mississippi at the same time.

7. Your hair looks like wire fence!

    a. Your hair looks like you haven't combed it in weeks!

    b. Your hair looks like an electric mixer went crazy on your head!

    c. You have cancha doncha hair—cancha comb it, doncha try!

    d. Spaghetti is what your hair looks like!

8. Your daddy is a girlscout!

    a. Your daddy is a brownie!

    b. Your daddy wears a dress and works as a maid!

    c. A butterfly girl is what they call your daddy!

    d. Your daddy is a sissy!

9. Your daddy is pregnant in the nose!

    a. Your daddy looks like he snorted a basketball!

    b. An elephant nose is what your daddy has.

    c. Your daddy has a fat face!

    d. Your daddy has a watermelon in his nose!

10. Your daddy so ugly that when he walk down the street, he gets a ticket for obscene exposure.

    a. Your daddy is public enemy No. 1 because he so ugly!

    b. Your daddy so ugly, when he sits down to eat, the dishes run away!

    c. Your daddy so ugly that when he walk down the street, people laugh at him!

    d. Your daddy so ugly that even blind people turn their heads!

Name _____ School _____

Period _____ Teacher _____ Date _____

Form J-1
Vocabulary

Find the word or phrase in the right column which you most easily associate with a word or phrase in the left column. Write the letter on the space. You can use each letter only once.

1. sanctified _____   a. straightened

2. bad hair _____   b. saved

3. pressed _____   c. jam

4. the devil's music _____   d. kinky

*5. I let my hair go back. _____   e. Uncle Tom

*6. What's up blood? _____   f. street smarts

*7. color struck _____   g. nappy

*8. oreo _____   h. signifying

*9. shuckin' and jivin' _____   i. a Black

                               j. high yellow

Tell why you chose each of the following:

5. _____

6. _____

7. _____

8. _____

9. _____

Name _____ School _____

Period _____ Teacher _____ Date _____

Form J-2

Read each of the following proverbs. Below each proverb write what you think it means in your own words.

1. The blacker the berry the sweeter the juice.

2. The Lord don't like ugly.

3. Grits ain't groceries, eggs ain't poultry, and Mona Lisa was a man.

4. If I tell you a hen dip snuff, look under its wing and find a whole box.

5. A hard head make a soft behind.

6. If you make yo bed hard, you gon have to lie in it.

7. You don't believe fat meat is greasy.

Form J-3

Write your name, school, teacher's name and FORM-J3 on a sheet of paper.

Read each passage below. On the sheet of paper with your heading, answer each question that follows a passage. Be sure to write the number of the question before your answer. Do not write the question.

The questions ask your opinion.

A. "Her hair is . . . Negro hair, but it's got a kind of white flavor. Like the piece of string out of a ham. It's not ham at all, but it's been around ham and got the flavor."

    1. Describe her hair in your own words.

B. "Josie came to know Mrs. Turner now. She had seen her several times during the season, but neither ever spoke. Now they got to be visiting friends.

    Mrs. Turner was a milky sort of woman. . . . JuneBug made a lot of fun about Mrs. Turner's shape behind her back. . . . But Mrs. Turner's shape and features were entirely approved by Mrs. Turner. Her nose was slightly pointed and she was proud. Her thin lips were a delight in her eyes. . . . To her way of thinking all these things set her aside from Negroes. That was why she sought out Josie to friend with. Josie's coffee-and-cream complexion and her luxurious hair made Mrs. Turner forgive her for wearing overalls like the other women who worked in the fields. She didn't forgive her for marrying a man as dark as JuneBug, but she felt she could remedy that.

    "Look at me!" Mrs. Turner said. "Ah ain't got no flat nopse and liver lips. Ah'm uh featured woman. . . . You oughta meet mah brother. He's real smart. Got dead straight hair. . . ."

    2. What would make Mrs. Turner feel the way she does toward dark skin and Black features?

C. "I stand looking at my[self] . . . in the looking glass. . . . My hair is short and kinky because I don't straighten it anymore. . . .

    3. How does this woman feel about herself? How do you know?

D. "Jerene and Darlene come help me with the business. . . . Darlene trying to teach me how to talk. She say 'us' . . . a dead country give-away. You say 'us' where most folks say 'we,' she say, and peoples think you _____. Look like to me only a fool would want you to talk in a way that feel peculiar to your mind."

    4. Fill in the missing word from the sentence above.

    5. How does Darlene want her to talk?

E. Jesse tell me all his love business now. His mind on Carol Butler day and night.
    "She pretty," he tell me. "Bright."
    "Smart?" I ask.
    "Naw. Bright skin."

    6. What does Jesse mean by bright skin?

F. "JoJo, she say, do you really love me, or just my color?" (This couple is African American.)

7. What does she probably look like?

8. Why might her color be an issue in her relationship with her boyfriend?

G. "Mamie and the prizefighter and all the children got in the prizefighter car and went to town. Climbed out on the street looking like somebody. Just then the mayor and his wife come by.

All these children, say the mayor's wife, digging in her pocketbook. Cute as little buttons though, she say. She stop, put her hand on one of the children head. Say, and such strong white teeth.

Mamie and the prizefighter don't say nothing. Wait for her to pass. . . Miss Millie finger the children some more, finally look at Mamie and the prizefighter. She look at the prizefighter car. She eye Mamie wristwatch. She say to Mamie, All your children so clean, she say, would you like to work for me, be my maid?

Mamie say, Hell no. . .

Mayor look at Mamie, push his wife out the way. Stick out his chest. Girl, what you say to Miss Millie?

Mamie say, I say, Hell no.

He slap her. . .

Mamie knock the man down.

The policies come, start slinging the children off the mayor, bang they heads together. Mamie really start to fight. They drag her to the ground. . . They beat Mamie. . .

What the prizefighter do in all this? I ask Mamie sister, Odessa.

He want to jump in, she say. Mamie say No, take the children home."

9. Why is the Mayor's wife called Miss Millie?

10. Why is Mamie called "Girl"?

11. What would likely have happened to the prizefighter if he had tried to help Mamie? Why?

Index

Abelson, R., 33, 160
Abrahams, R. D., 10, 153
Absenteeism, 74–76
Achievement tests, 49–50
Adler, M., 138, 153
Aesthetic reading, 77, 146
Afflerbach, P., 32, 34, 153
African American Vernacular English. *See* Black English Vernacular (BEV)
African-American Holocaust, 11
African American texts, teaching of, 2
Analogical reasoning, 14, 141
Anderson, J. D., 136, 153
Anderson, R., 33, 34, 54, 153, 154, 156
Anderson, R. C., 32, 36, 153, 160, 161
Anderson, Richard, 37
Andrews, M., 10, 153
Applebee, A. N., 2, 3, 50, 147, 153, 157
Assessment, 140–141. *See also* Measurement

Baker, H., 17, 150, 153
Baldwin, James, 7, 153
Bambara, Toni Cade, 52, 73, 78, 153
Baranes, R., 41, 42, 162
Baratz, J. C., 44, 153
Barr, R., 53–54, 153
Bartlett, F. C., 36, 37, 153
Beck, I., 1, 153
Black Aesthetic, The, 9
Black Aesthetic criticism, 150
Black English
  in the classroom, 14, 70
  in literature, 14, 15
  validity of, 140
Black English Vernacular (BEV)
  and reading comprehension, 44–45
  use of in literary works, 17, 21
Black Language Assessment Test, 44–45
Bleich, D., 145, 153
Bloom, A., 149, 153
Bloome, D. M., 45, 154
Bluest Eye, The, 6, 7, 56, 62
  examples of signifying in, 27–31, 95
Booth, Wayne, 13, 14, 15, 78, 128, 129, 143, 154

Bransford, J. D., 32, 34, 154
Brewer, W. F., 39–40, 154
Brody, P., 154
Brown, R., 10, 154
Bruner, J., 3, 154

Canon building, 149
Canonical texts, 141, 148
Cappin', 12
Carlsen, W. S., 120, 130, 138, 139, 154
Carraher, D. W., 42, 154
Carraher, T. N., 42, 154
Cazden, C., 120, 133, 154
Chiesi, H. L., 32, 154
Classroom research, 138–139
Cole, M., 3, 8, 161
Colker, L., 39, 161
Color Purple, The, 53, 54, 68, 70, 78, 79, 80
  as an example of signifying in text, 21–27, 95
  reason for title, discussion of, 115, 116–121, 123–126, 146
Comprehension. *See* Reading comprehension
Content knowledge, 35
Content schemata, 37
Constitutive questions, 119–120
Cooke, M., 10, 154
"Crayon enlargements of life," 19, 111–114
Critical thinking
  development of, 3, 144
  stages of, 34–35
Critical thinking theory, 34
Cross-cultural communication, 40
Cross-cultural studies, 8, 37, 39
Culler, J., 62, 143, 154
Cultural bias, 37
Cultural codes, 4, 47, 129
Cultural expectations, 37, 41
Cultural knowledge, 4, 5
Cultural schemata, 36–41
  influence of on interpretation, 38–39
Cultural self-definition, 10
Culturally sensitive texts, use of, 43–44
Culture and learning mathematics, 41–42
Culture-specific story properties, 39, 40

193

Author

Carol D. Lee is on the faculty of the School of Education and Social Policy at Northwestern University in Evanston, Illinois. She received her Ph.D. in Curriculum and Instruction from the University of Chicago. In addition, Dr. Lee has many years of experience as a classroom teacher at the elementary, high school and community college levels. She is a founder and former director of a twenty-year-old independent school in Chicago that integrates African American culture throughout its curriculum. Her research interests and publications focus on cultural contexts for literacy instruction.

Titles in the NCTE Research Report Series

NCTE began publishing the Research Report series in 1963 with *The Language of Elementary School Children*. Volumes 4–6, 8–12, 14, 17, 20, and 21 are out of print. The following titles are available through the NCTE *Catalog*.

Vol. *Author and Title*

1 Walter D. Loban, *The Language of Elementary School Children* (1963)

2 James R. Squire, *The Responses of Adolescents While Reading Four Short Stories* (1964)

3 Kellogg W. Hunt, *Grammatical Structures Written at Three Grade Levels* (1965)

7 James R. Wilson, *Responses of College Freshmen to Three Novels* (1966)

13 Janet Emig, *The Composing Process of Twelfth Graders* (1971)

15 Frank O'Hare, *Sentence Combining: Improving Student Writing without Formal Grammar Instruction* (1973)

16 Ann Terry, *Children's Poetry Preferences: A National Survey of Upper Elementary Grades* (1974)

18 Walter Loban, *Language Development: Kindergarten through Grade 12* (1976)

19 F. Andrée Favat, *Child and Tale: The Origins of Interest* (1977)

22 Judith A. Langer and Arthur N. Applebee, *How Writing Shapes Thinking: A Study of Teaching and Learning* (1987)

23 Sarah Warshauer Freedman, *Response to Student Writing* (1987)

24 Anne DiPardo, *A Kind of Passport: A Basic Writing Adjunct Program and the Challenge of Student Diversity* (1993)

25 Arthur N. Applebee, *Literature in the Secondary School: Studies of Curriculum and Instruction in the United States* (1993)

26 Carol D. Lee, *Signifying as a Scaffold for Literary Interpretation: The Pedagogical Implications of an African American Discourse Genre* (1993)